W0044195

Forging Capitalism in Nehru's India

Forging Capitalism in Nehru's India

Neocolonialism and the State, c. 1940–1970

NASIR TYABJI

OXFORD
UNIVERSITY PRESS

OXFORD
UNIVERSITY PRESS

Oxford University Press is a department of the University of Oxford.
It furthers the University's objective of excellence in research, scholarship,
and education by publishing worldwide. Oxford is a registered trademark of
Oxford University Press in the UK and in certain other countries

Published in India by
Oxford University Press
YMCA Library Building, 1 Jai Singh Road, New Delhi 110 001, India

© Oxford University Press 2015

The moral rights of the author have been asserted

First Edition published in 2015

All rights reserved. No part of this publication may be reproduced, stored in
a retrieval system, or transmitted, in any form or by any means, without the
prior permission in writing of Oxford University Press, or as expressly permitted
by law, by licence, or under terms agreed with the appropriate reprographics
rights organization. Enquiries concerning reproduction outside the scope of the
above should be sent to the Rights Department, Oxford University Press, at the
address above

You must not circulate this work in any other form
and you must impose this same condition on any acquirer

ISBN-13: 978-0-19-9457595
ISBN-10: 0-19-945759-X

Typeset in ScalaPro 10/13
by The Graphics Solution, New Delhi 110 092
Printed in India by Rakmo Press, New Delhi 110 020

To Meena, Shirali, and Rushika

CONTENTS

This book has taken a very long time to emerge from the scattered process of thought that provided the germ of the ideas that underlie its present form. This was principally due to two reasons. First, the ideas emerged disjointedly in the course of earlier work undertaken by me in a study of the underlying reasons for the technological torpidity displayed by Indian industry. It took me a considerable amount of time to appreciate the implications of the dialectical relationship between the potential embodied in Indian industrial companies and the stifling short-term perspectives of the owners of these firms, whether entrenched in the form of managing agencies, or later, in the form of closely held business groups. Evidence of these myopic perspectives came in the form of defensive statements by individual industrialists when they were confronted by instances of errant behaviour by some of their compatriots. When faced with specific challenges to their existing modes of business behaviour, such businessmen resorted to truculent modes of response, which signified an obsessive preoccupation with self-aggrandizement: the Liaquat Ali Khan and T.T. Krishnamachari budgets of 1947 and 1957 being key instances. The explanation offered, that the narrowly motivated behaviour clearly displayed was confined to 'businessmen' and not true industrialists, was indicative of an objective phenomenon.

Both the encapsulation of the precise distinction between businessmen and industrialists and a historical explanation of the emergence of this distinction seemed to me, increasingly, to constitute a subject worthy of study. It was a quite-by-chance re-reading of A.I. Levkovsky's study of the evolution of capitalism in India that led me to recognize how the businessman–industrialist distinction was to be conceptualized: it was to be approached both empirically, by considering the historical fact that Indian industrial firms were established by constituents of merchant communities who had accumulated their wealth through trade and moneylending; and, theoretically, through recognizing the unique modes of operation of the three associated forms of capital—merchant, usury, and industrial.

The second aspect of the phenomenon of the businessman–industrialist divide that required explanation was the reason for the overly long period taken for the transition from businessman to industrialist—a transition not entirely complete even at the end of the period under consideration here. It was an equally fortuitous return to Charles Bettelheim's study of Indian economic growth after Independence that provided a clue. Bettelheim insisted that the vast difference between the urban money market rate and the returns typically to be earned from rural moneylending could not be explained in dualistic market terms, even in its more refined variants. Rural moneylending operations did not constitute a market: each transaction was particular to the lender and receiver and the high rates prevalent here were precisely due to this characteristic. However, this decidedly did not mean that urban money flows had no nexus with the rural money lending sphere. This argument, when juxtaposed with the empirically based observations of the Banking Enquiry Committee in the 1930s, the Reserve Bank of India (RBI) Rural Credit Enquiry of the 1950s, and the Congress Parliamentary Party's Report on Bank Nationalization in the mid-sixties, provides a credible basis for concluding that the transition period seemed to have no end precisely because this nexus was enduring. The precarious nature of rain-fed petty peasant production would always provide a stable basis for the highly profitable use of urban funds for rural moneylending.

The second reason for this book's long gestation was that it proved difficult to find material in the public domain which would allow for an academic examination of the underlying issues. Access to the post-Independence papers of Jawaharlal Nehru enabled me to get a glimpse into the realm of operation of the principal political executives of the Nehruvian state. It was this that provided the context within which the material I found in the papers made historically grounded sense. It was, however, quite a task to read through the 800-odd volumes of the papers which had been filed purely chronologically; and an examination of every page of each volume, sometimes of 400 pages, was necessary before sufficient data could be assembled to provide for a coherent historical account. This exercise, then, spread intermittently over a period of many years, is the other related reason for this book's long gestation.

In the course of these years I found, in the reactions of participants at seminars where these ideas were presented, an important means of validating more or less formed propositions. Thus, ideas discussed in the first chapter were presented at the workshop 'Rethinking Economic History: Circulation, Exchange and Enterprise in India' at the Nehru Memorial Museum and Library (NMML), New Delhi, in March 2012. A preliminary draft of what has become the second chapter was presented in 'Business Culture in Post-War India: Evading Regulation or Evading Discipline?', presented at the 'Conference on Social Consciousness and Culture in Modern India', organized by the Indian Council of Philosophical Research (ICPR)–funded Project of the History of Indian Science, Philosophy and Culture (PHISPC) at New Delhi, February 2006. The third chapter is a modified and extended version of 'Jawaharlal Nehru, Big Business and the Liaquat Ali Khan Budget of 1947', originally published in *Thinking Social Science in India: Essays in Honour of Alice Thorner*.[1] The sixth chapter is based on material extracted from two papers presented earlier. The first was included in a seminar at the Institute for Studies in Industrial Development, New Delhi, held in June 2008. The paper was later published as 'Of Traders, Usurers and British Capital: Managing Agencies and the Dalmia-Jain Case' in *Indian Industrial Development and Globalisation*.[2] The second paper was presented at the conference 'Writing Indian Economic History: Trends and Prospects', organized by the Department of History and Culture, Jamia Millia Islamia, in February 2009 and also at a faculty seminar at the Institute for Studies in Industrial Development in March 2010. This appeared as 'Private Industry and the Second Five-Year Plan: The Mundhra Episode as Exemplar of Capitalist Myopia'[3] in *Economic and Political Weekly*, published later in 2010. Finally, a presentation of the arguments of the entire book formed part of the workshop on Nehru's India held at NMML in May 2014.

I must acknowledge here the emotional and intellectual support I received from the late Professor Ravinder Kumar, Director of the NMML, during the entire period of my formal association with the library, and also for the access he obtained for me to the Jawaharlal Nehru Papers. The Jawaharlal Nehru Memorial Trust complemented this support by awarding me a fellowship which permitted me to undertake the initial forays into the historical material which provides the empirical basis of this book.

* * *

Note on the bibliography: Reports published by the Government of India (GoI) have confusing and inconsistent formats (even those of a single agency such as the Tariff Board). I have tried to introduce uniformity in bibliographic references by treating the GoI as the 'author' of all documents; so the reference in all cases will be to 'India'. Reports of all subordinate agencies of the government are then listed chronologically. The same applies to documents listed under 'Great Britain'. Correspondingly, the Reserve Bank of India (RBI), which is not a subordinate office, is an 'author' in its own right.

---

3 *Economic and Political Weekly*, XLV, 32: 47–55.

From the mid-1960s up to the late 1980s, criticism had increasingly been voiced against the State's attempts in India to direct and regulate processes of economic development.[1] After the initiation of structural reforms in 1991, emphasis on the negative features of the policies followed from 1947 to 1991 has virtually precluded serious analysis of any enduring gains from those policies. This is largely because current analysis abstracts from the distinctive problems that attempting post-war economic growth posed for countries situated in the Third World, such as India. Thus, the criticism has ignored any consideration of the crucial role of State-sponsored structural change which accompanies economic growth (and industrial development, in particular) in predominantly agrarian societies.

Although the Indian economy was predominantly agrarian, it had specific features which possibly made it unique in the post-war world. With the development of the Indian cotton textile industry from the mid-nineteenth century and the involvement of Indians in large-scale trading activities associated with the imperial industrialized economies, a (large-scale) merchant and broker/intermediary community had crystallized.[2] The two world wars had allowed capital 'accumulation' in other ways, including blackmarketing and swindling in government contracts.

1 Streeten and Lipton (1968); Bhagwati and Desai (1970).
2 The formation of the Indian Federation of Chambers of Commerce in 1927 was the organized expression of this consolidation.

During the Second World War in particular, existing accumulations of money capital were further swollen by speculative activities, while entry into new industrial ventures which could have been facilitated by wartime import restrictions that relieved the pressure from international competition were, as the response to the Roger and Grady Missions shows, actively discouraged.[3] With the repatriation of British interests in jute, engineering, and the plantations at the time of Independence, and with a secure home market assured, the swindler and blackmarketeer 'accumulations' were invested in the associated enterprises, particularly in eastern India. Some of these accumulations were spent on acquiring managing agencies, while others were expended in buying large blocks of company equity.[4] A large number of very reputable firms thus came within the control of individuals or groups who had a tenuous connection with the industrial economy. The point to be emphasized here is that while the merchants and brokers/intermediaries had an appreciation of the imperatives of the process of industrialization, the other social groups had none.[5] They were overnight transformed from members of slightly risqué social groups into 'captains of industry'.[6]

The years between 1947 and 1966, covering the period from Independence to the end of the Third Five-Year Plan, provided the arena

3 The Roger Mission, led by Alexander Roger, was sent by the British Ministry of Supply in 1940 to survey the development of Indian industry. While it attended the meeting of the Eastern Group Supply Council held in New Delhi in October 1940 and provided impetus to the formation of the Council, it could do little to ensure that Indian industry had any substantial role in supplying defence requirements (Stevens 1941: 10, 15; Mitchell 1942: 18, fn 9; and Birla 1944: 124). The Grady Mission was a technical survey team sent by the United States Government in early 1942 to assess the potential for developing Indian industry for war purposes. The Government of India's lukewarm response is described in Grajdanzev (1943) and Birla (1944).

4 Goswami (1985: 245, Tables 4 and 5) shows that the large-scale entry of Marwari-controlled capital through the takeover of European companies took place between 1942 and 1945. Although he does not mention this, the initial impetus for the European exit probably came from the fears raised by the Japanese military advances into Southeast Asia.

5 The attitudes towards workers and the trade union movement, even amongst the long-established Mumbai textile industrialists, is discussed in chapter 4, 'The Unexplored Sources of Competitive Advantage: Contests on the Indian Shopfloor', and chapter 5, 'Managing Production and Managing the Shopfloor', of Tyabji (2000).

6 The term was introduced by Thomas Carlyle in 1843 in his book *Past and Present*.

for the most acute debates over the content of industrial development. In essence, these controversies centred on the form of ownership and control of the industrial undertakings which were already in operation and those which were to be established. Primarily at issue, thus, were the roles of the public sector and of the private sector on the one hand, and of Indian and foreign capital *within* the private sector, on the other. This book is based, however, on the proposition that industrialization in India involved not only the establishment of new enterprises by individual businessmen, or even by the government, but also measures of social engineering by the State. It was not simply a question of the State entering the industrial field in areas of high risk or those involving long gestation periods and/or large volumes of capital, leaving other fields to private enterprise. State activity, whether in the area of industry proper or in complementary spheres, was essential to nurture the development of entrepreneurs with a truly 'industrial' frame of mind.

The thrust of the argument presented in this book is that it is this major challenge—of achieving a large task of social engineering—which faced the political executives of the Indian State when planned industrialization became the proclaimed objective. And it is this challenge, both economic and social, that should form the context of a historical evaluation of State initiatives. It was not recognized in the early examinations of the planning process, such as those by the National Planning Committee, nor by contemporary or subsequent academic commentators. In other words, this factor has been largely, if not entirely, overlooked in discussions on Indian industrialization.

Levkovsky's work noted that in the colonial Indian context, there were marked differences with the processes underlying the Western European experience.[7] In India under colonial rule, the process of the emergence of the more complex forms of industrial organization through the increasing division of labour, demonstrated by the transition from independent artisanal production to (manually operated) manufactories, and, finally, to (power-driven) factories, did not take place.[8] Factories emerged directly in the nineteenth century in a form of organization imported from Britain. However, while in Britain

---

7 Levkovsky (1966: 44). See also Lamb (1955).
8 Levkovsky (1966: 229).

these institutions embodied concentration of industrial capital, in India, the factory form merely cloaked concentrations of merchant and usurer capital.[9] For a relatively long period, Levkovsky states, factory owners continued to engage in moneylending and trade alongside manufacturing operations. The process of an ever-increasing concentration on manufacture and organized forms of trade and banking (as opposed to moneylending) was long drawn out. In fact, until the world economic crisis of 1929–33, capital engaged in traditional trade and moneylending increased in absolute terms, though declining as a proportion of total non-agricultural economic activity.[10] Thus, while mercantile and usurious accumulations of money capital certainly formed the basis for the initiation of industrial enterprises, the influx of merchant and usury capital from associated enterprises continued alongside ongoing processes of industrial capital accumulation. Thus, even the growth of the assets in a manufacturing enterprise could not be taken to be entirely the result of industrial capital accumulation.[11] The critical point here is that if the *moment* in the process of development of industrial capitalism is to be assessed, the volume of capital invested in industrial enterprises can only be a proxy, though it is an important empirical measure.

This book's analysis is based on the political economy premise that industrial capital, merchant capital, and usury capital are distinct forms of capital, with identifiably different methods of accumulation associated with each. While merchant capital expands through profits made in the buying and selling of commodities, usury capital grows through the interest on the loans advanced by a moneylender. In the processes underlying the growth of merchant and usury capital there is a redistribution of value already in existence, from the consumer of the merchant's products or the recipient of the usurer's loan to the merchant or usurer, respectively. However, in the production process, new value is created by the application of labour power to the raw material purchased by the industrial capitalist, and it is this new value that (uniquely) underlies the growth of industrial capital. An index of the degree of industrial development is then provided by the relative importance of these three methods of accumulation within a

9   Levkovsky (1966: 229–30).
10   Levkovsky (1966: 231).
11   Levkovsky (1966: 243–4).

given economy during a specific historical period. In situations such as those that Maurice Dobb had examined in Western Europe, with industrialization the importance of industrial capital increased secularly, while that of merchant capital declined relatively.[12] Usury was also gradually reduced in importance as the role of peasant-based agriculture, with its related phenomenon of low and precarious incomes, declined. Capital engaged in commercial credit facilities geared both to production and consumption did, of course, become increasingly important, but this was decidedly an activity distinct to usury.

There have been substantial contributions to the understanding of India's industrial growth during the pre-Independence period. Starting with D.R. Gadgil, D.H. Buchanan, Vera Anstey, and P.A. Wadia and K.T. Merchant in the pre-Independence period, there were major additions to the scholarly literature from the 1970s, all of which addressed, explicitly or otherwise, the question of the impact of colonialism on the historical record of industrialization.[13] The most distinctive feature that differentiated the approaches, which were otherwise quite varied, was one of two underlying views: either that arrested development was an empirically demonstrable phenomenon with colonialism as its principal cause; or that colonialism, while being a historical reality, played no empirically significant role in the development of Indian industry.

Common to all these analyses, however much they differ in their approaches, is, quite naturally, a focus on industry (in Buchanan's phrase, on capitalistic enterprise). Perhaps the only exception was Andrew F. Brimmer's analysis of the 'setting' of entrepreneurship in India.[14] The institutional setting for entrepreneurship, in Brimmer's view, was not the industrial enterprise itself but the organization that actually held all operational control over it—the 'managing agency'.

---

12 Dobb (1963).

13 Gadgil (1971); Buchanan (1934); Anstey (1942); Wadia and Merchant (1957); Bagchi (1972); Ray (1979); Markovits (1985); Morris (1982); Roy (1999); Mukherjee (2002).

14 Brimmer (1955). What was particularly acute in Brimmer's observations was the distinction he made between British and Indian managing agencies. Although he does not analyse the material basis for these differences, it is a premise of this book that though the British firms generally displayed a behaviour associated with cut-throat merchant adventurers, the financial capital they embodied (discussed in Chapter 1 of this book) was qualitatively distinct to the merchant and usurer capital embodied in Indian managing agencies. Misra (1999) has an account of British expatriates in a colonial setting which well depicts the *Lord of the Flies* milieu of Calcutta.

In fact, his analysis made it clear that the issue was momentous for a serious study of Indian industrialization. It implied that if the *moment* (the precise stage) of development of industrial capital was to be truly assessed, it was to be clearly noted that the managing agency firm *was* the firm in the sense in which this term was known in institutional economics. If the firm was defined as the institutional setting in which entrepreneurial decisions were made, it was immediately clear why the managing agency should be so designated. To achieve the ends of expanding their capital, managing agents generally made use of the joint stock form of organization for the companies launched to undertake actual production and trade. These latter companies were then to be considered as operating units of the central, decision-making unit, the managing agency firm.[15] To understand the substance of economic activity encompassed by the managing agency system, then, it was critical to avoid a preoccupation with the managing agency merely as a legal entity, as also with the whole system of company law in India:

> With a few notable exceptions, the Indian [managing] agency firms seem to administer the operating companies under their control with a view to obtaining the maximum profit in the shortest possible time ... the detractions [to the reputation of Indian industry] made by Indian [managing] agency firms have been made by businessmen *still in the process of maturing.*[16]

The implications of this understanding are more profound than may be immediately apparent. If a manufacturing firm is merely an operating unit (or even only one unit of many) of a managing agency, which is itself an organizational expression of an accumulation of merchant or usury capital, then it cannot be held that the capital that is comprised of the agency and associated manufacturing units necessarily represents *industrial* capital as a whole. The situation is analogous to the historically familiar case represented by a handicraft establishment subordinated to a trader. The trader in this case, not

---

15 Papendieck (1978) has an interesting analysis of the major managing agency of Andrew Yule and Company and the operations of their coal enterprises. This empirical analysis bears out the general point being made in the text.

16 Brimmer (1955: 559). Emphasis mine.

the master artisan nominally in control of production, was the actual entrepreneur. There is extensive discussion in Indian economic history of whether enterprises of this type represented production of an industrial capitalist form or even provided the 'pre-conditions' for industrial capitalism.[17]

This book differs from earlier studies in that while its argument is firmly located within the view that colonialism did play the single most important role in retarding the growth of the Indian economy, its focus is on the development of industrial capitalism, in the sense that political economy views the process, rather than on 'capitalistic enterprise'. It postulates that for this reason the managing agency system, and not the enterprises that were established and controlled by these agencies, should be the focus.

The managing agency was a closely held firm, whether a single proprietorship, partnership, or limited liability company through which, under specific agreements, a variety of enterprises covering the field of industry, trade, and moneylending came under unified control. 'Agency Houses' originated in the late eighteenth century as partnerships of employees of the East India Company.[18] They provided the means for private business activities, whereby loans were advanced to indigo manufactories and manufactured dye received on consignment for sale in Europe. They were also the means through which surplus funds were invested in government securities, in shipping and docking services, and in sugar production. The bulk of international trade, including the shipping of opium to China, and the private trade between Bengal and Europe was channeled through their hands. In their time the agency houses held unchallenged control of the commercial life of Calcutta.[19]

The agency houses also operated the handful of joint stock associations founded before 1834. Though the joint stock form was limited to insurance and laudable societies, the employment of agency houses as managers provided the organizational model for the later managing agency system.[20] Use of the joint stock form of organization freed

---

17 Habib (1969); Chicherov (1971); Pavlov (1978).
18 Kling (1966: 38); Misra (1999), ch. 1.
19 Kling (1966: 38); Misra (1999), ch. 1.
20 Kling (1966: 38); Misra (1999), ch. 1.

the agency from the full risk of the new enterprise, while its agency agreement permitted it to maintain control over all management decisions.

In the subsequent 120 years of its unregulated existence, the managing agency survived despite criticism that was regularly voiced, as will be described later in this book. Various liberal commentators have claimed that although the managing agency system may have outlived its utility, it played an important role in supporting early efforts in industrial development: in particular, that industrial enterprises were floated at a time when there was little possibility of public participation in share issues, and that the managing agencies nurtured these firms until their viability and profitability had been demonstrated. What is not clear is whether the promoters took an exorbitant commission over an extended period in return for providing this time-bound initial support.[21]

The relationship between the managing agency and the associated enterprises remained unregulated, in any meaningful sense, by company law during the entire colonial period, and it was only in the 1950s that this nexus became subject to legislation. The book holds the view, further, that it was the institution of the managing agency that enabled the infusion of money capital, accumulated through varied non-industrial activities mentioned earlier, into industrial enterprises; however, it also allowed the reverse: the transfer of industrial surpluses into trade and rural moneylending.

The conglomerate nature of large Indian capital including its operation through the business group, comprising firms not only in varied industrial fields and modern banking, but also in trading and indigenous banking operations, had been widely noticed even before the first systematic exploration by Asoka Mehta in 1939.[22] However, beyond occasional references to the 'merchant' characteristics of industrial capitalists, the implications of such group structures on industrial performance were not fully appreciated. Typically, in what is still regarded as the classic account of industrial organization in the interwar period, P.S. Lokanathan did mention the fact that Indian

---

21 Cf. Papendieck (1978).

22 Originally published under the title 'India Comes of Age', the article was republished along with a similar study of the situation in 1949 in Mehta (1950).

managing agencies were generally firms which had had a financial, rather than an industrial, character; he also noted the critical point that rather than using the banking system, these agency firms often invested surplus cash in *hundis* (traditional forms of negotiable instruments through which prospects of earnings were of a greater order).[23] However, neither of these insights underlies his analysis. Vera Anstey also remarked on the shortcomings of managing agencies, and mentioned the charge that the surplus funds of firms were often cornered by *shroffs* (indigenous bankers) who were also their managing agents, but as the points were made in the course of acknowledging a litany of accusations made against them, she was not compelled to address this issue.[24] Much later, Brimmer characterized the Indian managing agencies as 'primarily financial in character'; at about the same time, the situation was described in more detail, but once again in a footnote disassociated from the analysis in the text:

> This [class of business leaders] is a new class of financiers, who have no traditions, except those of speculative finance and usury. Some of them earned their fortunes on the stock exchanges and commodity markets. But their spread of activities includes sowcari (village money lending), sarafi (urban indigenous banking and money-lending combined), dalali (intermediary finance, mostly on the stock exchange, bullion, and commodity markets), &c...[25]

There is recognized here the distinction between industrial capital on the one hand, and merchant (trading) or usury (moneylending) capital even when in ownership, control, and operation of *industrial* enterprises, on the other.

Trading or moneylending activities, empirically distinct from manufacturing, had, of course, been identified. However, the critical distinctions between these forms of existence of capital, *when in ownership of industrial enterprises* have generally been omitted from analysis. The ownership of a diversity of enterprises implies an obvious diversity of

---

23 Lokanathan (1935: 301, 303, 315). Managing agencies and their role in permitting unfettered business operations under the legal protection of limited liability are discussed in later chapters.

24 Anstey (1942: 114–15, 273–5, 501–5).

25 Brimmer (1955: 558); Rangnekar (1958: 123–4, fn 4).

economic interests which engaged the attention of the owners of the group, but also underlies the 'diversity' of their social identities, at various stages of evolution from speculators, moneylenders, and traders to industrialists. It was not, as has been implicitly assumed, that business group policies were neatly 'industrially oriented' when they concerned industrial firms in the group, and trader or moneylending oriented in the case of trading or traditional banking firms.[26] There was an integrated management philosophy that guided strategic decisions covering all the capital resources at the disposal of the group. Thus a

> typical Marwari family firm, unlike a European jute mill, was linked to several activities—from aratdari and kutcha baling in the up-country marts to manufacturing, baling and fatka in Calcutta—all controlled, like zaibatsus by the family patriarch and his ruling council and operating by consensus. Though the firms were nominally under different names and registered separately, the attempt was to maximise overall profits covering interdependent complementary and competitive activities. Thus, a Marwari firm's profit calculus was quite different from, and often at variance with, the norms of ... [the Indian Jute Mills Association] ... and the European mills.[27]

Again, empirically, it was recognized that in the jute industry some entrepreneurial interests, after accumulating capital through trading or moneylending, established entirely new jute mills (G.D. Birla and Sarupchand Hukumchand), while others bought controlling blocks of shares in existing mills and elbowed their way onto the boards of these companies, and even displaced the incumbent managing agents.[28] These quite distinct ways in which Indian industry grew were representative of equally clear distinctions in processes within the political economy. The first embodied the transformation, however partial and slow, of capital accumulated in trade and/or through moneylending

26 Rajat Ray is one of the few authors to have moved beyond merely noting the conglomerate nature of Indian business groups to granting that this implied the simultaneous engagement with manufacture, trade, and moneylending. He too, however, does not consider the accompanying dilution of the industrial imperative when undertaken in these combinations. See his discussion of the role of G.D. Birla's concern for 'real entrepreneurship' in the Introduction to Ray (1992: 58–9).

27 Goswami (1982: 154).

28 Goswami (1985: 231–4) describes these two processes.

into industrial capital as the enterprise grew, while the second signified the phenomenon of the parasitic control of an industrial unit by
representatives of yet incompletely transformed merchant or usury
capital.[29]

There were two further challenges little noticed or commented on,
academically, that faced the political executive. There was the lure of
quick and high returns available to urban industrial capital through
diverting its resources into the rural money market. One effect of the
colonial constraints on industrial development was that surplus funds
in the hands of capitalists found channels of high returns through
commercial operations in rural land transactions, and in extending
funds to rural moneylending. This phenomenon was empirically
substantiated by the investigations of the Central Banking Enquiry
Committee in the early 1930s.[30] Twenty years later, the All-India Rural
Credit Survey conducted by the RBI confirmed the continuing existence of links between urban large-scale capital and the rural money
market.[31] This flow not only bled the industrial sector of funds to
cover replacement costs of plant and machinery, but also provided
a stable base for an economic nexus between urban industrialists
and rural moneylenders. In this context, this book points attention
to an ignored aspect of the bank nationalization measures of 1969.
This was the effect of State control over credit disbursement that was
aimed at reducing the flow of urban money accumulations into the
rural money market.

Finally, the situation in India was unique in that the capitalists
who had emerged during the pre-Independence period were drawn
into the national movement, specifically into influential positions
within the Indian National Congress. This early support gave them

29 Thus: 'In the first place, the surplus funds of a concern are often taken over
by the managing agents as deposits with them, and although the usual interest may
be paid on them, they are utilized in their own agency businesses or loaned out to
allied concerns. Secondly, funds are borrowed in advance for the purpose of making
extensions, and till the time they are actually needed, they are employed elsewhere
in allied concerns or in the managing agent's own business' (Lokanathan 1935: 301).
Again: 'Some managing agencies had even utilized the funds of mill companies
for speculating in shares and securities, but they may be regarded as exceptional'
(Lokanathan 1935: 303).

30 India (1931: 99).

31 Reserve Bank of India (1954: 176–80).

not only privileged access to senior politicians, but also a moral authority to project policy measures which they could claim were not based solely on a narrowly focussed self-interest. The very close nexus long established between some sections of capital and the Congress Party made decisive political action problematical. This nexus is often overlooked when comparisons are made between the indecisiveness of Indian policies and the precision with which the government extracted appropriate responses from private entrepreneurs in East Asian societies.

The tricky point, as T.T. Krishnamachari, the then minister for commerce and industry, was to remind Jawaharlal Nehru, was that while they might privately agree that some industrialists were unsavoury, they were the only industrialists that the country had.[32] Business had to be done with them. However, doing business could not be coterminous with allowing the firms to be managed in any way the industrialists chose. Interestingly, there is also evidence that the necessity of administrative coercion in these matters was understood by the more advanced industrial entrepreneurs. Sumant Moolgaokar, of the Tata-promoted firm of Tata Engineering and Locomotive Company (TELCO), currently known as Tata Motors, pointed out to Krishnamachari that the government was the only agency through which the productive efficiency of the manufacturing sector could be increased.[33] As an industrial manager, Moolgaokar saw the problem

32 Letter dated 2 September 1954 from T.T. Krishnamachari to Jawaharlal Nehru, T.T. Krishnamachari Papers (subsequently TTK Papers), subject file 8 (A), pp. 120–4. T.T. Krishnamachari (1899–1974), initially elected to the Madras Legislative Assembly as an independent member, later joined the Congress. In 1946, he became a member of the Constituent Assembly and of the Constitution Drafting Committee. From 1952 to 1956, he was minister for commerce and industry and from 1956 to 1958, the finance minister. He became a minister again in 1962, holding the portfolio for economic and defence cooperation and then again the finance ministry, from 1963 to late 1965.

33 Letter dated 5 October 1953 from Sumant Moolgaokar to T.T. Krishnamachari, TTK Papers, correspondence with S. Moolgaokar file, pp. 1–2. Sumant Moolgaokar (1906–89) was an engineer trained at the City and Guilds Institute and Imperial College, London. In the pre-Independence period he worked in the cement industry and helped develop the ˙ manufacture of cement machinery during the Second World War. After the formation of TELCO in 1945, he was closely associated with its development until his death. He played an active role as a consultant in planning the development of the heavy engineering industry.

at the level of the individual firm, while the critical problem, of course, lay at the level of the social composition of the industrialists.

Theoretically, too, the importance of moving away from the firm to the social group is emphasized by a consideration of the role of the State in extending the time horizons of the business community. This, along with the appropriate technological educational inputs, helps in the problematical transformation of a class of merchant–usurers into industrialists.[34] In India, the major instruments for channelling resources into activities necessitating longer time horizons were, apart from the fiscal instrumentalities of the State, in the form of legislation, specifically the Capital Issues (Control) Act, the Companies Act, and the Industrial Development and Regulation Act (IDRA). All these acts represented potentially coercive administrative measures, aimed at strengthening the 'industrial' characteristics of private resource allocation decisions. In the event, the Capital Issues (Control) Act playing a subordinate role to the industrial licensing system, instituted by the IDRA, was of little independent significance. The IDRA, a key to social control at the level of the firm, did not ever achieve this goal.[35] Initially instituted during the period when the 'Economic Consequences of Sardar Patel' were most visibly present, it was finally legislated shorn of its more significant social and political attributes.[36] It was thus the Companies Act, identifying thereby the focus of social engineering as the *company* (a financial

---

34 Policy towards the small-scale sector has been examined in Tyabji (1989).

35 Chibber (2004: 137–42, 152–5, 173–8) provides a detailed account of the chequered path of the IDRA from the 1949 Bill to its actual passage in 1951.

36 The phrase is from the title of Asoka Mehta's pamphlet (Mehta 1949). Asoka Mehta (1911–84) helped organize the socialist wing of the Indian National Congress, along with Jaya Prakash Narayan, and was closely involved in the politics and government of the city of Bombay (present-day Mumbai). Mehta was an active participant in the Quit India Movement and was sentenced to rigorous imprisonment five times. After Independence, he helped organize trade unions in Bombay and was one of the founders of the Indian National Trades Union Congress (INTUC). Mehta retired from active politics in the early 1950s and wrote several books on his experiences, on India's independence movement and the importance of socialist-oriented reforms. He was a founder member of the Socialist Party, and when in September 1952 the Kisan Mazdoor Praja Party and the Socialist Party merged to form the Praja Socialist Party (PSP), Asoka Mehta became the general secretary of the new party. He was the Praja Socialist Party's president during 1959–63.

unit), rather than the *firm* (a productive unit), that provided the most effective legislative key to social engineering. And it is the Companies Act with which this book is mostly engaged.

A project to extend the time horizon of an entire social group, and that of the dominating social force at that, not only requires the acquiescence of the more advanced sections of this group of proto-industrialists in the necessity of such measures, it also requires the politically adroit combination of measures to ensure compliance with the accumulation norms of an industrial society.

At the beginning of this Introduction it was stated that criticism of the early post-Independence policies had abstracted from consideration of the requirements of State-sponsored structural change. It should be emphasized that the original, publicly stated, policy intention was equally silent on these issues. However, the silence must here be explained as a result of the blandness which necessarily characterizes State policy. It is precisely this silence that explains the choice of particular instances in India's history in this book, when crises of varying severity forced the disclosure of events and processes which otherwise remain within the privileged domain of the government. The episodes considered here—the capitalist initiatives towards presenting a plan following the Quit India Movement in 1942, the presentation of the Liaquat Ali Khan–Budget in 1947, and the drama surrounding the Dalmia-Jain and Mundhra cases—are all cases in point.

In February 1958, musing over just how a situation had arisen by which an outstanding minister, T.T. Krishnamachari, was likely to be forced to resign over the fallout of the 'Mundhra Episode', M.O. Mathai had an explanation to offer.[37] In a note to Jawaharlal Nehru, Mathai argued that the great jubilation amongst some Gujarati and Parsi businessmen over the situation was basically due to the fiscal policies that Krishnamachari had pursued. Continuing, Mathai explained that based on various kinds of information available to him, including messages from 'decent' businessmen, it was apparent that the campaign was the first attack on (Nehruvian) socialism. It was, indeed, also an indirect attack on Nehru. Opponents of this ideology were openly proclaiming that socialism would disappear with

---

37 M.O. Mathai was Special Assistant to Nehru. Secret note, 2 February 1958, Jawaharlal Nehru Papers (subsequently JN Papers), File no. 590, p. 82.

Krishnamachari's exit. Further, so the argument went, as the head of the government Nehru should also resign. A week later, bowing to the inevitable, Mathai pointed out that if Krishnamachari had to go, as seemed certain by then, there was an uncomfortable fact to be faced: that he had been sacrificed for implementing policies that he had introduced as a loyal comrade of Nehru.[38]

This book, based on contemporary records, reaches the conclusion that while this was indeed so, there was a more viscerally felt reason for the opposition to Krishnamachari. This lay in the Rama Rao episode. Though less glamorous, this drama had led to the resignation of the RBI governor, B. Rama Rao, in December 1956 over his inability, in his perception, to prevent the infringement by the government of the RBI's autonomy in determining monetary policy. Actually such a perception of events trivializes the historical importance of the episode: it was part of a strategy to institute an effective industrial policy by subordinating monetary policy to the demands of industrial development. Further, this book argues that Krishnamachari tripped in attempting, through the stewardship of the finance ministry, an ambitious programme of social engineering: he tried to force a section of the dominant bloc of businessmen who had acquired control of industry to behave like true industrialists, rather than engaging in moneylending, speculation in stocks and commodities, or asset stripping. In this, his political fall from grace provides an object lesson in political economy: the deadly consequences of misreading the limits to the relative autonomy of the State.

More successful was the effort to unravel the Dalmia-Jain Group's mode of operation. This book postulates that the group represented one of the largest concentrations of largely unreformed merchant/ usury capital, and that their methods of using the nexus between their managing agencies and associated manufacturing firms quintessentialized the behaviour of this form of capital. Ultimately, the disclosures of the Dalmia-Jain investigation led to the abolition of the managing agency system in 1969. It should also be noted that despite the dramatic aspects of the Haridas Mundhra case, his operations were stock market speculations, unconcerned even with gaining management control except in the very short term; much more corrosively,

---

38 Note, 11 February 1958, JN Papers, File No. 593, pp. 241–3.

the Dalmias specialized in devising means of squeezing all the liquid assets out of well-functioning industrial enterprises which came
under their control.

To recapitulate, the thrust of the argument of this book is that the
existence of a class of businessmen does not automatically mean the
existence of a group of industrially oriented entrepreneurs, because
the development of industries is not necessarily the only money-mak-
ing activity available to them. Even acquiring the position of being in
charge of industrial ventures does not automatically convert businessmen into industrialists because they could very well use their control
to divert resources into other non-industrial activities.[39] It therefore
requires a historical process of a definite nature for a class of true
industrialists to come into being. In the Indian case, colonialism and
'arrested development' formed the context within which emerged the
group of businessmen responsible for managing industrial ventures
after Independence. They were part of an imperfectly formed group
of industrialists possessing characteristics that reflected their background of engagement in non-industrial activities—activities with
which they continued to be involved, even as they acquired control
over industrial companies. In 1949, the Bombay Shareholders' Association in a memorandum listed questionable practices by managing
agencies owned by Birla Brothers, Dalmia-Jain, Karamchand Thapar,
Jaipuria, Walchand, Surajmull Nagarmull, Sarupchand Hukumchand, Kamanis, and Bajoria amongst the more prominent business
groups. This made them all, as will be argued in this book, prone
to a particular kind of fraud greatly inimical to the industrialization
effort.[40] It also meant that the State had to play a crucial part in transforming this group into a class of true industrialists. The 1950s and
1960s are naturally important in this regard being the critical early
years of post-Independence industrialization.

39 The possibility of such moves (admittedly in the short term) even in a fully
industrialized economy has been suggested by Dillard (1980: 259).

40 Bombay Shareholders' Association (1949: 74–82). Further empirical evidence
for this proposition is available in Bombay Shareholders' Association (1936); see also
India (1958a, 1958b, 1963).

CHAPTER ONE

Capital Accumulation under Colonial Economy and Company Law

THE PROBLEM IDENTIFIED

By the start of the First Five-Year Plan in 1951, the four years of experience since Independence had reinforced in the government's perception several dysfunctional features of the operations of private capital in the industrial field.[1] In this perception, speculative commercial practices which flourished during the Second World War had left legacies which impeded the industrial development of the country. In fact, attempts to deal with illegal wartime accumulations and to prevent the siphoning of resources through manipulated share price rises had been a feature of the budget presented by the Congress Muslim League Interim Government in early 1947.[2] The tax proposals in this budget, the formation of an Income Tax Investigation Commission, and the continuation of wartime controls on the issue prices of shares with the Capital Issues (Control) Act were then presumed to be able to deal effectively with what were conceived to be temporary, war-situation-created anomalies.

---

1 This was the thrust of the speech in Parliament of the then minister of state for finance, Mahavir Tyagi, when introducing the Indian Companies (Amendment) Bill 1951. Indian Companies (Amendment) Bill 1951, Parliament of India Debates, vol. XIV, part II, 16.8.51 cols 711–12.

2 The Interim Government's budget and related proposals are discussed in detail in Chapter 3.

In 1947, then, these undesirable practices were viewed as a one-time effect of the war, and it was assumed that investigations, and subsequent prosecutions, would address the issue. However, by 1951, it was recognized that these were enduring and widespread features of private capitalist behaviour. Manifestations of this behaviour were found in specific grey areas of operations. Included amongst these were the diversion of companies' investible funds towards trading in managing agency rights and the accumulation of shares in the open market, the object being that of merely acquiring control over other well-established firms. The progressive expansion or development of these undertakings, let alone the development of new lines of manufacture, was not the intention here. It was simply the furtherance of narrow group advantage, to the detriment of existing investors, and the interests of the companies themselves. The object was to grasp the cash resources and liquid reserves built up by these companies, in order to utilize these for gaining control over other companies, and to engage in speculative activities in share and commodity markets.[3]

In the ensuing debate, several larger issues connected with this mode of financial manipulation, which affected not only industrial development but also the very ideological premises of a capitalist economy, were identified. The most critical of these issues to be voiced by a member of the Parliament (MP) was that the industrial revolution which the country was experiencing, if not accompanied by a *moral* revolution, risked creating more tensions than poverty and ignorance had done.[4] Large industrial firms concentrated great power in the hands of a few people, and to wield so much power, in the absence of an underpinning of the ethical values of an *industrial* society, could lead to an explosive situation.

In other words, while speculation might be publicly tolerated in commodity and share markets, its spread to the instrumentalist pursuit of control in the industrial sphere would lead to widespread

3 Tyagi, speech in the Parliament in August 1951, Indian Companies (Amendment) Bill 1951, Parliament of India Debates, vol. XIV, part II, 16.8.51 cols 711–12.
4 K.C. Sharma on Companies Bill, Parliament of India Debates, vol. VI, 1955, 17.8.55 col. 10258.

outrage.[5] While this MP's view was driven by concern over the long-term public acceptability of the institutions of a capitalist society, it also hinted at a more incisive analysis. Apparently, indiscriminate extension of the *mores* appropriate to operations in the money and commodity markets to the industrial sphere denoted a fundamental inability of the capitalists concerned to comprehend the distinctions characterizing these activities. In actual fact, it is argued here, this inability to discriminate was due to the placement of many capitalists in the grey area of evolution from moneylending and trading activities to the sphere of industry proper.

COLONIAL ORIGINS OF CONGLOMERATE BEHAVIOUR

It is important to emphasize the historical roots of this situation. Neither the management philosophy nor the practices that emanated from this philosophy were Indian in any essentialist way.[6] Rather, they flowed from the specifics of the colonial Indian economy and the ways in which Indian capitalists had emerged and evolved. There were three aspects to the context in which capitalist evolution in India proceeded.[7]

Primarily, what made the situation in India unique in the colonized world was the absence of plantation crops from the greater land

5 In an ingenuous account of the way in which he made the first instalment of his fortune, Ramkrishna Dalmia shows that it was neither skill nor even acquired market knowledge that enables accumulation by speculation, rather it is inside information about the impending operations by dominant players in that market (Dalmia 1948). See also footnote 46.

6 The sole scholarly work that has addressed this issue so far, and in considerable detail, is Levkovsky (1966).

7 The ideas, largely the data, and even many phrases for this section (given their appropriateness for the flow of the argument here) are drawn from Rajat K. Ray (1988). The ideas are corroborated by the books on indigenous banking by Jain (1929) and Krishna (1959); and regional studies by Baker (1984: 233–333) for the Tamil districts and Satyanarayana (1990: 74–98) for the Telugu Districts of Madras Presidency; Mridula Mukherjee (2005: 31–54) for Punjab; Bose (1986: 98–145) for Bengal Presidency; and Hardiman (1996) for the Gujarat districts of Bombay Presidency. The official reports on marketing of the main commercial crops, jute, rice, wheat, cotton, and groundnuts given in India (1938, 1941a, and 1941b), Indian Central Jute Committee (1938), and Indian Central Cotton Committee (1928a, 1928b, 1928c, and 1928d) have also been examined.

mass of the country—the plains.[8] Here, both indigo and jute were overwhelmingly grown on peasant farms. Genuine plantation crops like tea, and to a certain extent, coffee (but even this was substantially a peasant crop), grew in the hills. Thus, tea was the only crop which was exclusively produced on plantations, and which the British managing agencies could control right from its cultivation through its dispatch by rail to its shipment for final sale in London. But leaving aside hills in the northeast and southwest of the country, where intensive peasant agriculture had not previously been established, and where conditions were favourable for capital-intensive tea plantations, nowhere else could planters compete with peasants in terms of costs. New capital inputs were small in Indian agriculture, while labour and cattle inputs were massive and largely household-based. Systematic efforts by Western machinery manufacturers to sell tractors and other unsuitable machinery to Indian peasants ran quickly aground; and one possible means of remote control of Indian agriculture through agricultural machinery supply was denied to colonial manufacturing interests.

Furthermore, peasant-operated small farms not only excluded the introduction of potential plantations, but also the peasants were themselves part-time artisans, and employers of artisans in agricultural work in peak seasons. The controllers of the colonial economy could not displace peasant agriculture with plantations, nor artisan industries entirely with factories. It was the tenacity with which peasant farming and artisan activity–based economies continued, however precariously, that provided the base for the accumulation of capital. To assemble the produce from dispersed peasant farms, and even more atomized artisans, required a network of merchants and moneylenders. These arrangements generated the essential flows of credit for an economy characterized by high risks due to the poverty of the population and uncertain seasonal agricultural conditions. India was incorporated into the world capitalist economy through the operations of numerous agents gathering in and financing the produce of peasant farms and artisan households.

Second, given the scale at which industrial enterprises operated by the mid-nineteenth century when the first cotton mills were

8 Habib (1988: 285).

established in India, it was inevitable that it was only accumulations attained through large-scale trade and moneylending that would have achieved the minimum mass required for establishing a new factory. The sparse artisan population that survived the onslaught of overseas imports could not conceivably have been able to accumulate the required capital through the meagre retained earnings from production.[9] Thus, it was the trading and financing network operated by the merchant and moneylender communities from which an industrial capitalist class struggled to emerge.[10]

Large international trading concerns—Ralli, Volkart, Shaw Wallace, Sassoons, and Mitsui Bushen Kaisha—dominated the exports of India's agricultural produce, principally rice, wheat, cotton, jute, and groundnuts; and also imports of piecegoods, kerosene oil, sugar, and other manufactured goods. All maintained extensive purchasing organizations in the *mandis*, the main assembling centres of agricultural produce. The method of direct purchases from the mandis to reduce the *arhat* or commission of the *arhatiyas* (commission agents) was initiated as a systematic policy by Ralli and Volkart before the First World War, and they extended the policy after the war by pushing still further into the countryside during the 1920s.[11] They set up a number of agencies at key points which supervised the buying operations of grains, seeds, and cotton by a large number of sub-agencies staffed with the exporter's own personnel.

Competing with these operations lay the sphere of indigenous bankers and merchants, operating through their financial nexus of commission agencies (arhatiyas) and bills of exchange (hundi). It was they who increasingly enabled inland produce and credit transactions

9 The only recorded instance of entrepreneurs emerging from artisan backgrounds and from manufactory owners seems to have been in Bombay. Parsi mechanics trained at the Bombay dockyards provide notable instances of this transformation, but the enterprises they established did not survive and become enduring features of the industrial world (Guha 1984: 128–9). For further accounts of Parsi enterprise, see Guha (1970a, 1970b) and Desai (1968).

10 Habib (1988: 293). Raman Mahadevan has brought to my notice some exceptions to this trajectory, particularly in Madras Presidency where the Coimbatore-based textile industry was established in the 1930s by rich peasants and landlords drawn from peasant backgrounds.

11 Ralli and Volkart's activities, together with those of A & F Harvey in Madras Presidency, are detailed in Baker (1984: 253–8).

to take place on an all-India basis.[12] The linking of widely dispersed mandis through these traditional business devices, now successfully geared to the railways and the telegraph, produced an integrated indigenous exchange system.[13]

The bankers (shroffs) and commission agents (arhatiyas) who constituted the bazaar used the term in a specific technical sense, meaning the market for indigenous credit they drew upon to sustain domestic traffic in produce, manufactures, and bullion. Thus, the bazaar rates recorded by the Controller of Currency meant the rates at which inland bills of exchange (hundis) were discounted by the shroffs.[14]

There was clear evidence of the distinction between rural credit and urban finance.[15] The involvement of the big merchants and bankers in the cycle of agricultural loans was indirect. They did not operate within the social and political power structure which allowed the village mahajan to lend money to the overwhelmingly impoverished peasantry. The mahajan could draw on the town moneylender who, being considered credit worthy, received accommodation from the big bankers.

It was the difference between the mode of operation of the rural credit system and that of the bazaar that led to an apparent paradox. During the monsoon, there was a slack in the urban money market while the villages experienced stringency. The kharif season advance, taken from June onwards, was repaid after harvest in December or January. The rabi advance was taken in October and repaid after marketing the following April. From May to August, rural moneylenders needed more funds than they controlled themselves to make advances to cultivators for sowing the kharif crop.[16] However, the

---

12 Baker (1984: 276–301) has a detailed account of indigenous banking in Madras Presidency.

13 Within Madras Presidency, the expansion of paddy-based trade is described in Baker (1984: 241–3).

14 Ray (1988: 268).

15 There is a detailed account of the process by which paddy reached the market in Madras Presidency in Baker (1984: 239–41), and of cotton in Bombay Presidency in Dantwala (1937: 10–62, 107–235).

16 The kharif crop, being the main crop, demanded considerable financial outlay, which was more than the rural moneylenders could provide out of their own resources

funds available in the bazaar at the end of the grain-trading season in June could not be easily transferred to these rural moneylenders: the whole rural economy lay outside the sphere of the hundi-based money market. A money market can be said to exist only when negotiable instruments are in use and hundis did not circulate through the rural economy. In their absence the bazaar money moved to the country through the device of book credits which prevented the expansion of mobile credit, the sort of credit which could have eased the seasonal stringency in the villages. This entire agricultural credit was extended through book entries, and not by means of hundis. The system of book credits was sustained by the nature of the rural economy—a chronically deficit and insecure one in which mobile credit simply could not develop. It also secured the special status of the village moneylender, who could not be displaced by the urban indigenous banker.

The hundi bazaar run by the shroffs sustained, amongst the spot and forward trade transactions of the arhatiyas, the grain and seeds bazaar, the raw cotton bazaar, the piecegoods bazaar, the gold and silver bazaar, and the *fatka* (futures trading) bazaar. The size of bazaar operations still exceeded, between the two world wars, modern banking, export–import trade, and factory industry. It was the bazaar, through its twin instruments of the hundi and the arhat, which assembled, distributed, and financed the produce of close on 360 lakh small dispersed peasant households.

Finally, there was the vast rural hinterland which was served by seasonal fairs and weekly or biweekly markets dispersed over the countryside.[17] The fairs were annual or seasonal gatherings, one of the most critical functions of which was to enable the peasants to buy cattle from the stock breeders and livestock traders. The more regular rural markets, known as *shandies* in Madras (present-day Chennai), *painths* in northern India, and *haats* in Bihar and Bengal, assembled once or twice a week for retail transactions in agricultural produce and urban manufactures. The typical *shandy*, which unlike the urban

---

(even when all loans from the previous cycle had been repaid). Of course, this is the official version as many loans were not repaid at all and were simply recycled. The rabi crop did not require the same order of advance, and could be met from the moneylenders' own resources.

17 R.K. Ray (1988: 274).

retail market had no permanent market structure, was held on the roadside or in a grove, where the producer brought his produce to sell in small quantities to the shopkeeper or petty trader, and purchased with the cash thus obtained, a wide range of articles imported from towns for household use, such as cloth, salt, and brass vessels.[18] Even the portion of the crop retained in the villages entered into a well-established nexus of exchange and credit, comprising both market transactions by cash or barter through the shandies, and important non-market transactions such as crop sharing (*batai*) between peasant, labourer, and landlord, and ritualized exchanges (*jajmani*) between peasant and artisan, regulated by hereditary custom and conducted on an annual basis.

Although the market-based exchange economy had penetrated the country deeply through its hierarchy arranged in three distinct layers, rural periodical markets, market towns, and the financial and commercial centres, foreign imports and exports did not form a significant part of rural exchange. The amounts passing into the urban retail market were many times more, and the produce traded in the country fairs and markets at least one-third more than that handled by the mandi-based bazaar. While the proportion of the total produce of the country that never reached the market was well below half, that reaching the higher commercial world of the bazaar was somewhat over a third.

The export–import figures of Indian trade and the allied volume of exchange bank operations reveal only the international dimensions of India's economy. Indian trade and finance broadened when viewed at each level of internal trade. In 1928–9 there were, at the peak, 90 lakh tons of imports and exports, mainly through eight ports—Karachi, Bombay, Cochin, Tuticorin, Madras, Vizagapatam, Calcutta, and Chittagong. At the second level, there were these 90 lakh tons moving along the railway lines to and from the ports, and in addition, something like 760 lakh tons of goods moving along the railway lines between market towns. Finally, at the base of this trading system was the movement of these 850 lakh tons of goods on carts along the roads running to the railheads, plus the indeterminate volume of goods marketed or exchanged through traditional means within

18 R.K. Ray (1988: 274).

the localities away from the railheads, perhaps an additional 500 lakh tons.[19] Thus, at the three successive levels of the market, the tonnage of traded goods increased from 90 lakh to 850 lakh to 1350 lakh.

The predominance of small peasant agriculture and household industries in the Indian economy was the key factor in explaining the development of Indian capitalist enterprise. Compared to most colonial countries, where plantation agriculture was fully established, India was able to develop a large capitalist class, in fact the largest in the decolonized Third World. This was because colonial rule could not replace peasant agriculture with plantations, nor entirely displace household industries with mills. To assemble, then, the produce from dispersed peasants and artisans, a substantial part of the economy had to be conceded to the bazaar. It was this that provided an enduring basis for the growth, albeit slow and extended, of an indigenous industrial capitalist class out of the communities which dominated this system. Only the bazaar could deliver the goods from the bottom to the top by the use of a set of complex financial arrangements that interlocked its successive layers. These arrangements generated the essential flows of credit without which the economy could not function. In an economy characterized by high credit risks at the base, the bazaar represented a set of financial methods which effectively exploited the poverty of the population and the uncertain seasonal agricultural conditions. Necessarily, India fed into the world capitalist economy, not through direct British control of the labour process through mills and plantations financed by banks, but through the operations of numerous shroffs and arhatiyas gathering in and financing the produce of countless farms and households.

The progenitors of this class of merchant and usurer capitalists had concentrated in their hands the largely autonomous indigenous money market that had incorporated widely dispersed market operations into their credit operations.[20] Before the Depression,[21] for

19   R.K. Ray (1988: 273).

20   Some of the methods by which this was achieved are described by Baker (1984: 256–62).

21   Although the beginning of the Depression is conventionally associated with the spectacular New York Stock Exchange crash of October 1929, its roots lay in the interwar economic setting: the handling of the war debt and reparations problems, the general climate of financial and economic instability accentuated by self-seeking US strategy, and the failure of the major industrial powers to coordinate their policies.

instance, the Multani bankers were sending money from Shikarpur in Sind to Madurai, or to take another example, the Marwari bankers were remitting funds from urban centres in Bikaner and Shekhawati to the Brahmaputra valley.

The specific form of commercial organization in India, the arhat or indigenous commission agency system, took the place of wholesale trading. Firms operating on the scale of wholesale trade were almost invariably commission agency organizations. They bought and sold not on their own account but on behalf of actual buyers and sellers, whom they financed to the extent of three-quarters or more of the goods and produce which they handled on the firm's behalf. Under the commission agency system, losses in transit would never fall on the wholesale trader, but would be borne by the consignee. However, bad debts could fall on the large trader who had made advances to village-level dealers operating in a chronically deficit economy, who could give no guarantee of repayment of loans. The only safe form of credit was an advance against a crop or against goods in transit. The wholesale trader, variously a mahajan, a *sowcar*, or a shroff, was in a position precisely to locate the produce which could be used to secure a loan. However, while trading in the identified amount of produce whose value had been advanced, the wholesale merchant had to share the risk of an unpredictable monsoon fluctuation with both the producer and village dealer. Thus, wholesaling was substituted by commission agency operations, a far more advantageous form of business for the big trader.[22]

The stored produce could change hands as many as twelve times during a season; storage was used not merely for raising credit, but for speculation as well. An important feature of the bazaar, which distinguished it from the rural economy, was the presence of produce exchanges. The produce exchanges in the port towns and the big mandis of Punjab and western United Provinces were mainly for speculative transactions, as distinct from spot and forward transactions. They were controlled by a particular group among the traders who were aware of the seasonal and world movement of prices and who specialized in taking commercial risks. It was their business that linked the daily market prices to movements in supply and demand as

22 R.K. Ray (1988: 303).

they varied from season to season. The futures options in inland mandis such as Hapur, Meerut, Muzaffarnagar, Hathras, and Agra were concentrated in the hands of that important group among the dealers which controlled the warehouses—the pucca arhatiyas.[23]

The volume of speculative transactions can be estimated from the fact that though at a time when 10 million tons of wheat was produced, it was traded in futures to the extent of 70 million tons. Such speculative transactions had long been a part of the Indian commercial scene, but their volume had been far less before the First World War. Law court records showed that *teji-mandi* gambling had been in vogue for a very long time, so were futures.[24] But formerly their volume had been kept down due to the fact that up to this period, the greater proportion of the export trade in grains and oilseeds, and a considerable part of the cotton and jute export trade had been in the hands of a few international trading houses, especially Ralli and Volkart. They needed price stability to sustain their large international operations and their impact was to stabilize, or at least to coordinate, prices in different markets.

Futures trading in cotton and some other agricultural commodities had taken a kind of organized form in Bombay, where indigenous traders had indulged in it before the First World War. Simultaneously, this widening activity was threatening to disrupt the supply lines of the dominant European business in Calcutta, too. As Goswami notes:

> The raw jute trade up to the up-country secondary markets... [was]... teeming with Marwari aratdars (commission merchants with storage sheds or

---

23 R.K. Ray (1988: 297).

24 'The buyer of an option has to pay some money to secure an option to buy or sell during a specified period a specified quantity of produce at the current rate. The money is commonly known as *nazarana* or premium. The party which takes the premium is known as the "eater" (*khanewala* or *khanar*) and the party which pays the premium is known as the "supplier" (*laganewala* or *lagandar*). The buyer of a *teji* option is a "bull", that is, he believes that the prices are likely to rise. If he finds that the price has not risen, he does not demand delivery of the produce purchased by him and forgoes the consideration money paid by him. The buyer of a *mandi* option, on the other hand, is a "bear", that is, a person who expects the price to fall. If he finds that the prices have not gone down, he keeps quiet and allows the premium paid by him to be forfeited. The buyer of a teji-mandi option secures the option to buy or sell as it suits him. The buyer of a double option is both a "bull" and a "bear". In other words he expects the market to fluctuate appreciably.' Quoted by R.K. Ray (1988: 295–6).

arats) and kutcha balers from the last quarter of the nineteenth century. However, the most notable index of Marwari presence even in the pre-war years was the meteoric rise of fatka (or speculation) and its impact on spot trade from the first decade of the twentieth century. Fatka, almost exclusively a Marwari institution, was introduced by six Marwari traders in 1905–6 and by 1911, it ha[d] so influenced spot prices that IJMA (Indian Jute Mills Association) appealed to the Bengal Government to ban all future trade on the ground that it was '...making legitimate trade something of a huge gamble...' with the result that '...the price of jute was maintained at a level above its proper value...'[25]

In Calcutta (present-day Kolkata), a small jute futures trading association had been formed in 1912. The authorities suppressed it on charges of pure gambling in 1927, and suppressed two more such associations in the next two years.[26] In 1927, the Birlas took the lead in organizing the much bigger East India Jute Association, which gradually secured control of the jute futures market in India. In Bombay, where the indigenous business element had always been much stronger than elsewhere, there had been several cotton produce exchanges before the First World War. These were replaced in 1922 by the more organized East India Cotton Association established by statutory authority. A few years later a smaller and more *indigenous* cotton produce exchange, the Shree Mahajan Association, sprang up, operating a smaller unit of transaction and giving formal recognition to teji-mandi gambling, which caused acrimony between organized business and the bazaar in the Bombay cotton trade. Soon the activity extended beyond Bombay and Calcutta. The first step towards organ-ized inland trading was taken in 1920 with the formation of the Sugar and Grain Merchants Association of Amritsar, which was later con-verted into the Indian Exchange Ltd.

As a result of speculative activity, in the course of the First World War, there was a large increase in accumulations of money capital, which qualitatively changed the significance of these forms of capital

---

25 Goswami (1982: 143), where the author quotes from Indian Jute Mills Association (1912): 91–103; also R.K. Ray (1988: 287–8). Sinha (1929) has details of the evolution of fatka.

26 R.K. Ray (1988: 296–7).

in the Indian economy, and correspondingly, resulted in an increase in the influence of their controllers.[27]

Although data for this period is necessarily based on a number of assumptions, it may be noted that compared to an estimate published in 1924 of Rs 400 crore of moneylending capital, and Rs 100 crore of trading capital, the paid-up capital invested in Indian operated joint stock companies was of the order of Rs 63 crore in 1920, rising to about Rs 100 crore in 1925.[28] Although precise estimates of the growth of these accumulations are problematic, there seems to be a general consensus that the aggregate size of moneylending capital continued to increase.[29] The total sum which was invested by mahajans, sowcars, and shroffs in agricultural advances around 1930 was estimated by the Central Banking Enquiry Committee at roughly Rs 900 crore, of which at least Rs 400 crore was short-term seasonal loans for seed, cattle, and so on.[30]

However, the essence of colonial policy lay in preventing the large-scale development of industrial capital from these merchant and usurer accumulations. This was evident in the pursuit of fiscal and trade policies that were, in their most favourable interpretation, not conducive to encourage industrial ventures.[31] Industrial enterprises

27 Goswami (1985: 231) notes that '....Marwaris made fortunes by speculating on jute as well as on company shares. Ghanshyamdas Birla, Sarupchand Hukumchand, Kesoram Poddar, Mangiram Bangur, and Baldeodas Doodhwawalla made millions on the bullish stock market and on hedge transactions in raw jute and gunny and, in the process, multiplied the capital that was soon to be sunk into industries'. Unfortunately, he does not (again) follow on the implications of this application of speculative gains on industrial management.

28 See Shah and Khambata (1924) for the estimates of moneylending and trading capital; Venkatasubbiah (1940: 118) for the estimate of corporate capital.

29 Wadia and Merchant (1957: 270–82).

30 R.K. Ray (1988: 280).

31 This subject, of course, is at the very centre of controversy over Indian industrial performance in the colonial period of the twentieth century. Politically, it arose in the context of discussions at the sixth Congress of the Communist International (Comintern) in 1928, where the thesis of British decolonization as evidenced by Indian industrial growth, propounded by M.N. Roy, was challenged and outvoted. There are important documents related to this in Adhikari (1982: 455–606). The central texts pertaining to this are Bagchi (1972), Morris (1974), Morris (1982), Habib (1985), and Gupta (1987). This work is forthrightly based on an understanding that supports the broad Comintern/Bagchi/Habib/Gupta approach.

arose only in fields which had the fortuitous leeway created by the exigencies of the overall colonial balance of payments system, made evident by the growth of cotton and jute textiles and the subsequent concession to sugar manufacture.[32]

The first wave of entry into the industrial field outside of Bombay and Ahmedabad took place during this period, as mentioned earlier, broadly through two methods. The first, more noticed in existing literature, was the initiation of new industrial ventures; the second was through the purchase of significant blocks of shares in existing firms.[33] To repeat, the choice between these two paths of entry into the industrial sphere may have been part of alternative business strategies. Critically, however, they represented different historical paths of evolution of the capitals in question. The case of 'greenfield' ventures signified the initial stage of transformation of merchant/moneylending capital into industrial capital; the second, a market transaction by which ownership of preexisting industrial proprietary rights were acquired, implied a more speculative use of liquid capital, and not a transformative process, the hallmark of an industrial revolution.

Large volumes of futures trading and teji-mandi gambling went on in India in the interwar period.[34] During the Depression, as European control over the trade in agricultural commodities collapsed, bazaar speculation in the inland mandis increased enormously.[35] During

32 For jute, Tara Sethia (1996) has a systematic account of the international factors that provided a leeway for the growth of the industry in Bengal. In the case of cotton textiles, see Habib (1975) and Misra (1987). Levkovsky (1967: 273–83) discusses the considerations underlying the decision to grant tariff protection to the sugar industry.

33 Goswami (1989: 293). The theme of the decline of British managing agencies was earlier discussed by Tomlinson (1981) and, subsequently, by Misra (2000).

34 R.K. Ray (1988: 296).

35 The Government of India's response to the challenge of the Depression was an orthodox one, of retrenchment and extreme caution as far as any financial commitments were concerned. This approach would by itself have been enough to accentuate the effect of the Depression, but the government was obliged by its colonial obligations to adopt a deflationary policy to maintain rigidly a high rate of exchange of the rupee. Furthermore, the government appeared as a competitor in the Indian money market and raised large sums mainly in order to tide over its current financial difficulties and to repay old debts. It is important to note that the government did not raise loans for development projects in India, which could have helped to create employment and to prime the pump for future economic growth. See Ulyanovsky (1981); Rothermund (1992).

1932–3, more than 60 speculative produce exchanges were formed in the Punjab alone. Their main business was trading in wheat futures, with some marginal speculation in gram, barley, and rapeseed. By 1934, many of these badly organized produce exchanges had collapsed. The better organized exchanges in Bombay and Calcutta, though fewer in number, showed greater tenacity.[36]

It was not merely the supply lines of the international trading firms and the industrial managing agencies that the bazaar threatened by its rampant speculation. In active trade seasons or times of political uncertainty, violent fluctuations were caused in the market by futures and teji-mandi options. Such fluctuations, besides involving the speculators in losses, forced many consumers and shippers to withdraw from the market, so that peasants found their market options narrowing at such times.

During the Depression, imports and exports became even more marginal in the total production and distribution of agricultural produce in India (see Table 1.1).[37] Because the banks had few branches outside urban centres, the shroffs and arhatiyas necessarily financed the overwhelming part of inland trade.[38]

Table 1.1 Agricultural Exports as Percentage of Total Agricultural Production

Crop	1900–1901 to 1904–1905	1910–1911 to 1914–1915	1920–1921 to 1924–1925	1930–1931 to 1934–1935
Rice	9.2 (100)	7.1 (132)	5.9 (143)	6.2 (146)
Wheat	11.2 (100)	12.4 (126)	5.0 (117)	0.5 (122)
Raw Cotton	50.5 (100)	56.8 (136)	63.6 (152)	61.4 (149)
Raw Jute	53.1 (100)	44.4 (129)	50.6 (90)	45.4 (114)

Source: Venkatasubbiah (1940) Table III, p. 82 for index of production and Table IV, p. 83 for percentage of exports.

Notes: (1) Figures in brackets refer to total production with quinquennium 1900–1 to 1904–5 as base 100. (2) For groundnut, the quinquennium 1905–6 to 1909–10 as base 100.

36 R.K. Ray (1988: 297).

37 An observation based on the reports for rice, wheat, and linseed in *Agricultural Marketing in India*, Marketing Series, published by the Agricultural Marketing Adviser to the Government of India (R.K. Ray 1988: 272).

38 Even in the case of large urban areas, in 1928–9 it was estimated that of the total capital invested in trade in Madurai of Rs 140 lakh, Rs 94 lakh was provided by indigenous bankers and the balance by the organized banking sector (Baker 1984: 289).

It was with some reason that the Bombay Shroffs' Association asserted that the total turnover of cash during a working day in their Bombay exchange far exceeded the corresponding figures of all local banks taken together.

The Depression hit at the foundations of the widespread inland buying organizations of the international export houses. As exports fell, costs had to be reduced. Consequently, most of the inland procuring organizations were closed: direct sub-agency buying in small lots from producers who were represented by smaller commission agents (*kutcha* arhatiyas) was no longer profitable. The volume of direct small-unit purchases, which had formed a large portion of the total purchases in the 1920s, fell to insignificant proportions in the 1930s and were practically replaced by 'port pass contracts' with big commission agents (pucca arhatiyas) acting as guarantee brokers.[39] This alternative method of purchase, which had been less in vogue in the pre-war and early post-war years, regained ground in the 1930s. The commission agents guaranteed at a pre-arranged rate of commission the fulfilment of all contracts made by the mandi merchants to the export houses. The big arhatiyas were keen enough to win the valuable position of *guarantee brokers* by putting in a substantial security deposit. This financial and marketing network, tied at two ends to Bombay and Calcutta, emerged from the Depression more closely intermeshed than ever. It consisted of twelve money exchanges and 1,718 produce markets, all linked to each other by daily transactions operating through the telegraph, each pulling into its orbit the local rural economies of its hinterland, linking them by its wide-ranging hundi and arhat operations to the European banks and firms at the ports.[40] It was on this basis that the bazaar operators gradually asserted themselves in the sphere of the central money market which controlled India's international economy.

Indian merchants suffered, too, as the total volume of domestic trade declined perceptibly in the 1930s. But they were willing to continue trading within the contracting domestic market at far lower

---

39 Under the port pass contract, the mandi-based merchant received an advance of 80 to 90 per cent of the value of the consignment railed by him to the shipper. In return he undertook to accept, without question, the shippers' analysis and weighing of the produce at the port of loading. After analysing the quality of the produce and weighing it with his own weights, the shipper paid the balance of the value of the consignment with such deduction as he thought fit (R.K. Ray 1988: 287).

40 R.K. Ray (1988: 267).

profit margins than the export houses with their reduced international operations were prepared for.[41] Furthermore, Indian merchants had the means of reducing their losses, at a time when the domestic prices of industrial products were holding up better, through diverting part of their resources to the urban sector, including a certain amount of industrial investment.[42] In the 1930s, there was thus a second wave of industrial entry, strengthened by the concessions given by the colonial government to the sugar industry.[43]

The growth of industrial firms during the post-Depression phase has been noted and explained as the movement of capital from the agrarian to the industrial spheres as a result of declining returns to agriculture. What has not been equally noted is that this did not necessarily imply the initiation of an organic cycle, whereby the reinvestment of surplus generated through industrial production, within the sphere of industry itself, became the preferred avenue for accumulation.[44] In the case of the light industries which depended on agricultural raw materials, cotton and jute textiles and sugar, many of the new entrants into industry were drawn from the intermediary/moneylending groups who had traditionally dealt in those very agricultural raw materials.[45] Despite their new industrial investments, they continued to operate in their earlier activities of speculation, moneylending, and trade by diverting part of the industrial surplus.[46]

41 Parry's withdrew because they found the groundnut market speculative to a degree that made it difficult to compete in international markets (Brown 1954: 235–6).

42 Baker (1984: 309–18) discusses the situation in detail with respect to the Madras Presidency.

43 Levkovsky (1966: 273–83) describes, at some length, the considerations that lay behind the tariff concessions granted to the sugar industry. See also Amin (1981) and Baru (1983).

44 As late as 1954, an official survey (Reserve Bank of India 1954) demonstrated the same phenomenon of flows of urban industrial surpluses into the rural moneylending sphere, first noticed by the Central Banking Enquiry Committee in the 1930s. See Bettelheim (1971: 74–9).

45 In the case of sugar in 1932, virtually the entire cane crushing capacities of Indian operated mills was owned by Marwari and Bania groups known to be engaged in speculative agriculture-related trades (Baru 1983: Table 1).

46 This is exemplified by an official account of the opaque origins of the Dalmia-Jain Group. According to this version,

the Dalmias had an unpretentious beginning, and it was only in 1932 that they came into the lime-light, by starting the South Bihar Sugar Mills with *borrowed capital*.

As the export houses began to withdraw their agencies from the inland mandis during the Depression, and domestic trading came to represent practically the entire trade of India, the bazaar established an independent command over the Indian economy. Not only did it occupy the void created by the withdrawal of Ralli and Volkart to the ports, it also penetrated deeper into mandi operations to compensate for the falling profits from trade. A series of investigations by the Punjab Board of Economic Enquiry into wheat marketing in the nine mandis of Lyallpur, Ferozepore, and Attock districts showed that the arhatiyas were now buying between 66 to 77 per cent of their wheat purchases directly from the peasants. Direct dealings between the peasants and the commission agents had been pushed up by the Depression, which had largely eliminated the small trader who had hitherto mediated between the mandi and the peasant producer.[47] At the same time, the organized modern business sector had been compelled to withdraw from the mandis. In the nine mandis surveyed, there were 438 arhatiyas, 25 European firms, and 12 flour mills amongst the large buyers.[48]

When the Indian economy emerged from the Depression and commercial activity once again entered into an upswing, merging with the speculative boom of the Second World War, there was a clear divergence in the role of international firms in the trade in wheat and groundnuts. While the withdrawal from the wheat mandis became a permanent feature with the practical extinction of the export market (Table 1.1), in groundnuts the export firms, though reduced in number, also tightened their hold on the market. They too bypassed

Their income tax record for the period 1932–39 did not even suggest that they were possessed of big capital; in fact, their assets fell far short of their liabilities during that period. It was asserted by Mr Ram Krishna Dalmia that in 1935, he made a huge profit of some 50 lakhs in speculation in silver, done through Shanghai in London, but he could not produce any documentary evidence in support of his statement. According to Mr Dalmia these profits were gradually invested in shares. Thus by 1939, they acquired controlling interest in twelve concerns, the share capital of which was nearly Rs 393 lakhs. [Emphasis mine] (JN Papers, File no. 81, p. 260, para 2 of 'Gist of the Report by the Income Tax Investigation Commission on the Dalmia Group of Cases' enclosure to letter no. 640-PSF/51, 20 April 1951 from C.D. Deshmukh, finance minister, to Jawaharlal Nehru.)

47 The position of the smaller landlord and the village money lender is described in Baker (1984: 251).

48 R.K. Ray (1988: 289).

the mandis, buying directly through their agents and transporting the produce to the ports.

The market network in India had thus achieved a fuller articulation, exhibiting in clear outlines the shape of a pyramid. The knitting together of financial and commercial transactions at the higher levels of the network had created a national market in which indigenous capital was the integrating factor. At the base of the pyramid were the weekly or biweekly markets and seasonal fairs dispersed over the countryside and serving the peasant population. There were in all 1,733 main fairs, about half of which assembled annually along a strip of plain stretching from central Punjab to north Bengal along the Gangetic valley, and 22,080 shandies, haats, and painths, which dotted the countryside at intervals of 6 miles or so from one another. At the middle tier of the structure, there were 1,718 mandis, among which closer relations had been established by constant movements of goods and credit. These regularized interchanges, that were made possible by the hundi facilities provided by Bombay, Calcutta, and ten other exchanges on the coast and inland, had integrated the commercial economy of the country.[49]

Thus, the large volume of internal trade in the country became substantially independent of foreign capital. Added to the colonial constraints on investment in industrial activities were the high returns from agrarian moneylending which made the movement of liquid resources, even from industrial surpluses, into the urban money market and, ultimately, into rural moneylending entirely a logical use of funds.[50] Thus, by the time of the Second World War, there was

49 R.K. Ray (1988: 289–90).

50 'Another far-reaching abuse of the system was the practice of managing agents taking huge loans or advances from the companies they managed. The allegation that many managing agents took such loans or advances was hotly denied by the Bombay and Ahmedabad Millowners' Associations before the Indian Tariff Board Cotton Textile Industry Enquiry of 1932, but the Bombay Shareholders' Association proved in 1935, with the help of facts and figures, that the evil existed. Nor was this evil confined to the cotton textile industry' (Das 1956: 87).

Earlier, Jain (1929: 46–9) had noted that indigenous banking was combined with industrial operations such as the operation of sugar and flour mills, and glass factories in the United Provinces, Central Provinces, and Delhi; in Bombay Presidency and the Central Provinces, indigenous banking was combined with trading in cotton and in speculating in produce and share markets.

not only a greatly strengthened presence of industrial capital, but also the simultaneous presence of money capital *within* the same blocs of capital.[51]

DEPRECIATION FUNDS: THE MARKER OF INDUSTRIAL CAPITAL

The characteristic feature of the financial management of companies which marked the disconnection between the imperatives of industrial evolution and the attitudes of their proto-industrial capitalist controllers was a disregard of the necessity of accumulating reserves for industrial modernization. In the 1920s, the Tariff Board noted that the Bombay textile industry did not adhere even to the minimum allocation for depreciation that was permitted as per the norms laid down by the Income Tax Department.[52] Their aggregate reserve accumulation was about 73 per cent of the expectations based on these conservative norms (which made no allowance for technological obsolescence or for price rises), the remainder being dissipated through dividends.[53] In Ahmedabad, the other major centre of the textile industry, there was a similar nonchalance about provisioning for maintenance and modernization.[54]

When these facts are counterpoised with the average dividend paid, the scene is of a situation where post-World War I, industrial growth, measured in terms of increases in looms and spindles, is accompanied by degradation of existing industrial assets through the squeezing of their value by excessive dividend disbursements. This led to a situation where twenty years later, in 1944, the *Eastern Economist*

---

51 The number of joint-stock companies registered in India and at work increased from 4,708 in 1921 to 11,114 in 1939 and the paid-up capital from Rs 164.5 crore in 1921 to Rs 290.4 crore in 1939. However, these figures included banking, loan and insurance companies, trading companies, and land and building companies. If the figures for these are excluded, the increase in specifically industrial enterprises is from 1,701 companies with a paid-up capital of Rs 76.1 crore in 1921 to only 3,278 companies with a paid-up capital of Rs 154.7 crore in 1939 (Das 1956: 6, fn 1).

52 This was at the rate of 2.5 per cent of the value of buildings, 5 per cent of the value of spinning and weaving machinery, and 7.5 per cent on bleaching and dying machinery and electrical equipment per year (Samant and Mulky 1937: 158).

53 Samant and Mulky (1937: 158).

54 Samant and Mulky (1937: 149).

could report that 11.5 per cent of the blow room equipment used in cotton textile mills was installed before 1890, 11.1 per cent between 1906–10, 18.6 per cent between 1921–5, and 11.4 per cent between 1936–40. Similarly, 35.5 per cent of the draw and speed frames were laid out before 1910.[55]

In addition to this, there were typically fraudulent practices evidenced by the admission that, in actual fact, no resources were actually allocated for depreciation reserves, that is, it was a paper exercise for tax purposes.[56] Of equal significance was the stated position, of both the Bombay and Ahmedabad Millowners Association, that it was financially impossible for the industry to allocate funds to depreciation reserves at rates higher than prescribed by Tax Laws. That these statements were made following the high dividend payments that characterized the post-World War I period indicates the prevailing management philosophy. There was a similar situation in the paper and coal mining industries.[57]

Compounding these predilections were the effects of the practice of payment of commissions to managing agencies on the basis of profits earned by the enterprises controlled by them. This, when combined with the ways in which permissible expenses were deductible, created a favourable atmosphere for financial manipulation. Thus, while depreciation charges were included in the estimate of profit on which commission was paid, allocations for maintenance and repair were subtracted from the profit. The managing agencies would, therefore, instruct their accountants to transfer these allocations to the depreciation account, thereby increasing their commissions. This led to situations where the company was incapacitated from making adequate provision for maintenance, let alone long-term modernization.[58]

55 *Eastern Economist*, 7 July 1944, quoted in Palme Dutt (1970: 174).

56 Oral evidence given to Tariff Board on Cotton Textile Industry, cited in Samant and Mulky (1937: 166).

57 An observation based on the Tariff Board enquiries into the paper industry and evidence by the Bengal National Chamber of Commerce before the Central Banking Enquiry Committee (Samant and Mulky 1937: 160–1).

58 Twenty-five years later, in 1953, despite the growth of industry during the Second World War, capitalist comprehension of the link between allowing for adequate depreciation and modernization, that is, the future of an industrial unit, were as little in evidence. See Kapoor (1953).

INCUBATION PROCESSES IN MANAGING AGENCIES

This widely prevalent management philosophy, though stemming from the merchant/moneylending–generated attitude of the capitalists, whose origins were outlined earlier, was given free reign by the managing agency system. This institution, whose origins have been traced to the 1830s, predated the first Companies Act in the 1850s.[59]

Following the passage of the English Companies Act of 1844, an act for the registration of joint-stock companies was enacted in India in 1850.Under this act every partnership in which the shares were transferable without the consent of all the partners became entitled to registration as a company, although limited liability was not conferred on the members. Another act was passed in 1857 for the incorporation and regulation of joint-stock companies with limited liability of the members. It was not until 1866, however, that a comprehensive act was passed affirming the principle that no member of a joint-stock association should be liable for more than the unpaid portion of his share. Between 1882 and 1913, five amending acts were passed in India, but these related to minor amendments only. Finally, in 1913, a comprehensive act was passed, following the English Companies (Consolidation) Act of 1908.

Critically, even after successive revisions to the Companies Act in 1882 and 1913, there was no clause introduced to allow even legal recognition of the managing agencies. Managing agencies have, of course, been much discussed in the literature.[60] However, the operational significance of the system for the colonial economy has been little noticed.[61] Its function was to provide the channel for British capital flow into India; however, its crucial *structural* purpose was to provide the institutional channel by which the commodity and capital markets

---

59 Rungta (1962).

60 Lokanathan (1935), Basu (1958), National Council of Applied Economic Research (1959), Goel (1961), Kling (1966), India (1966). Chapman (1985) introduced the concept of 'investment group' to describe the structural role of the managing agencies in the colonial system. However, in his attempt to use this concept to cover *all* British overseas investment, he overlooked the specific nature of the economic relationship between Britain and India; critiques of Chapman's approach are in Vicat Turrell and Van-Helten (1987), in Jones and Wale (1998), and the response in Chapman (1987). However, these do not take us forward theoretically.

61 McQueen (2008).

in the city of London could exert direct influence on the Indian economy.[62] This was achieved by permitting the managing agency to superimpose on the companies within its ambit untrammeled power to direct all managerial functions.[63] The contract between an agency and the managed system could only be challenged when the terms of the contract itself were infringed. As the contract was framed in such a way to preclude any normative evaluation, there was effectively no recourse for the company's shareholders at all. Up to 1913, there was no requirement for a company even to have a board of directors, let alone a board able to act effectively as the representative of the shareholders, and assert the claims of the company, when the managing agents attempted to use their position to the detriment of the company.

The Act of 1913 had not taken into account this system which was in vogue in India but unknown in England—company management through managing agents. Indian company law had followed the English law closely and remained silent about this important economic institution in India. The result was that unscrupulous persons had begun to take advantage of the loopholes and omissions in the law, and abuses and malpractices by some managing agents had become a common phenomenon.

Senior British officials in the colonial Indian government were fully aware of the manipulations possible under the unregulated managing agency system. Thus, the then secretary of the commerce and industry department wrote in 1913:

> It is possible, and not uncommon, that the managing agents, as a firm, should buy a very large quantity of jute, cotton, coal or other such commodity without indicating, at the time the transaction is completed, whether they purchased for their firm or for one or more of the companies for which the firm acts as Managing Agents. Hence it may occur that, after making

---

62 Visible evidence of this occurred, apart from the instance discussed in the text later, around 1910, when James Mackay, chairperson of the Binny Managing Agency in the Madras Presidency prevailed on the secretary of state for India to order an end to the Madras Government's efforts to develop, amongst other handicrafts, the handloom industry. See Dewey (1979: 225–6). It is also significant that the Swiss Volkart and the Greek Ralli firms operated through the London money market (R.K. Ray 1988: 285).

63 For 'biographical' accounts illustrating this aspect, refer to the case of the Finlay Group in Jones and Wale (1998) and of the Bird Heilger Group in Tomlinson (1981).

a large purchase of this description, if the market becomes unfavourable, the Managing Agents are tempted to represent the transaction as effected on behalf of one of the managed companies while, similarly, if the market improves there is nothing to prevent them treating the transaction as the property of the firm, and thus become entitled to the profit.[64]

Thus, he concluded,

> to pass a Bill [the 1913 Companies Act] regulating the constitution and management of companies in India and to fail to deal with the notorious irregularities of the Managing Agent system would surely be to lay the Government open to serious criticism. It has to be recognised that English Company Law when imported into this country requires special modifications if it is to deal with conditions which do not exist in England.

Clearly, if legislation continued to bypass such obvious grounds for abuse which had been noted in writing at the highest levels of the government, the managing agency system must have had, as noted earlier, crucial importance for the colonial system.

This was made evident from the exchanges following a question raised by a retired Indian Civil Service official, John Rees, in the House of Commons in June 1913.[65] Rees drew the attention of the British Government to the bill to amend the Indian Companies Act, 1913, which had been introduced into the Legislative Council of the governor-general. Not only did this bill concern the interests of British business firms, but certain provisions of the bill, he asserted, particularly those relating to the appointment of directors, would also injure British interests, both in India and in Britain. In response, the secretary of state for India, Edwin Montagu, reassured the MP that the bill had not been introduced into the Indian Legislative Council and would not, in fact, be considered until the end of the year. In any case, he said reassuringly, publication of the draft bill would give British firms whose interests might be affected an opportunity of studying its provisions and of representing their views to the Government of India. When pressed, he also agreed to forward to the Government of India any representation submitted to him.

64   Enthoven (1913).
65   Great Britain (1913).

In 1913, the main issue was the board of directors, until then not required at all by English Company Law—usually the model for Indian legislation. Not only were British interests opposed to any change in the law, but the Indian Merchants Chamber and the Bombay Mill-lowners' Association supported them in this position.[66] Evidently, though introduced as a device permitting imperial aggrandizement, Indian businessmen, too, reveled in the complete absence of legislative supervision that the managing agency system allowed. It was left to Ibrahim Rahimtullah, the then member of the Central Legislative Council and future chairperson of the Fiscal Commission, to argue the case for a provision requiring that the majority of the members of the board of directors of a company should be accountable to shareholders. Such a step, which would have prevented gross forms of misuse of industrial assets for speculative, unconnected trading purposes or their diversion into the rural moneylending markets, would have been an important step towards the industrial transformation of money accumulations. However, the odds against such a proposal (opposed by British and Indian capitalists for quite separate reasons) were overwhelming at the time.[67]

After the First World War, malpractices indulged in by a number of managing agencies, which resulted in the collapse of several companies, created so much public resentment that a move for the abolition of the system gained momentum. From the 1920s, an opposing force of organized shareholders' movements arose.[68] Although the shareholders movement began in 1921 in Calcutta, the Bombay Shareholders' Association, founded in 1928, was the most organized.[69] This public opposition was accompanied by acknowledgement of its existence voiced in official reports, notably by the Tariff Board on

66 Sen (1966: 101–2).

67 Sen (1966: 103). See, also, Anstey (1942), Appendix E, 'The Legal Position of Managing Agents'.

68 The stock exchanges in India were unregulated until 1925 when the Bombay Securities Contracts Act was passed. Generally, the functioning of the exchanges remained as opaque as the functioning of companies themselves in the entire period leading to the passage of the Securities Contracts (Regulations) Act, 1956. There are important details of the functioning of the exchanges in the reports of three committees: Bombay (1924, 1937) and India (1948).

69 The association was formed under the chairpersonship of Ibrahim Rahimtulla, who had chaired the Fiscal Commission of 1921–2 (India 1960a).

the textile industry.[70] Common to these criticisms was a demand for greater transparency in the reporting of the performance of individual companies and the removal of managing agencies, or at least a considerable reduction in their power so that a company would be truly under the control of the board of directors. The Bombay Shareholders' Association, in particular, put forward cogent arguments in favour of abolition.[71] However, the government decided in favour of retaining the fiction of shareholder regulation.

Agitation for removing the defects of the Indian Act escalated after 1930, and in September 1934, the Government of India placed a lawyer with experience in the administration of company law on special duty to examine the materials collected and to make proposals for the amendment of the Indian law. This lawyer's report was published in January 1935.

In the run-up to the proposal to amend the Companies Act in 1936, the Bombay Shareholders' Association presented a detailed memorandum on the proposals.[72] They were a sufficiently organized force and not only did their memorandum gain wide publicity, but also their representative was actually invited to a round table chaired by a member of the Viceroy's Council. At this meeting, where the viewpoints expressed otherwise were those of large British and Indian capital, the procedure adopted was of accepting or rejecting amendments by voting. On many clauses both big Indian and British capital were opposed to the measures suggested by the Shareholder's Association. On issues of the power of managing agencies, both British and Indian agencies were united in opposition.[73] Within the Central Legislative Assembly, where the bill was debated, while there was a recognition that corporate behaviour had been such as to cause a serious loss of confidence in the managing agency system, there was a simultaneous disapproval of the government taking any effective steps to change the situation.[74] The Companies Act was merely modified to ensure

70 Although in 1927 the Tariff Board, India (1927: 85–90) remained agnostic, by 1932 the tone was more sharply critical and the need for legislative changes in company law was explicitly mentioned (India 1932: 77–93).

71 Bombay Shareholders' Association (1934).

72 Bombay Shareholders' Association (1936).

73 India (1936).

74 India (1960b).

that in future, the appointment of a managing agent could only be made after the shareholders had passed a resolution at a general body meeting. The revisions of the 1913 act, passed in 1936, thus, recognized and regularized the system without imposing any substantive regulation.[75]

There was, thus, not only an organic relationship between the overarching powers of the managing agents over companies in diverse areas, and the varied sphere of operation of the merchant/money-lending/industrial capitals, but the untrammeled powers provided to the agencies also gave scope for the grey areas of operation that underlay the trade and moneylending routes to vast accumulations of liquid capital. Rather than regulating these activities so as to channel the capital increasingly towards industrial investment, company law remained under the thrall of the managing agency system.

A later commentator referred to a view prevalent amongst advocates of State regulation '...which is difficult to shake off from one's mind, viz., that businessmen or, for that matter, any set of men can be made honest by force of statute'.[76] While this proposition may be debatable, there is little doubt that the Government of India, by acceding to influential lobbies, both British and Indian, adopted a cavalier approach to regulating corporate business practices in the entire period leading up to Independence. And it was the legacy of this nonchalance that the government of independent India had to address with a clear recognition of the scope of the problem, if not of its root causes, that the then minister of state for finance expressed in Parliament in 1951.

75 Das (1938: 94–6) has a detailed account of the progress of the 1936 Amendment Bill.
76 Das (1956: 95).

CHAPTER TWO

Inculcating Corporate Responsibility

The Bombay Plan as Social Engineering

FURTHER MONEY ACCUMULATIONS DURING THE SECOND WORLD WAR

There were three striking features of the development of the wartime economic situation in India: the first was the government's indifference to the profits accumulated through industrial, trading, and speculative activities; second, there was a fresh display of hostility to the use of these accumulations in further industrial investment, even if this could aid the munitions effort.[1] Finally, as a corollary to the first, was the government's unwillingness to take steps to safeguard the living standards of the civilian population.

During the early war years, the government evidently believed that India would remain safely distant from the then European-based theatres of hostilities. Thus, under the impression that the demands on its physical and financial resources would not lead to an inflationary situation, it made no effort either to obtain adequate knowledge of wartime economic controls in other countries, or to evolve suitable procedures of its own. Regulation of the wartime economy, therefore,

---

1 As mentioned in the Introduction, the Roger Mission, which visited New Delhi in October 1940 and a`.ended the meeting of the Eastern Group Supply Council with the purpose of strengthening war supplies from the countries of the British Empire, could do little to ensure that Indian industry played an effective role.

proceeded with the adoption of ad hoc controls to meet pressing needs and these were extended as new emergencies arose.[2]

To the unpreparedness of the government to institute controls, and the haste with which these had then to be introduced, was added the inability of the government to take a firm stand against propertied interests. This factor affected its response to the ever rising price levels of both agricultural and industrial products. In the case of agricultural prices, the central government encountered provincial opposition: governments of provinces with surplus agricultural produce, like that of Punjab could not, on political grounds, be forced to moderate the demands of their producers. In consequence, prices and procurement operations affecting a basic commodity—food grain—remained uncontrolled. Similarly, the central government was equally unable to resist pressure from business interests in controlling industrial prices.[3] Until 1942, it did not contemplate controlling the prices of even the most important commodities for civilian needs. The prices of cloth or coal were controlled for government orders and were fixed at what the government considered to be a reasonable level.[4] Prices of all commodities in the civilian market, however, were allowed to rise without limit.[5]

Only when the inflation grew to such proportions that it threatened to obstruct the war effort itself did the government introduce control of civilian prices. The prices of cloth rose to more than five times the pre-war levels before the government intervened, and when intervention came, it was only on terms which assured the industrialists' cooperation.[6] Cloth prices were, for example, put under the control of a subcommittee of the Textile Control Board, the overwhelming

2 Desai (1970) describes the ad hoc accretions to import-control procedures, starting from 1939.

3 Kamtekar (2002: 201–4).

4 By the end of 1942, the government's Supply Department was procuring 35 per cent of textile production for official use (Grajdanzev 1943: 196, fn 18).

5 Gadgil (1949: 115–16).

6 '[In the area of cloth control] the ordinary government official) was not particularly successful. That he should seek non-official co-operation was undoubtedly desirable but that he should seek it, and seek it almost exclusively, from the parties most intimately concerned and should establish them in the position of arbiters in their own cases was an error of the first magnitude. The initial mistake vitiated the whole control' (Gorwala 1952: 17).

majority of whose members were manufacturers. Subsequently, there was some decrease in prices but it was still far from sufficient. An article in the *Times of India* stated that 'The present reduction of about thirty per cent in the peak level of [textile] prices is not enough, and a further reduction is absolutely essential in the interests of consumers, at least to the level of between 250 and 300 per cent of the pre-war level'. According to the *Vanguard*, 'No doubt the upward trend of cloth prices has been checked. A small reduction in prices is also secured. But in view of the four to five hundred per cent rise which had taken place the small reduction of thirty to forty per cent is hardly any help to the consumers'.[7]

A rise in prices to five times the pre-war level would suggest that the profits of the mill owners would be enormous. Two-thirds of these profits should have been absorbed by the excess profits tax yet the receipts from tax collections, not only from the textile industry but also from all industries and trades, were small.[8] On the basis that at least 80 per cent of the total proceeds of the tax was realized from the cotton textile industry, tax collections in 1943–4 amounted to Rs 62.25 crore (as compared to the expected Rs 40 crore) and the expected yield of the tax in 1944–5 was Rs 78 crore.[9] With the rate of excess profits tax set at 66.67 per cent, this implied that the profits in excess of the base-line pre-war levels were about Rs 93 crore in 1943–4 and were expected to reach Rs 117 crore in 1944–5. This may be compared to figures from a rough calculation on costs and sales price increases in textiles from the pre-war years. While the average price of one yard of cotton goods in 1939–40 was 4 annas (Rs 0.25), by the middle of 1943, the prices of cloth were four and even five times as much. By June 1944, they were reduced in the open market to a level three times that of 1938–9, while in the black market, they were sold at prices which were 50–60 per cent over the controlled prices. In the meantime the

---

7 Quotations from *Times of India*, 15 March 1944, and *Vanguard*, 15 April 1944, from Grajdanzev (1944: 464).

8 The Excess Profits Tax Act (No. 15 of 1940) imposed a levy on 'excess profits', that is, those over and above 'standard profits', either profits earned during a 'standard period' in the past (the assessee could choose any one of five such periods) or, where computation of such profits was impossible, a percentage on the capital (Cornelius and Wickenden 1943).

9 Grajdanzev (1944: 465).

costs of production had risen to roughly two and a half times the pre-war cost.[10] According to a contemporary observer, this suggested that the excess profits in the textile industry alone should have been above Rs 300 crore in 1943, and above Rs 200 crore in 1944.[11] These calculations provide an order of magnitude of the degree of undeclared profits, about Rs 100 crore in both years.

According to the chairperson of the Textile Control Board, Bengal was being supplied more cloth than any other province in the country. He expressed surprise at the campaign led by some newspapers in Bengal which asserted that Bengal was not getting enough cloth. In fact, he declared that Bengal was supplied 12 yards per head per annum. After asking rhetorically that if, indeed, this was the situation, then where the cloth supplies were, he concluded, 'The answer is simple, they melt into thin air—they disappear from the market the moment they arrive.'[12] It was also reported that 'under the Hoarding and Profiteering Prevention Ordinance prices of a number of articles in common use have so far been fixed and the upward trend of prices in the civilian market has been arrested.... Experience, however, has shown that with the control of prices of a particular commodity its available supplies have a tendency to go underground'.[13]

Other newspapers carried items like this: 'The Government cancelled sixty licenses of the prominent dealers in cotton textiles, freezing thereby the huge stocks held by them and by four textile factories in Bombay, Ahmedabad and Coimbatore after surprise raids on secret cloth go-downs' or 'Delhi: It is learnt that 1,860 cotton cloth bales worth about Rs 3,500,000 have been exported by rail between July 1 and 15, in contravention of the Government's order'.[14] They mentioned the discovery of unstamped cloth, surreptitious dealings in yarn and cloth, hoarding, and so on. The textile commissioner was invested with fresh powers for compelling declaration of stocks, for

10 According to the statement of the Textile Commissioner, Government of India, reported in the *Times of India*, 26 June 1944, quoted in Grajdanzev (1944: 465).

11 Grajdanzev (1944: 465). Though the methodology used for this rough and ready calculation is not clear, it does provide an indication of the order of undeclared profits.

12 *Dawn*, 16 July 1944, quoted in Grajdanzev (1944: 467).

13 A press note quoted in *Dawn*, 16 July 1944, from Grajdanzev (1944: 467).

14 *Vanguard*, 1 June 1944, and *Dawn*, 23 July 1944, quoted in Grajdanzev (1944: 467).

freezing stocks, for inspecting account books, for regulating stocks. But the temptation to get extraordinarily high profits was so great, that goods, instead of reaching the consumer at prescribed prices would just 'melt into thin air'.[15]

Consumer access to many other consumer goods passed through the same phases that cotton textiles had—a fantastic rise in prices, government regulation, some fall in official prices, and the appearance of the black market. In July 1944, an order for the display of maximum retail prices for shoes was issued by the government. However, press reports expressed the fear that the result of this regulation would lead to the disappearance of goods from the open market, and because of the same loopholes in the control procedures, shoes would follow textile goods into the black market.[16]

The prices of coal were similarly fixed in consultation with an advisory board whose membership consisted chiefly of producers. There was no attempt to fix price levels in the light of any objective considerations such as those of costs or profits. All prices were negotiated prices, that is, prices which industrialists were not reluctant to accept. The fixing of industrial and agricultural prices in wartime India thus offered a sharp contrast to the work of the Canadian Wartime Prices Board, the Ministry of Supply, and other control agencies in the United Kingdom, or the Office of Price Administration in the United States.[17]

Early in 1942, the United States government sent a special technical mission to India under Dr Henry Grady to investigate how India could become completely a supply base for the Eastern front. The full report of the mission was never published, but in the press it was reported that the mission's general impression appeared to be that India's industrial centres were still working on a peacetime basis and there was great scope for expansion. With proper planning, rationalization, and the use of equipment from America, India's production could be increased by 200 to 250 per cent.[18] In the following month, a summary of the preliminary recommendations of the mission included the following passage:

15 Grajdanzev (1944: 466–7).
16 Grajdanzev(1944: 468).
17 Gadgil (1949: 116).
18 *Capital*, 21 May 1942, quoted in Grajdanzev (1943: 190).

Assessing the possibility of increasing output, the Mission recognizes at the outset that most of India's engineering workshops are ... jobbing shops, by which they mean establishments existing in order to maintain other plants in repair.... To remedy this ... it is necessary to provide new equipment, to transfer equipment from one shop to another and rearrange equipment within existing shops. Another recommendation is the institution [in the words of the Report of the Mission] of 'high-powered controls, independent of established government agencies, on the American model'.... Specifically it advises further investigations into the possibility of producing power alcohol; measures to extend the availability of electric power and to rationalize its use; the expansion of the steel industry; the rationalization of plants producing munitions; concentration in respect of aircraft and ships upon repairs rather than new construction; greater production of aluminium; the conservation of tin and rubber; and acceleration of the production of refined sulphur.[19]

However, in November amidst rumours that the report of the mission was shelved, the viceroy referred to this question:

We welcomed during this year the visit of the American Technical Mission, which was a very useful stimulant and most helpful to us in every way. The far-reaching scheme of industrial expansions recommended by the Mission would, if accepted in full, have involved the earliest supply to India by the United States of large quantities of materials and equipment and of large numbers of technical personnel. The United States Government has found it impossible to implement this program in full in present conditions. But they have generously offered to consider any projects which are essential for the war effort and to which the Government of India attaches particular importance—and we are already receiving very significant assistance from the United States in the form of materials, machinery, and plants. [20]

Thus, from the 'far-reaching scheme' of general industrial expansion, the Government of India turned to the piecemeal expansion of plants mostly needed in particular fields, and some of the blame for the inability to adopt the mission's proposals was put on the United States. The Indian press reacted differently:

19 *Capital*, 11 June 1942, quoted in Grajdanzev (1943: 191).

20 In a speech before the Chamber of Commerce and Industry in Calcutta on 17 December 1942, quoted in Grajdanzev (1943: 191).

But the fact remains that powerful interests also are operating abroad for the purpose of throttling further industrialization of this country, so that in the postwar world there would not be any dangerous competition to the West from the East.... The Indian business community has long been demanding the immediate publication of all the recommendations of the Grady Mission Report, a request which has not been conceded by the authorities on account of military or strategic reasons. But the Indian demand is based on some sort of a suspicion that the Government of India does not possess initiative but also finds its hands tied up from London. [Shelving of this report] is bound to create further misapprehensions.[21]

To seek advice on industrial policy, in November 1942 the Government of India created three panels of industrialists at Bombay, Calcutta, and Madras. According to an announcement, the

government would advise ... [potential industrial suppliers] ... of their possible requirements or future demands, and the panels, in their turn, would tell the government which of the existing plants could be expanded or where new plants could be directed and which firms were interested in taking up new projects. On receiving this information, the government would negotiate with the firms concerned.... The industry would put up the capital, but the government would take full responsibility in arranging for the imports of plants from abroad and for priorities and shipping.[22]

Thus, instead of a plan of government-sponsored general industrial expansion, the government turned to private initiative. But when faced with a necessarily temporary opportunity for expansion, industrialists, not satisfied with wartime profits (which in India were taxed very mildly as compared with Great Britain), wanted guarantees for the post-war period.[23]

In December 1942, it was reported that standard cloth suitable for the use of the poor and the urban lower middle class was to be made available within three months throughout the country at a uniform price. The cotton textile industry was to execute the initial

---

21 *Commerce*, Bombay, 28 November 1942, quoted in Grajdanzev (1943: 191).

22 *Times of India*, 30 November 1942, quoted in Grajdanzev (1943: 192).

23 For example, 'the glass industry in the Deccan pleads for protection during the postwar period in view of the additional investment that it would have to make to meet the demand of the central government for war purposes' (*Times of India*, 12 December 1942, quoted in Grajdanzev 1943: 192).

order placed by the Government of India on behalf of certain provinces and Indian states for 15 million yards to meet the immediate requirements of the rural population in the provinces.[24] However, as the annual per capita consumption of cotton piece goods in India was between 10 and 15 yards, the 15 million yards ordered by the government would have satisfied the demand of only 1 to 1.5 million persons.[25]

Apart from military demands, export possibilities and the rising purchasing power of some groups of the population attracted the attention of textile manufacturers away from the production of standard cloth for the poor. Standard cloth, thus, became either unavailable or available only at extremely high prices. While millowners offered to devote 5 per cent of their capacity to the production of standard cloth, this was in a situation where total cloth production for 1942 was expected to be 30 to 35 per cent below the average, supposedly because of labour problems which were left unspecified.[26]

THE RESPONSE FROM THE CAPTAINS OF INDUSTRY

It was in the context of the evidence of substantial accumulations of capital during the early stages of the war, and the government's disregard of the political and social implications of unethical business behaviour, that the initiative to formulate the Bombay Plan arose. The report of the planners was published in two parts: Part I, published in early 1944, dealt with the economic and financial aspects of the plan;[27] Part II, which appeared at the end of 1944, was concerned with the issues of distribution and with State intervention in more general terms. It is the second part which is of interest here.

24 *Times of India*, 11 December 1942, quoted in Grajdanzev (1943: 197).

25 Grajdanzev (1943: 197).

26 *Foreign Commerce Weekly*, 14 November 1942, quoted in Grajdanzev (1943: 196, fn 17).

27 Contemporary academic commentaries are available in Anstey (1945), Lokanathan (1945), Shenoy (1944), and Wadia and Merchant (1946). Recently, the Bombay Plan has been the focus of renewed attention as in Chibber (2004), Zachariah (2005), Sanyal (2010), and Lockwood (2012). The focus in these latter studies has been on the political intent behind the formulation of the plan, and also on its excision from public memory as a precursor of the national planning effort from the 1950s. The emphasis here is on Part II of the plan and its role as a blue print for social engineering.

The implications of Indian public opinion on widespread evidence of antisocial practices, speculation, hoarding, black-marketeering, and the like had begun to exercise the minds of established industrialists by 1942. Thinking along these lines coincided with the period of uncertainty that followed the Quit India Movement and the arrests of the members of the Congress Working Committee in August 1942. Thus, it was in a letter to G.D. Birla in September 1942, that Purshottamdas Thakurdas informed him that J.R.D. Tata had asked for Thakurdas' cooperation in preparing an economic development plan.[28] In reply, Birla agreed that Tata's proposal was constructive and welcomed Thakurdas' support in the effort.[29]

Following these feelers, in December, John Matthai, now employed by the Tata Group, circulated to some of the most senior industrialists and businessmen—Purshottamdas Thakurdas, G.D. Birla, Kasturbhai Lalbhai, and Sri Ram—a letter on behalf of the Tata Group.[30] An omission from this group, worthy of further investigation, was that of Walchand Hirachand.[31] Apart from these four businessmen, J.R.D. Tata, Ardeshir Dalal, A.D. Shroff, and Matthai himself represented the Tata Group.

In Matthai's letter, it was foreseen that when a national government eventually came to power, there would be widespread demand

28 Purshottamdas Thakurdas Papers (subsequently PT Papers), File no. 239, part IV, p. 329; 27 September 1942, p. 332.

29 Birla, Thakurdas, and Sri Ram were the joint founders of the Federation of Indian Chambers of Commerce and Industry, and the latter two continued to work closely together until the late 1940s (Kochanek 1970: 1295, 1306).

30 John Matthai, of the Indian Educational Service, had earlier been president of the Indian Tariff Board (PT Papers, File no. 291, part I, pp. 266–7; pages 6–7 of General Note enclosed with John Matthai's letter to Thakurdas and others dated 8 December 1942, pp. 262–3).

31 Mehta (1950) mentions that by 1940, Tata, Birla, and Dalmia-Jain, the largest conglomerates, were comparable in scale to the British managing agencies; the Walchand Hirachand and Thapar Groups were close to joining this league. Walchand Hirachand, advocating the cause of Scindia Shipping, had been in the forefront of opposition to colonial concessions to imperial shipping interests, and he would seem a natural candidate for membership of the planning committee. A clue to his exclusion is provided in an indication that his temerity in attempting to establish an aircraft manufacturing plant (later Hindustan Aeronautics Limited) had aroused Tata's enmity (M.A. Master Papers, Subject file 164, 'Note re: interview of Mr M.A. Master and Mr G.L. Mehta with Mr J.R.D. Tata on Wednesday, 14th June, 1944, at 4 P.M. dated 15.6.1944 Confidential draft', pp. 4–9).

for a comprehensive programme for tackling the problem of poverty in India. Proposals would be made for immense and far-reaching changes affecting every aspect of the organization of the Indian economy. It was then to be expected that when a democratically elected government was confronted by a loud and insistent demand for action to remedy the negative effects of the existing socio-economic structure of society, they would be tempted to adopt measures that found strong popular support. Equally, these actions were likely to be taken without serious consideration of the damage they might inflict on the institutions of private property. For this reason, Matthai argued, it was of great importance that a well-considered and impartial scheme of economic development should be prepared in advance by those who could claim the requisite knowledge and experience. Such a scheme would provide a steadying influence, both upon the government and upon public opinion, by focusing thought on the more essential elements of the problem and by suggesting practical ways of meeting them.

Whatever plans industrialists made, Matthai continued, had to allow for the changes in world conditions and in movements of thought that had occurred in recent years. Among these changes, there was probably none that was more likely to have a direct bearing on privately owned economic organizations in India than the reaction, which had been in evidence, against the capitalist system. The movement against capitalism was not confined to Europe, but had also made headway in Eastern countries, particularly in China. The inevitability of a change in the direction of a socialist economy, even in a country like India, had to be recognized.[32] Leaders of industry would then be well advised to take this into account, and to prepare to make such adjustments as might meet all reasonable demands before the socialist movement assumed the form of a full-fledged revolution. The most effective way in which extreme demands in future might be obviated was for industrialists to deliberate, while there was yet

---

32 It is likely that the proposals that had been made in the course of the deliberations of the Congress' National Planning Committee about the imperative of a predominant public sector presence in the industrial sphere had influenced the reasoning underlying this letter (Lockwood 2012: 107). It is significant that a similar line of argument was followed a year later in a compilation of articles on planning in the Birla-supported *Eastern Economist* (1943).

time, as to the best means of incorporating into the capitalist structure whatever was sound and feasible in the socialist movement.

Matthai, on behalf of the Tata Group, suggested that a planning
committee of senior industrialists should be established. This would
formulate an economic plan, in which one of the principal tasks of the
committee would be to examine how far socialist demands could be
accommodated, without capitalism surrendering any of its essential
features. The extensive adoption of 'controls' in one form or another
during the Second World War had meant, in effect, the partial introduction of a nationalized economy. To that extent, the current circumstances would make it less difficult for the committee to devise a practical method of approach to the question.

As Matthai was later to say, the work of science did not end with
the production of industrial and agricultural commodities. It was
in distributing this great wealth, which science helped to produce,
among common men that science could do the best service to society.[33] According to Matthai, science also had its role to play in the
changes in world view that accompanied the industrial revolution.
During the nineteenth century, scientific ideas had shattered the arbi-
trary foundations of religion. This was indicated by the emergence of
three ideas in the sphere of philosophy which had traces of a scientific
origin: the idea of the unity of the human race, the idea of the worth
and greatness of the individual, and the idea of public service as a link
connecting the individual to humanity.[34]

As Matthai's letter, and his views expressed on other occasions
show, the question of the dangers to the social order emanating from
the delinking of the 'moral revolution' from the industrial revolution
was recognized early by the more farsighted capitalists.[35] Their credentials for initiating a discussion on the procedures for overcoming
this hiatus, albeit under the guise of preparing an economic plan, was

33 Report on John Matthai's Presidential Address at the Royal Institute of Science,
Bombay, annual social gathering reported in Bombay Chronicle, 7 February 1945, p. 4.

34 Matthai, Presidential Address.

35 In the contemporary context of controversies over the political intent of the
framers of the Plan, that is, whether it was merely a capitalist plot, more or less
subtle, it should be emphasized that the point of interest here is the evidence of
the comprehension of the effect of unethical business operations in weakening the
hegemonic hold of capitalist ideology.

discussed in an exchange of views between the secretary of state for India and the viceroy when the issue of the 'Transfer of Power' arose a few years later.[36] Referring to criticism of the behaviour of Indian industrialists during the war, the then secretary of state, L.S. Amery, wrote,

[T]hat section of the Indian community [big industrialists] seems to be the ablest and most enterprising and I cannot see anything very much wrong in enabling them to do for India today what men of the same type did for this country a hundred years ago or for America in the last 50 years, more especially as we now have social standards to enforce which the economic theories of 1840 believed to be misguided.

The Viceroy replied:

....(From my reading of social history, Birla and Co. are in many respects better than the industrial magnates to whom we handed over our own people in the last century)

Foremost amongst the problems the Committee had to address, in its search for socialist measures that could be incorporated within capitalism, was the fact that a considerable part of Indian labour drew its inspiration from the Soviet Union.[37] When coupled with the undeniable fact that the Soviet Union enjoyed great prestige amongst its allies, the rights of labour in post-war India had a special importance. This was so because the formulation of the rights of labour and the recognition of these rights had been rather slow in India. One of the principal reasons for this was the comparatively slow growth of a social democratic consciousness amongst industrialists—surely, it may be noted here, an index of the contemporary stage of the 'moral revolution'. The pressure of public opinion on industrialists had been less marked in India than abroad, the note added, although there had been insistent discussion about the need for a national minimum for every human being in areas such as nutrition, education, and housing.

Thus, on the one hand, it was clear that the 'moral revolution' would not come about through the market: State intervention on fairly

36 Great Britain (1974: 1282), exhibits 628 and 631.
37 From the note on 'The Rights of Labour', p. 220, prepared for the meeting on 21 July 1943.

unorthodox lines was essential; on the other hand, such a degree of active State intervention had never been welcomed as a long-term feature of an economy by industrialists. The draft paper for discussion in the planning committee had, therefore, proceeded cautiously. It was usual, it stated, to classify the opinions of those who differed in their views regarding the economic function of the State into two sharply defined categories—capitalist and socialist. There was, the paper continued, perhaps no more striking instance of the confusion of thought which resulted from the indiscriminate use of economic labels than a clear-cut distinction made between capitalism and socialism. The principle of laissez-faire which, the paper asserted, was regarded as the dominant note of capitalism, had during the previous hundred years been so largely modified in the direction of State intervention in various spheres of economic activities, that in many of its characteristic aspects, capitalism had been transformed almost beyond recognition. It was stated that as a result of these developments, the distinction between capitalism and socialism was ceasing, as a matter of fact, to have any fundamental significance.

In the view of the draft prepared for the planning committee, no economic organization could function effectively or possess lasting qualities unless it accepted, as its basis, a judicious combination of the principles associated with each school of thought. These principles might be summed up as follows—first that there should be sufficient scope for the play of individual initiative and enterprise, and second, that the interests of the community should be safeguarded against individual abuses by the institution of adequate sanctions.[38] It was from this angle that the committee approached the problem of determining the place of the State in a planned economy in India. They believed that capitalism, insofar as it afforded scope for individual

38 In the final report it was stated:
Briefly, we plan for change but we also plan for stability and orderly development. It is our firm belief that if the future economic structure of the country is to function effectively, it must be based on these twin foundations. It must provide for free enterprise but enterprise which is truly enterprising and not a mere cloak for sluggish acquisitiveness....
In effect, they argued that State intervention in the internal operations of firms was the means towards generating habits of thought appropriate to the industrial era (Thakurdas et al. 1944: 1).

initiative, had a very important contribution to make to the economic development of India. At the same time, unless the community was endowed with powers for restraining the activities of individuals seeking their own aggrandizement regardless of public welfare, no plan of economic development would succeed in raising the general standard of living or in providing the common good.[39] Well-directed and effective State control was, the note continued, bound to put important limitations on the freedom of private enterprise as it was presently understood. Legal ownership would lose some of the essential attributes which were attached to it, especially in respect of the use and disposal of economic assets. The right of private property would naturally be greatly circumscribed.[40]

Significantly, G.D. Birla did not share the perspective that the proposed intervention, through an exercise in planning, was necessitated by the increasing influence of socialism as an ideology. Although he had agreed to be a member of the planning committee, his reservations about granting an ideological concession to socialism as the inspiration for an interventionist State was spelt out in a note addressed to Matthai and copied to some other members of the committee.[41] The question of a better distribution of income and the elimination of gross inequality was very important. Yet, the note added, it had to be borne in mind that without increased production, a mere elimination of inequality could hardly help. Equally distributed, Rs 65, the per capita income of India at that time, would only be a distribution of poverty and misery. On the other hand, he pointed out, a minimum income of Rs 100 per capita even with some degree of inequality (which was viewed as not undesirable for social progress) could be a credible target to achieve.[42] Birla's point was that the post-Depression failure of capitalism to induce economic growth in the

39 Pages 1–2 of draft section on 'The State and Economic Activity' circulated with John Matthai's note of 9 June 1944, Thakurdas et al. (1944: 27).

40 Para 4, pp. 4–5 of 'The State and Economic Activity', Thakurdas et al. (1944: 27–8).

41 Enclosure to G.D. Birla's letter of 3 October 1944 to John Matthai, copied to Kasturbhai Lalbhai, Purshottamdas Thakurdas, and Sri Ram. Kasturbhai Lalbhai Papers (subsequently KL Papers), reel 59.

42 Birla had in mind here the incentive which persons with higher than average incomes enjoyed in return for their supposedly greater talents or hard work.

advanced countries, rather than any ideological reaction to it, was the reason behind the disenchantment. The plan was necessary so that incomes in India would rise adequately and quickly so as to remove the grossest inequalities.

In a publication issued a year earlier, which Birla endorsed by contributing a foreword, it was asserted that it was the very evolution of capitalism that required the expansion of the role of the State.[43] In his note he elaborated this point: economic progress was not conditioned by any one unique form of organization, be it capitalism, fascism, or socialism.[44] Democratic America and England, a Bolshevik Russia, a Nazi Germany, or a militarist Japan, could all increase their wealth, some with a 'planned policy' and others with a 'plan'. This demonstrated that what was needed was not any particular 'ism' but a government which was bent on increasing its national wealth by all legitimate means at its disposal, whether through a 'planned policy' or a 'plan'. Such a government could, with its stability and popularity, carry its people with it in such planning. Having said that, Birla conceded that while a mere planned policy may have been adequate in the past for advanced countries, planning had become a necessity for a backward country like India in view of the great and compelling problems it faced. No country could achieve a high standard of living unless it was largely industrialized through a process of growth of small- or large-scale industrial units, and had increased its efficiency in every field of production. Agriculture alone, Birla argued, could not make a country very prosperous. The model pattern, perhaps, would be 25 per cent of the population working in the fields, the rest in secondary and tertiary occupations. Every country that raised its standard of living had to invariably transfer its population from the field to the factory.

Sri Ram had a position closer to Matthai's, in its appreciation of the currently weakened ideological authority of capitalism.[45] This was

43 It must be presumed that he was not opposed to the ideas expressed in the pamphlet in chapter VII, 'The State and the Private Sector', *Eastern Economist* (1943: 50–4).

44 Enclosure to G.D. Birla's letter of 3 October 1944 to John Matthai, copied to Kasturbhai Lalbhai, Purshottamdas Thakurdas, and Sri Ram, KL Papers, reel 59.

45 Letter from Sri Ram to John Matthai, 5 October 1944, copied to Kasturbhai Lalbhai in KL Papers, reel 59.

made apparent when some time later he wrote a note criticizing the draft of the second part of the report of the planning committee. He pointed out that the section on 'The State and Economic Organisation', paragraph 3, mentioned the record of capitalism in the nineteenth century and described the improvement in national income and in the general standard of living under the capitalist system. Sri Ram felt that although the facts could not be denied, their discussion so early in the chapter might create the impression that the design of the authors was merely to generate propaganda for the continuance of the system, and might prejudice people against it. This paragraph could more appropriately find a place in the latter part of the chapter. In other words, Sri Ram was aware that, particularly in the context of the record of wartime operations of many businessmen, the committee needed to be sensitive to public reactions to a capitalist-inspired economic plan.[46]

ASSESSING THE PUBLIC MOOD: REACTIONS TO THE PLAN

The first part of the economic plan was released in January 1944. As one of the first commentators was to say, any one of the seven Indian business magnates who were members of the planning committee could have written the 49-page pamphlet, even given the considerable effort involved in collecting the statistics it contained. But the joint authorship gave additional authority to the booklet on a subject on which there had been a great deal of speculation, combined with substantial disagreements in the past.[47]

Indeed, it was pointed out that there was the additional fact that the plan, if implemented, would reinforce the dominant position of industrialists within Indian society.[48] It was argued that there was a point of view that the industrialists in India had already displaced the princes from their pre-eminent position in the country. The

46 In one of the few detailed responses to Part II of the Plan, Wadia and Merchant (1946: 16–48) provide a devastating critique of business pretentions towards social concern.

47 *Bombay Chronicle*, 18 January 1944, p. 4, Walchand Hirachand Papers, File no. 143 (I).

48 *Madras Mail* quoted in *Free Press Journal*, 25 January 1944, p. 24.

implementation of the Rs 10,000 crore plan would surely strengthen the position of the industrialists yet further, unless the people decided that if India was to be rejuvenated it were better that the beneficiary should be the State, as in the Soviet Union.

It was precisely because of the authority that the combination of the seven industrialists commanded that reactions to the plan, presented in January 1944, were on broadly three bases. The dominant response was critical of the credentials of industrialists whose business fraternity had alienated public opinion by its self-seeking mode of profit making. Further, the viewpoint maintained, owing to the manner in which some industrialists and members of the commercial community had bled the country white during the war, the people had lost all faith in the capabilities of the so-called industrialists and commercial magnates to salvage the country from its economic ills.[49] Another criticism brought the focus back to the question whether the State, in the absence of a 'moral revolution', would remain a 'soft state', incapable of tackling the task of planning the economy. It was argued that India was unlikely to emerge with a strong central government composed of elements with a common ideology in political, economic, or social matters.[50] There were thousands of professional politicians who had not only unsatisfied ambitions, but were also reactionaries, selfish and treacherous to a degree where they might conceivably barter their country in return for concessions granted in their own narrow interests, and towards their self-aggrandizement. Uprooting of these elements would take at least a generation. If, therefore, Indians were to face the facts, they would have to realize that they were likely to inherit a democracy with all its weaknesses. Such a government would surely not be by itself an appropriate authority for planning even if it was quite representative.

Also expressed was the consumer's resentment:

> You are the only Nationalist Paper [*Bombay Sentinel*] that has had the courage to write something which is very true against this humbug scheme of selfish capitalists. You are the only Editor, who has come forward to state that there is no industry in this country which can be called a National Industry in its true sense....

49 Shah (1944: 47).
50 Shah (1944: 41–2).

The example of the Textile and Steel industries, which you have given in the said article are worth studying. The interest of labour has at times been given some consideration by industrialists in this country, because labour in certain parts is organised but I do not remember any time in my 20 years' experience that interest of the consumer has ever been cared, attended, and looked after by anyone. We used to get cheap article made in this country not because the industrialists wanted us to give cheap but he had no alternative, except to sell it cheap as the foreign goods were being dumped every week....

I, as an average consumer ... [am] ... willing to judge any Scheme not by future promises, but by past experience of last three years of my own Industrialists and their Associates ... I am sorry for buying nothing but Indian Made Goods all these years at high prices, and inferior quality, thinking they are our National Industries. I supported them as a Tax-Payer by tariff, subsidies and royalties. And all this for what?[51]

It is an index of the prevailing mood at the time that Purshottamdas Thakurdas felt the point raised by the letter would have sufficient resonance in the public mind to warrant a response. In his reply, he admitted that the existence of profiteering by both manufacturers and middlemen was not in dispute.[52] However, he added, profiteering had been allowed because the government was incapable of controlling the situation effectively. It was precisely because of the chaotic state of affairs that those who had put forward the economic plan had indicated the necessity of a national government responsible to the legislature.

The second strand of reaction to the plan was of the section of middle class opinion which was distrustful of the large industrialists' ability to look beyond their own specific concerns.

India's hungry, naked, suffering millions cannot wait for five years after the war, for the formulation of a Plan, and wait again for the morsel of food, for a piece of clothing and other necessaries of life, for the major part of the planned fifteen years.... We grudge none of the crumbs that they [a few] can pick; we grudge, however, even a remote risk of the misguidance of

51 Jamnadas Meghji's letter to *Bombay Sentinel*, 17 March 1944, p. 4.

52 Purshottamdas Thakurdas's reply addressed to the editor of *Bombay Sentinel* under the pseudonym 'A Consumer', 18 March 1944, PT Papers, Press Clippings, File no. 21, p. 216.

even a single person.... To impart a popular character to the Planning, the principle objective is stated to be to double the present annual per capita income and to raise the net output of agriculture to a little over twice the present figure, at the end of fifteen years. The barrenness of the objective is revealed, when it is recalled, that, on the basis of 1939 figures, as against an annual per capita income of Rs 1,406 in USA and Rs 980 in the United Kingdom, the per capita income in British India is Rs 65. No nation of four hundred millions can uplift itself, while struggling to keep body and soul together, on an annual per capita income of Rs 65, increasing in fifteen years, to Rs 130, assuming the miscalled Planning yields its maximum results. The Plan is really in the nature of a scheme of Barter. The entire concept is based on the realisation, that, in Britain and America, the two Big Powers that count today in the counsels of the world, it is MONEY or in other words, Big Business that governs and not Democracy.[53]

V.M. Tarkunde, secretary of the All India Radical Democratic Party, pointed out that the experience of the textile industry in India illustrated the fallacy that lay at the root of the plan.[54] For several years, the textile industry was protected from foreign competition; capital, labour, raw materials, technical advice were all available in adequate quantities, and yet, vast numbers of people in India, who were too poor to purchase cloth, continued to go half naked. He posed the question of why the industrial magnates did not develop the textile industry and provide the Indian people with adequate clothing. The whole plan amounted to an ill-concealed claim that a so-called national government dominated by the manufacturing and commercial interests of the country could promote the prosperity and well-being of the people, Tarkunde concluded.

The passage of several months in between the release of parts I and II of the plan allowed a longer view to be taken of the proposals in part I. The London-based *Economist* pointed out that the Bombay Plan had had the most significant double effect on Indian politics, particularly Congress politics.[55] On the one hand, its conception of State planning attracted support from many Congress followers and

53 *Free Press Journal*, 20 January 1944, p. 16 and 19 January 1944, p. 7.

54 *Free Press Journal*, 25 January 1944, p. 24. Vithal Mahadeo Tarkunde was a prominent lawyer, civil rights activist, and humanist leader. He was a founder of the Civil Liberties Movement in India.

55 The *Economist* quoted in *Bombay Chronicle*, 16 May 1944, p. 37.

other nationalists who were disillusioned with liberal nationalism, on the other hand, the plan caused great anxiety among convinced democrats.[56] The planning project, the *Economist* continued, fitted other tendencies in contemporary Indian thought and politics. The Second World War had brought increasingly authoritarian rule, both at the centre and in the provinces, it had increased the planned utilization of Indian resources, and also enabled the growth of Indian industry.

Another foreign commentator, Fenner Brockway, examined the plan from a left wing position. In a sentence, he wrote, the authors of the industrialists' plan were the core of the capitalist and financial interests associated with the Independence Movement in India.[57] They represented the 'vested interests' which had been challenged within Congress during recent years by the inpouring of peasants, industrial workers, and socialists. It would be a mistake, however, he continued, if their report was dismissed as merely a conscious design to further their own economic interest. In contrast to many Indian industrialists and financiers, most of them had proved over the years that they were not prepared to be the 'yes-men' of the British authorities. Some of them, at least, had shown by their association with movements of education and social progress a real desire to see the people of India lifted from destitution, disease, and ignorance. Admittedly, he continued, their report had the fundamental and fatal limitation of any capitalist document, but the passion for a resurrected and independent India had led to two unprecedented features in any plan that had previously emerged from capitalist sources. First, it approached the problem from the perspective of 'the needs of the people' and, because the authors wished to be free from foreign financial domination, it dismissed prevailing conceptions of money. In other words, Fenner Brockway suggested, 'created money' in the form of deficit financing of the plan was a notable departure from the strict canons that guided Indian budgetary policies.

56 Evidently, in the view of the *Economist*, to these 'convinced democrats' laissez faire was the hallmark of democracy.

57 Fenner Brockway in *New Leader* quoted in *Free Press Journal*, 24 August 1944, p. 74. Brockway was a British anti-war activist, politician, and humanist. As the editor of the *Labour Leader*, the newspaper of the Independent Labour Party, he was arrested three times during the First World War. During the Spanish Civil War and the Second World War he supported armed resistance to fascism but continued to serve as Chair of the Central Board for Conscientious Objectors until his death.

S.A. Dange, president of the All India Trade Union Congress, belonged to the India League's Economic Committee that was established in order to study the Bombay Plan and to facilitate the work of the industrialists who proposed to visit Great Britain in the near future.[58] In an interview he said that the League's Committee had three objectives: first, to popularize the plan in Britain; second, to show its patriotic outlook, and third, to answer those critics in England who thought adversely about the plan.[59] While staying in London at the Trade Union Congress Headquarters, Dange sent a telegram to Sri Ram saying that the plan had aroused a great deal of interest in trade union circles and that the projected tour by industrialists was essential to consolidate the political gains earned by the plan.[60] Evidently, Dange considered that the show of self-confidence displayed by the formulation of the plan had impressed some sections of the British public who were sceptical of India's state of preparedness for independence.

The publication of Part II of the plan led seasoned observers to speculate on the new trend in philosophy which seemed to have infused the minds of senior industrialists.[61] Particularly interesting were the following statements:

58 The India League was a Britain-based organization whose aim was to campaign for full independence and self-government for India. The activist, lawyer, and editor V.K. Krishna Menon was the driving force behind it. It evolved from the Commonwealth of India League (established in 1922) which, in turn, evolved from Annie Besant's Home Rule for India League (established in 1916). Menon became joint secretary of the Commonwealth of India League in 1928 and radicalized the organization, rejecting its objective of Dominion Status for the greater goal of full independence and alienating figures such as Besant in the process. The India League sought to raise consciousness among the British people of the injustice of British colonial rule in India and to mobilize them to protest against it.

59 *Hindustan Times*, 4 July 1944 in PT Papers, File no. 21, p. 6.

60 Enclosed with Sri Ram's letter of 20 June 1944 to J.R.D. Tata, copied to Kasturbhai Lalbhai.

61 There was also an element of scepticism, of doubt whether the contradictions between the stated principles outlined in the plan could be reconciled to the empirical behaviour of the industrialists evident in the companies they managed:

> Every signatory to the Bombay Plan is a member of one or more of the [Government] Planning Committees, even though, the entire basis of the Economic Planning by the Government of India, has no relation to any of the principles enumerated by the authors of the Bombay Plan. Nor is this all; there is no relation to the principles on which the signatories to the Bombay Plan conduct themselves in regard to their management of industries and the principles enumerated in the second volume of the Bombay Plan. (*Free Press Journal*, 17 January 1945, p. 57.)

We have, however, to deal with another and a more specific set of functions which are being advocated by important sections of enlightened opinion both in this country and beyond. These functions centre round i) ownership ii) control and iii) management of economic enterprises. A widening of economic functions of the State in these directions is advocated on the ground that unrestricted private enterprise, under the capitalistic system of production, has not served the interests of consumers and of the community generally as satisfactorily as it should have.... State control of this character is, however, bound to put important limitations on the freedom of private enterprise as it is understood at present. Legal ownership would lose some of the essential attributes which are attached to it at present, especially in respect of the use and disposal of economic resources.... The rights attaching to private property would naturally be greatly circumscribed.[62]

The *Economist* editorially referred to the second part of the Bombay Plan and pointed out that the authors had accepted the principle of State control, which, it said, was an important statement of creed from the 'Kings of acquisitive society'.[63] Even though it was balanced by an equally firm belief in the contribution to be made by capitalist enterprise and initiative, it was an indication of a remarkably radical turn (from whatever motive) in educated Indian thought, the journal commented. However, the fundamental queries already set against the Bombay Plan, raised by the *Economist* in 1944, still remained unanswered. Some other questions concerned the political and social conditions necessary for overall economic planning, with which the plan had never attempted to deal.[64] The easy assumption that there

62 Thakurdas et al. (1944: 27–8).
63 Quoted in *Bombay Chronicle*, 12 February 1945, p. 1.
64 The *Times* had similar doubts:
The planners have made insufficient allowance for the difficulty of modifying, in a statically ordered society, time honoured customs which obstruct economic progress—for example caste restrictions, impeding mixed farming and subsidiary industries, social obligations entailing exaggerated display and crippling expenditure. They seem content to rely on the prestige of the National government to wean the masses from their ancient ways. Assuredly something more will be necessary.... The planners must enlist the help not only of politicians, administrators, and of Scientists but also of religious leaders if their efforts are to elicit an adequate response from the masses. For in India custom is king, and it is custom enshrined in the socio religious texture of life divorced both from politics and economics as understood in the west. There seems only one way of changing it quickly and that is through the agency of outstanding personalities whom the masses will follow, not because they understand

would be an Indian Government, both responsible to the nationals and efficient, was the biggest 'If' of all. Without it and without the confidence of Indians behind it, the plan might turn out merely to be another (though valuable) blueprint, the *Economist* concluded.

According to the *Bombay Chronicle*, there were several features in the second instalment of the Bombay Plan, prepared by half a dozen leading industrialists in the country which, considering the authorship, marked a definite advance in liberal economic thought.[65] All in all, the paper felt, the programme outlined in this pamphlet was clearly more advanced, reasonable, and equitable than their first production appeared to be. If, however, both parts of their plan so far published were taken together, the *Bombay Chronicle* doubted whether there was specific room provided in the plan for all the adult inhabitants of India to be fully employed, with adequate remuneration, subject to a predetermined and irreducible minimum wage. The industrialists recognized that a considerable enlargement of the function of the State, both positive and preventive, was essential to any large-scale planning. At the same time, the paper felt they seemed to be such confirmed believers in the utility and necessity of private enterprise that in all that they said about the need for public control they left out the question of initiative altogether. It was only the private entrepreneur, who, in their view could most advantageously as well as profitably, initiate enterprise, and work it through the experimental stage. This last was, indeed, not explicitly stated in their pamphlet, but its implications appeared inevitable from a general survey of the remarks, concluded the *Bombay Chronicle*.

Not only was the role of the State controversial, but different members of the committee had distinct agendas to pursue through their association with the committee. In August 1942, the Congress Working Committee had been jailed due to their opposition to India's involvement in the war. As the end of the war drew near, the end of hostilities brought the prospect of the release of the Congress Working Committee closer. It was then that those members of the

---

but because they revere. If such leaders are forthcoming the transformation of India into a modern State is possible. But without them even plans so admirable as those now under discussion in India are likely to prove sterile. (*Times*, 27 February 1945, quoted in *Bombay Chronicle*, 28 February 1945.)

65 *Bombay Chronicle*, 12 February 1945, p. 1.

planning committee, closer to the Congress, began to argue for the need to involve prominent Congressmen in the formulation of the conclusions of the committee. Both through the successful generation of discussions on the first part of their report, and with the evolving political situation, the industrialists were no longer alone in the task of keeping public opinion within a 'responsible' groove.[66]

So, in a letter to J.R.D. Tata with a copy to Kasturbhai Lalbhai, G.D. Birla suggested that discussion of Part II of the plan be postponed from September to November 1944:

> I think, on the other hand, that meeting after November would be advisable for more than one reason. The war is going to terminate now very soon. And perhaps the members of the [Congress] Working Committee may also be released in the near future. We have to discuss the question also with Gandhiji. Don't you, therefore, think that it would not be advisable to make any commitment before we have met some of these men [?] I would like to have your own reaction in this matter. Perhaps you would like to consult Sir Purushottamdas and Kasturbhai in this matter. In any case, if you finally decide that the meeting must be held on the 11th September, I will be prepared to come.[67]

66 'A comparison between the enthusiasm which greeted the first part of the plan on its publication 12 months ago and the almost perfunctory reception accorded to this final instalment provides the measure of the advance of public opinion during this interval—an advance for which the authors are themselves entitled to due credit' (*Times*, 27 February 1945, quoted in *Bombay Chronicle* dated 28 February 1945).
The first part was a pioneer document which broke fresh ground. A vision was set before the Indian people to show them what their country could be made to look like under planned economy. As a result men's minds were turned into new channels:
[P]lanning is now a settled feature of Indian policy. But the conception has now lost the charge of novelty.... The solid and factually based labours of the Member for Planning and Development, of the Reconstruction Committee of Council, of the Provincial Governments and numerous expert bodies have put a stamp of orthodoxy upon what was once a new and invigorating gospel.... (*Bombay Chronicle* dated 28 February 1945.)

67 Letter dated 21 August 1944. More interesting still is the '*Economist's* view that, though medical grounds are obvious for Gandhiji's release, "... perhaps the most significant reason is a political one". We are left to infer—it is, indeed, broadly suggested—that to the British businessman Indian industrialism is a greater menace than Indian nationalism and that Gandhiji, who is, "... in effect a political dictator of Indian nationalism" is released to counteract the growing influence of the industrialists' (*Bombay Chronicle*, 16 May 1944, p. 36).

The reasons for Birla's reluctance to discuss the draft early lay in his anxiety to ensure that industrialists were in step with the current perspectives of the leadership of the Congress.

Differences in political strategy were also made apparent when the government took the initiative to arrange a conference with the authors. Some members were then prepared to risk the possible odium of associating with the colonial government.[68] Those present were Purshottamdas Thakurdas and, in effect, the Bombay House group, J.R.D. Tata, Sri Ram, Ardeshir Dalal, A.D. Shroff, and John Matthai. Neither G.D. Birla nor Kasturbhai Lalbhai, both close to the Congress, took part in this meeting. In fact, in a letter to the convenor of the conference, and member of the Viceroy's Executive Council, J.P. Srivastava, Lalbhai said that he could not attend the meeting in Delhi to discuss the Bombay Plan as he had a wedding in his house![69]

The conclusions reached at the conference were unorthodox in the role they assigned to the government. It was stated that effective government control would be essential through the planning period, and the tradition of control built up during the war should be sustained. Control of industry should be secured through the continuation of most of the wartime controls, the introduction of controls implicit in progressive labour legislation, and on the institution of the kinds of supervision contemplated by the Fiscal Commission for a permanent Tariff Board.

Although the financial allocations projected in the Bombay Plan have recently been demonstrated to be remarkably similar to those of the first three of the post-Independence Government of India plans covering the period 1951 to 1966, the Bombay Plan itself has faded from public memory.[70] It is a justified exercise to conjecture why this is so, but for the concerns of this work the Bombay Plan's importance lies in its recognition of the problem of the distinction between 'enterprise which is truly enterprising and not a mere cloak for sluggish

68 Reconstruction Committee of Council, brief record of an informal conference with the authors of 'A Plan of Economic Development for India' on Thursday, 20 April 1944 (File No. 260, p. 262, PT Papers).

69 9 April 1944, File no. K 135, reel 58, KL Papers.

70 Sanyal (2010).

acquisitiveness....'[71] This was another way of indicating the problem of the incomplete transition of a significant bloc of capital from its merchant/moneylending/speculative origins to industrial capital proper.

71 Thakurdas et al. (1944: 1).

CHAPTER THREE

Liaquat Ali Khan's 1947 Budget and the Corporate Response

Despite the formulation of the Bombay Plan and the government's response in establishing a (short-lived) Department of Planning and issuing an Industrial Policy Resolution, the situation with regard to the uncoordinated and often contradictory packet of controls remained unchanged. At the end of the war, there was, in India, roughly the same system of controls as there was in other major countries. There was a detailed procedure of rationing food, and probably a larger foodgrain procurement progamme than in most countries. There were controls on capital issues, imports and exports, and on prices of most agricultural and industrial products. However, these steps were unaccompanied· by any attempt to fix price levels on objective considerations such as that of costs or profits. All prices were negotiated at a level that industrialists were not unwilling to accept. Inevitably, the price level was much higher than in any other country with similar controls. The standard of living of the people had worsened to a larger extent than elsewhere; profiteering by industrialists, traders, and speculators was enormously greater and the lack of a common policy of coordination much more stark. This was because of the peculiar ad hoc additions to wartime controls. Thus, despite having the same formal structure as in other countries, the system had operated quite differently.

This was the situation when the Interim Government (Congress–Muslim League) assumed office in the third quarter of 1946. The government could have chosen either of the two courses of action:

either to correct the mistakes of the previous government, to integrate and coordinate controls, and to pursue an intelligent and firm policy regarding prices under control; or to lift the existing controls and to let economic forces operate at will. That a definite choice was not made for more than a year may be explained chiefly by the mixed composition of the Interim Government.[1] The Congress party, one of the two parties that constituted this government, had received considerable help in its growth from Indian business interests and was controlled by political leaders who had many connections with these businessmen; the other political party, the Muslim League, whose base lay substantially with the dominant zamindars (feudal landlords) of north India, was indifferent to the fortunes of the capitalist group.[2] The leaders of one political party, therefore, openly talked and worked against the regime of controls, while the representatives of the other party favoured, through the departments in their charge, all measures which would control Indian capitalists.[3]

It was in this context that the finance department in the Interim Government, in response to the rise in prices from the middle of 1946, had appointed a Commodity Prices Board in February 1947.[4] Although the board suffered from the inherent tensions over economic issues within the government and was not given guidelines to help it with a perspective, it produced twelve reports before it ceased to exist in October 1947, when both of its members resigned. This first step towards developing a procedure whereby prices, distribution, and profit levels could be controlled in an integrated and rationalized manner was taken forward by the 1947 budget proposals, whose fate is discussed in detail later. Both were victims of the factional conflict

1 Gadgil (1949: 116).

2 Cf. 'The growth of trade, commerce and education had begun much earlier in Bombay, Calcutta and Madras, that is, in the Hindu-majority areas, than in the Muslim areas of the North.... Hence with the rise of the Indian bourgeoisie conditions of sectional rivalry existed which could easily assume a communal guise. The great landlords who formed the main basis for the Muslim upper class, viewing with displeasure the advance of the trading and industrial bourgeoisie, regarded that advance as "Hindu"—the menace of the "hindu bania" etc.' (Palme Dutt 1970: 458).

This pithy formulation has generally been supported by subsequent detailed historical research, such as by Alavi (2002), and from alternative perspectives, Papanek (1972), and Jalal and Seal (1981).

3 Gadgil (1949: 116).

4 Sovani (1948).

between different sections of the Indian propertied class, complicated by differing ideologies concerning the future of the Indian State.

Even before Liaquat Ali Khan, finance member in the Interim Government, had finished his 1947 Budget Address to the Central Legislative Assembly, some 'well-dressed' observers had left the visitors' gallery.[5] Leading the walkout was G.D. Birla, a recognized patron of the Congress, and one of the big five of Indian industry.[6] The well-dressed visitors' on-the-spot reaction was ominous. It indicated the prospect of canalized and well-organized opposition to the budget proposals. In fact, over the three weeks that followed, the protest was to extend from prolonged closure of the Bombay, Calcutta, Delhi, and Madras Stock Exchanges, to sustained campaigns in both the national and regional press. It was to result in the co-option of the Congress Legislature Party (CLP), led by Jawaharlal Nehru, into the position of the unabashed advocate of a narrowly conceived point of view solely favouring big business, and it was to make the 1947 budget into an early post-war cause célèbre.

With the momentous events of 1947 and 1948 following, the budget of the short-lived Interim Government became a document of passing interest, apparently no longer representing any phenomenon of enduring historical concern. However, with the publication of Maulana Azad's biography, in 1959, the budget became a matter of controversy again.[7] In Azad's account, the budget was mischievously conceived, of a piece with the entire record of the Muslim League's disruptive attitude to working a coalition Interim Government with the Congress.[8] While incorporating Congress ideals, the budget

---

5 *Statesman* (New Delhi Edition) 1 March 1947, p. 1.

6 *Independent India* (Ed. M.N. Roy, V.B. Karnik, Mng Ed.) 9 March 1947, p. 139.

7 Azad (1959).

8 The Muslim League's overall ideology in economic matters has not been as yet satisfactorily elaborated. Referring to proposals in its Planning Committee Report of 1945, it has been remarked that the proposals made by a team handpicked by Jinnah 'would not be out of place in Congress Socialist Party Publications' Talbot (1994: 884). However, it has equally been noted that

> [a]t the same time, it is difficult to imagine that a political movement in whose Council the two largest groups were landlords (163 out of 503) and lawyers (145) would take a particularly radical stance on economic issues. Efforts in provincial Leagues to introduce resolutions calling for the nationalization of public utilities, public control of private industry, and a tax policy directed to a sharp equalization of incomes were not made part of the general policies of the Muslim League at the national level. (Papanek 1972: 9.)

proposed an impractical set of taxation measures, which would have ruined Indian industry if they had been accepted and implemented. Azad also blamed Sardar Patel for suggesting that the Finance port-folio be offered to the Muslim League, as this gave the league the opportunity to interfere in the functioning of all the departments of the government.

Following the publication of Maulana Azad's biography, there have been a number of attempts to 'set the record straight'. These have generally concentrated on absolving Sardar Patel of any responsibility for saddling the Interim Government with an irresponsibly function-ing finance department.[9] Further, they have reinforced the view that the Muslim League had entered the government with the sole pur-pose of demonstrating the impossibility of governing a united India.[10] In this view, the 1947 budget was the supreme example of the Muslim League's approach to coalition government.

In the midst of this controversy, the version of events provided by H.M. Patel, member of the Indian Civil Service, and at the time joint secretary to the cabinet, has gone unnoticed and unremarked. This account is so much at odds with the received versions that it is worth describing in some detail. According to Patel, officials in the cabinet secretariat were bemused by post-budget developments, because spe-cial care had been taken by them to explain to members, and particu-larly to Nehru, the conventions which governed cabinet scrutiny of the budget. According to these conventions, the principles underlying the budget proposals would be explained in the cabinet, but no details would be provided. If there was any query, it had to be raised during the cabinet meeting. Failing this, it would be presumed that everybody had accepted the proposals. It was also explained to members that the pro-posals formulated by the finance member would be brought before the cabinet after they had been fully explained to the viceroy. According to Patel, the budget proposals were explained to everybody in the cabinet, and to the best of his recollection, there was no major objection.[11] Com-menting on the reaction to the budget proposals, Patel felt that it was

9 A. Ray (1968); Gandhi (1989).

10 There is an interesting exception in the political biography of Liaquat Ali Khan by Kazimi (1997).

11 H.M. Patel (1971: 10–11).

purely emotional. Although he was not then directly connected with the formulation of the budget, he certainly was concerned with explaining the budget proposals to members. At no time did the idea enter Patel's head that there was something sinister underway to undermine the Congress' prestige, or the country's economy.[12]

The attempt here is to provide a new perspective that imbues the budget with far greater significance than historical accounts have attributed to it. It incorporates the views propounded by contemporary observers:

> Mr Liaquat Ali Khan appeared to have grasped the problem [of transition from a war to a peacetime economy] and to have taken the first step towards the framing of a clear-cut economic policy but before he could take any effective steps his term of office came to a sudden end by the partition of the country.[13]

and

> The budget for 1947–8 presented by Mr Liaquat Ali Khan had many elements of corrective policies and innovations, but as a whole it proved too much of a shock, particularly to the business and industrial community. It was in severe contrast with the previous budget and while its points were recognised, their motives were questioned. In any case it focussed attention on the generally unhealthy and difficult state of the economy....[14]

In the process, this book re-examines the trajectory of Congress co-option in order to demonstrate the influence of concurrent political events on Nehru's declining ability to forge a consensus on key features of the budget. Within the new perspective, this failure is shown to defeat the objectives set by G.D Birla himself who, with his colleagues, had advocated very similar goals to those that the budget pointed to, in the Bombay Plan barely two years previously.[15] This

---

12 H.M. Patel (1971: 12–13).

13 Sovani (1949: 30).

14 Deshmukh (1957: 18).

15 Chibber (2004) argues that the Bombay Plan was not meant as a serious policy prescription. In this view there would be no contradiction between Birla's position in 1944 and in 1947. An account more sympathetic to the large capitalists' bonafides suggests that when confronted by the prospect of Nehru as Prime Minister, they

suggests that Birla felt that some larger political objectives could be attained by a campaign of virulent opposition, even though he might have both understood and supported the budget measures under other circumstances.[16]

THE BUDGET PROPOSALS AND EARLY RESPONSES

The proposals themselves principally involved the introduction of a tax on business profits, on capital gains, and an increase in super-tax scales and in corporate tax. As the Dalmia-Jain–controlled *Times of India* noted, this emphasis on direct taxes in the revenue-raising exercise was a natural corollary to the Congress' proclaimed ideal of reducing inequalities in society. There could equally be no valid objection to the investigation proposed into the private accumulations of wealth during the war years. Within all strata of society, public confidence in private enterprise had been weakened by the suspicion that black market operators and other anti-social groups almost always 'got away with it'. The setting-up of the Commission of Investigation could be expected to help in reversing the tendency to think that authority and the common good could be flouted with impunity.[17] All in all, there was a marked consensus in the media in the first two post-budget days that the proposals met the requirements of the situation.[18]

Agreement on the objectives of the budget and the means proposed to achieve them was seemingly widespread, and more significantly, vocal. In Bombay, the same evening as the budget speech, the prominent businessman and executive committee member of the Federation of Indian Chambers of Commerce and Industry (FICCI), Chunilal Mehta, welcomed the proposals. Significantly, this was despite the

---

became concerned that State intervention could take a decidedly anti-capitalist turn (A. Mukherjee 2002: 423–5). This is supported by Venkatasubbiah (1977: 70). It could be added here that the post-war period of working class militancy added to the capitalist's brief period of anxiety. For this, see Chibber (2005).

16 This somewhat coy formulation actually has a firm historical basis in Birla's long-standing belief that a united India was not politically feasible. He probably felt that a Congress–Muslim League breakdown over the budget would hasten a partition he viewed as inevitable. See Kudaisya (1998).

17 *Times of India*, 1 March 1947.

18 Examples of the Indian press' opinion of the budget are available in the *National Herald*, 8 March 1947, p. 4.

fact that from the viewpoint of the commercial community, he felt that the proposals were 'very drastic and discouraging'. He explicitly welcomed the proposals to control speculation on the stock, commodity, and bullion exchanges, and the appointment of a special commission to investigate the large accumulations of wealth.[19] The *Times of India* provided a rationale for the proposals. In the last year before the full transfer of power to Indian hands, India's financial position was not strong. It was expected that the Interim Government would pursue every legitimate and far-sighted means of improving it in the succeeding twelve months.[20]

The left-of-centre nationalist press, of course, was fully (and consistently) in support.[21] Both the *National Herald* and the Nagpur-based *Hitawada* also saw a major political gesture by the Muslim League in the budget. It would be too much to expect a Leaguer, stated *Hitawada*,

to cease to be a Pakistani but should Pakistani fanaticism be toned down to the practical requirements of the country even that would be a consummation devoutly to be prayed for. Mr. Liaquat Ali Khan can, with his practical

19 *Statesman*, 2 March 1947, p. 5 (Statement in Bombay on 28 February 1947).

20 *Times of India*, 1 March 1947.

21 'The Interim Government's budget is a budget of social objectives and the various proposals to achieve those objectives are unexceptionable although stiff opposition is likely to be encountered from those sections which are directly affected.... The plea for tackling urgent economic problems like inflation, unemployment and production of goods will find a ready response from all, irrespective of party or community' (*National Herald*, 2 March 1947, p. 4).

'The reactions among the public in general to the first budget of the Indian National Government are indicative of great hopes of a new order of social justice and economic progress. A century of foreigner's budgeting for this country had kept India severely aloof from those ideals of national finance that the present Finance Member has proclaimed in no uncertain account. We must sincerely congratulate the first Indian Finance Member of the Government of India, free from any bureaucratic taint or alien influence, on his budget, not only as to the actual content but also the spirit that animates his pronouncement about principles and projects.... In marked contrast to this, [Matthai's railway budget] Mr. Khan announces his policy of social justice, seeking gradual equalisation of incomes and standards of living by means of direct taxation by the State. War is declared on excessive wealth and privilege. The distribution of wealth is no longer to follow the law of the jungle, nor the vagaries of price [sic] the system of grab and grasp ... the soundest proposals a Finance Member ever put forward on behalf of the Government. The... Masses of the poor and the disinherited will at last have a glimpse of hope and happiness. It is to be hoped that the attempts made in certain interested quarters to the discredit of India will not succeed' (*Bombay Chronicle*, 3 March 1947).

experience as a finance member, play an important role in bringing the Congress and League together. His budget is admirable and there is that in it which still makes us hope that he can bring about a working agreement between League and Congress.[22]

The *Bombay Chronicle* added that, at the very least, it could be said of the proposals that they put the necessary burden on those who could bear them. Further, by conceding that the items of expenditure were essential, the *Bombay Chronicle* argued, the most vociferous critics of the proposals of taxation shifted the terms of controversy to that of a choice, of the degree of reliance on direct, as opposed to indirect taxation.[23]

However, there was a major problem in the underlying political uncertainty, and in the Muslim League's unwillingness to concede any ground in the area of long-term planning.[24] It was the *Statesman* again that correctly gauged that the problem with the budget lay in that it transferred the political impasse into an economic stasis, and that could alienate businessmen. It noted that both markets and industry itself were likely to draw the inference from the finance member's speech that the government was both lacking in intention and resources to push ahead with many of the large planning and development schemes. It was upon these that the conception of an expanding Indian economy had been built up, and the future prospects of a number of industries correspondingly assessed. This conclusion, it stated, was inescapable.[25]

THE REACTION GROWS

Although Congress legislators remained publicly in support of the budget proposals for another week, an astonishing assertiveness by

22 *Hitawada*, 2 March 1947.

23 *Bombay Chronicle*, 1 March 1947.

24 'The Finance Minister, it is pointed out, has expressed himself strongly in favour of regional planning and has frankly admitted inadvisability of long term development plans in advance of constitutional settlements.... The lobbies have reacted well to the finance member's viewpoint, but would like to follow the logical consequence by deferring all development till June 1948, by which time all constitutional issues are bound to be settled. This aspect of the question is expected to loom largely during the Assembly discussions on the Finance Bill and demand for grants' (*Pioneer*, 2 March 1947).

25 *Statesman*, 1 March 1947.

the big business community became apparent at the FICCI Executive Committee, which met over the following weekend. The outgoing president, Gurusaharan Lall, the incoming president, M.A. Master, Purshottamdas Thakurdas, G.D.Birla, Sri Ram, Padampat Singhania, and, significantly, Chunilal Mehta were expected to attend.[26] In the meantime, on 1 March, the Bombay Stock Exchange had closed down, and it was made clear that it would not be reopened until 'clarifications' on the budget proposals were made available. The Calcutta Stock Exchange also closed on 2 March.[27] The Madras Exchange and the Delhi Exchange followed these, both on 4 March.[28]

It was Birla's *Hindustan Times* that provided the most graphic account of the new mood. It reported that the consternation that had been caused by the budget proposals found its echo among businessmen assembled for the annual session of FICCI, and also among the legislators who examined the budget in detail. It said that if the outspoken criticism of the budget made by several members of the executive committee of FICCI were to be made public, it would astound the Interim Government. It hinted that the cabinet as a whole had no say in the formulation of the budget proposals, and that at the pre-budget presentation meeting, the proposals were merely mentioned for the information of the cabinet. The reason for this procedure, the *Hindustan Times* explained, was that the responsibility for scrutiny of the budget proposals had been delegated to a subcommittee of the cabinet consisting of Nehru, Matthai, and Liaquat Ali Khan, the finance minister. The newspaper had no doubt that Liaquat Ali Khan had embarrassed his two colleagues by the manner in which he elaborated his proposals, and by the justification he gave for them. Apparently, the feeling in unnamed circles was that even a 'right proposal would look wrong in the way it was presented by the finance minister who made the budget political with the League bias'. In the same circles it was being openly said that in most of what Liaquat Ali Khan had propounded, he spoke only for himself and 'certainly not for the majority of his colleagues'. Further, it was not known as to what extent the cabinet subcommittee was in a position to examine

26 *Pioneer*, p. 6.

27 *Hindustan Times*, 2 March 1947, p. 12; 4 March 1947, p. 8; and 5 March 1947, p. 10.

28 *Hindustan Times*, 4 March 1947, p. 8 and 5 March 1947, p. 10.

the full implications of the budget proposals. But it was clear that the cabinet as a whole took it for granted that Nehru and Matthai had satisfied themselves on the various aspects of the budget before sanctioning it.[29]

Three days after the budget was presented, Nehru gave the inaugural address at the annual session of FICCI, held in Delhi on 3 March. This was to be the occasion when Nehru would outline the Interim Government's policy towards industrialization of India.[30] In the process he would make clear his position on what was characterized by the United Press of India agency as the 'all too sudden, ultra-socialistic approach' of the central budget.[31]

Following the weekend meetings of the FICCI Executive Committee, the Congressparty in the Central Legislature held a three-hour meeting on Sunday evening to consider the budget proposals. Backbench opinion was evidently sufficiently in favour of the proposals and it was considered desirable to establish a subcommittee to examine the financial proposals '.... in the light of criticism that might be voiced during the next two days general discussion on the budget as well as public criticism and to make recommendations to the party'. The reaction of the big business community had been transformed within a day, in these words of the Associated Press of India agency, into public criticism. Even the *National Herald* announced that the decision to refer the bills dealing with the Business Profits Tax, the Capital Gains Tax, and the Income Tax Investigation Commission to a select committee was a gesture to *public* reactions.[32]

Both the *Times of India* and the *Hindustan Times* worked to widen the wedge that had evidently been created within the leadership of the CLP. The *Times of India* substituted its cautious welcome to the

---

29 *Hindustan Times*, 2 March 1947, p. 1.

30 'The reaction hitherto available to the taxation proposals of the Interim Government are exceedingly pessimistic ... Mr. Liaquat Ali ... is hardly likely to turn from the path he has chosen. Nor will his colleagues in the Interim Government break with him under the pressure of big business, since considerable odium will attach to any section which initiates a surrender.... The next few days will reveal whether Indian business will adjust itself to the new conditions, or whether it will attempt to resist the Interim Government's financial policy' (*Free Press Journal*, 3 March 1947).

31 United Press of India report in *National Herald*, 2 March 1947, p. 6.

32 Associated Press of India report in *National Herald*, 3 March 1947, p. 1.

budget with a much more negative view. The paper noted that what it called the 'country wide' reaction to the budget confirmed its fear that the drastic new taxation would arrest development and stultify private enterprise during one of the most vital phases of India's history. It claimed that arguments supporting the opposition were too strong for any government to dismiss them as the mere outpourings of moneyed sections reluctant to be parted from their wealth. It suggested that the proposals should be revised to lessen the enormous burden placed on business and to remove the threat to private initiative. If they were not, it warned, great harm might be done to India's economic structure. The *Times of India* was unable to criticize the unexceptionable aim of the budget proposals—the 'social uplift of the masses... [and to achieve] ... this laudable end by vast development schemes...'. It had also to grant that a major effort of resource mobilization required to fund these schemes had, implicitly, been accepted by the cabinet. Despite this, the *Times of India* now attempted to isolate Liaquat Ali Khan within the cabinet by criticizing the corollary of this initiative—higher taxation of the corporate sector and wealthy individuals. It showed surprise that he should have gone on to introduce a taxation policy which would, it declared, act as a brake on that industrial progress which would be one of the surest ways of raising the standard of living. The paper granted that the central government needed more revenue, but reliance on direct taxation would, it argued, stall the wheel of progress. Dramatically changing the position it had held two days previously, the *Times* concluded that while India's finances needed careful husbanding during the difficult days ahead, it was all the more unfortunate that the Interim Government's budget should have weakened internal confidence. It was business confidence, above all, that was the country's great need during the transition period.[33]

The *Hindustan Times* made no bones about the exact nature of the public opinion that the *National Herald* and the *Times* had referred to. It reported that, parallel to the meeting of the CLP, some of the most prominent businessmen had analysed the budget proposals. Their intention was to make the nature of business objections comprehensible to the legislators who would consider the Finance Bill the

33 *Times of India*, 3 March 1947.

following week. These objections were to be forwarded not directly to the Congress backbenchers but to a subcommittee of senior Congress leaders. This subcommittee had been appointed not only to analyse the budget proposals, but also to recommend modifications.[34]

So, on Sunday, 2 March, two days after the budget was presented, the Congress had taken a momentous step by thus establishing the subcommittee's terms of reference. It had further weakened the conception of the Interim Government as a coalition government. According to the Congress there was no cabinet that bore collective responsibility for the proposals. It was then a question of whether Nehru and John Matthai could prevail over their Congress colleagues in what was still technically the Viceroy's Executive Council.

The problem lay in the limited franchise under which the elections to the Central Legislative Assembly had been held and the social composition of its members. The *Tribune* noted that while the Congress and the League backbenchers, including a few politically prominent figures, had been enthusiastic about the new taxation proposals, it was clear that Liaquat Ali's scheme of scaling down business profits had thrown a bombshell among the big capitalists. The fact that Nehru and Matthai were associated with Liaquat Ali Khan during the formative stages of the budget proposals would, the paper felt, deter destructive criticism during the debates, but it was likely that the proposals would be modified and made less stringent. The *Tribune* indicated the strategy likely to be used by big business in order to widen their base of support. The 25 per cent special tax on individual profits might, it argued, be tolerated for development plans but when it affected dividends payable to shareholders, the paper felt that already large numbers of the assembly members would have been seriously prejudiced. Evidently, in the FICCI-inspired briefing to Congress legislators, the politically significant urban middle classes were asserted to be amongst those who invested in shares and were likely to be affected by the Business Profits Tax.[35]

Nehru's speech at the FICCI inaugural session was clearly a key indicator of his willingness and ability to stand firm. Left-wing critics,

---

34 *Hindustan Times*, 3 March 1947.

35 *Tribune*, 3 March 1947, p.10. Unlike the wartime Excess Profits Tax, the Business Profits Tax was applicable on professions and occupations, in addition to industry (*Hindustan Times*, 3 March 1947, p. 7).

both contemporary as well as later historians, have seen in this speech early signs of capitulation.[36] According to M.N. Roy's *Independent India*, there was some relief that Nehru did not say anything that would imply lack of moral support to the budget proposals. While assuring businessmen that it was not the intention of the Interim Government to injure 'industry', he asked them to see things in the larger context, rather than from a narrow quick-profit perspective. Other remarks by Nehru, however, possibly signalled a different message. He said, 'If we find we have committed a mistake, we will change that'; and again, 'It [the Interim Government] must react to popular will.' These statements, argued *Independent India*, addressed to the particular audience to which he was speaking gave the impression that Nehru was not wholeheartedly with the budget proposals. The paper elaborated that, evidently, the 'mistake' consisted of encroaching on private profits, and the 'popular will' referred to the opposition by big business and their press. If the assurance about not injuring industry meant not harming industrial interests, then *Independent India* was sure that Nehru would soon yield and be on the side of the vested interests on the issue raised by Liaquat Ali's 'bold' proposals.[37] On the other hand, the *Statesman* reported that Nehru's speech was generally interpreted to mean that the budget proposals continued to have his support, and crucial evidence from private correspondence would support this interpretation.[38]

C. Rajagoplachari, then in charge of industry, also referred to criticism of the budget during the discussion on a resolution moved by G.D. Birla on the centrality of increasing production. More critically, it was Rajagopachari who hinted to the FICCI audience that Congress'

36 Chattopadhyay (1986, 1988). It may be noted that an author who evidently enjoyed FICCI's confidence writes that M.A. Master, in responding to Nehru's speech, said that there was no longer any need to think that the industrial future of India was doomed (Venkatasubbiah 1977: 71).

37 Volume XI, 10, 9 March 1947, p. 129.

38 *Statesman*, 4 March 1947, p. 1. In a letter to Liaquat Ali Khan written on 1 March 1947, the day after the budget was presented, Nehru did not mention any disagreement over the taxation proposals. He expressed reservations about references in the budget speech to proposals for regional planning and nationalization of the Reserve Bank. The correspondence between Liaquat Ali Khan and Nehru on the budget shows no sign of differences on central issues until 17 March 1947. On this day, Liaquat Ali Khan protested against the lobbying by Satya Narain Sinha against the taxation proposals (JN Papers, Second Instalment, File no. 144A).

support could be gained if they proposed alternative measures that would preserve the revenues at the budgeted level. While nominally conceding the Liaquat–Nehru–Matthai viewpoint that the corollary of private enterprise economy was high direct taxation, he also admitted that there were grounds for arguments against the budget proposals. These lay in the assertion that since the nation depended on individual enterprise and management, there should be some incentive to profit, which the taxation proposals allegedly destroyed.[39]

In the two-day debate in the Central Legislative Assembly, before the taxation bills were referred to the Select Committee, John Matthai spoke forcefully on behalf of the proposals. Representing what *Independent India* referred to as the 'Voice of Enlightened Capitalism', Matthai spoke against the narrow profit-seeking mentality of the industrial and commercial interests of the country. He posed the question whether the supposed virtues of private enterprise would not cost the country too much if it was to have the high rates of profits demanded, and whether 'it is in India's interest that capitalism should have a longer lease of life'. He warned the capitalists that they were asking for higher returns than they were entitled to, and that their attitude implied an unconcern with the dangerous repercussions on the country's internal and external credit which 'monkeying with a deficit budget' would have. The paper disagreed with Matthai's implicit assumption that Indian capitalism was capable of behaving in a less profit-grabbing way than it was doing, and that if it only would behave more sensibly, capitalism might work. *Independent India* understood that Indian capitalism had no legacy of traditions which arose in the course of a normal capitalist evolution. It operated in a country whose problems could not be solved within the framework of purely a profit-oriented economy. Confronted, then, with a situation where broad-based growth (which incorporated the peasantry) was inherently infeasible, a psychological reaction had congealed in the minds of Indian capitalists: this led them to follow a course where reckless maximization of profits, to the detriment of the interests of the bulk of the people, was the logical and, indeed, the sole way to operate.[40]

---

39 *Bombay Chronicle*, 4 March 1947, p. 5; the speech is also in the *National Herald*, 6 March 1947, p. 4.

40 *Independent India*, 9 March 1947, pp. 129–30.

The problem of dealing with the speculators, it turned out, was that they were not organizationally distinct to the industrialist. Even within the Tata Group, while John Matthai represented the 'Voice of Enlightened Capitalism', his colleague in the Bombay Plan Committee and one-time fellow employee of the Tata Group, A.D. Shroff, played perhaps one of the most active roles in mobilizing opposition to the budget.[41] FICCI was probably correct when it expressed regret at the bitter attack which Liaquat Ali Khan made on the behaviour of the stock exchanges, which it felt was due to a lack of his understanding of the nexus between finance and industry.[42] All in all, the two-day debate in the CLA had left on the *Hindustan Times* the impression that the treasury benches had been shaken from their original stand. If the captains of industry could convince the Select Committee that the taxation proposals should be modified in the interests of industrial development, they were likely to succeed in their object, the paper concluded.[43]

Nehru, along with Vallabhbhai Patel and C. Rajagoplachari met the FICCI delegation consisting of G.D. Birla, Sri Ram, G.L. Mehta, and A.D. Shroff, after the assembly debate on 6 March, but despite an eloquent exposition of the businessmen's case by Birla, they expressed no views.[44] Birla was reported by the *Times of India* to have said that the formation of the national government, earlier than he had anticipated, had given rise to high hopes about the implementation of the Bombay Plan, of which he was one of the authors. While the industrialists were eagerly looking forward to the opportunity to serve the country on the economic plane, he was sorry to find that the whole atmosphere had been vitiated by what was proposed in the budget.[45]

41 Nearly ten years later, income tax officials were to disclose the startling basis of this opposition. In the 'single greatest tax evasion' in the history of the levy of income tax, written evidence was allegedly available to show that J.R.D. Tata, Ardeshir Dalal, and J.D. Choksi had been personally involved in systematic falsification of the Tata Iron and Steel Company's declared profits, between 1940 and 1946 (JN Papers, First Instalment, File no. 410, pp. 197–8).

42 *Hindustan Times*, 5 March 1947, p. 1.

43 *Hindustan Times*, 5 March 1947, p. 1. The paper was also surely aware that Patel, Nehru, and C.H. Bhabha had submitted notes to the viceroy dissenting from the cabinet minutes that recorded that the budget proposals had, in fact, been approved (Moon 1973: 425).

44 *National Herald*, 7 March 1947, p. 7.

45 *Times of India*, 8 March 1947, p. 7.

THE TURNING POINT: CONGRESS WORKING COMMITTEE RESOLUTION ON PUNJAB

On 8 March, the Congress Working Committee (CWC) met to consider the political situation in Punjab and suggested its division into western and eastern wings under a single governor.[46] The implications of this stand in terms of the long-term viability of the Interim Government, and consequently, the erosion in Congress' willingness to honour its commitment to the budget proposals must have been clear to Nehru. He took the unusual step of sending the CWC resolutions to Liaquat Ali Khan and suggested a meeting to discuss their political differences at an individual level.[47]

Meanwhile, as the budget demands under different heads were to be debated in the Central Assembly from 10 March, the Congress members in the assembly met to consider the attitude which members of the Congress party should adopt towards the budget demands. Significantly, even at this stage, it was reported by the *National Herald* that the view was that the budget had been presented by the finance member on behalf of the Interim Government as a whole. It was decided that Congress members would be allowed to raise discussion on important issues through token or economy cuts that should, however, be withdrawn on receiving satisfactory assurance or a reasonable explanation from the finance member. The trend of talks among Congress members of the central legislature showed that they proposed to concentrate on two issues. The first point was the advisability of laying stress on regional planning instead of central planning as recommended by the Planning and Advisory Committee. The second issue was the expediency of imposing taxation on a flat rate without laying down any criterion of what were called standard profits, as was done in connection with the Excess Profits Tax.[48]

Simultaneously, there was another political trajectory evident within the official structure of various Congress committees, where Vallabhbhai Patel seemed securely in charge. Before the sessions of the Select Committee began on 10 March, Congress leaders took stock

---

46 CWC resolution on the partition of Punjab in the *National Herald*, 9 March 1947, pp. 1, 8.

47 Nehru–Liaquat correspondence, JN Papers, Second Instalment, File no. 144A.

48 *National Herald*, 9 March 1947, p. 3.

of the situation at a meeting held at Patel's residence the previous afternoon. Nehru and other ministers of the Interim Government, the subcommittee of the Congress party in the assembly that had been studying the budget, and the Congress members of the Select Committee attended the meeting on the taxation bills.[49] The following day, a United Press of India report in the *National Herald* conveyed a growing hegemony of the party machine over individual members' political behaviour. Congress members of the assembly met Matthai and other members of the Select Committee, and were also put in touch with the FICCI commercial and financial experts. The report hastened to clarify that the Congress party itself did not appear to be influenced by capitalist complaint that the budget proposals were likely to hamper the growth of industrial enterprise.[50]

By 13 March, while there was talk of a compromise on the Business Profits Tax in the lobby of the assembly,[51] A.D. Shroff at a meeting of the Progressive Group[52] had 'held out a threat that businessmen would strongly agitate against the new budget proposals'.[53] In fact, as the *Pioneer* reported, the ceaseless attacks by big business and its supporters on these bills since they were introduced on 28 February had apparently driven a wedge into the Congress party itself. With the socialists and former labour leaders vying to be among the most fervent supporters of FICCI's point of view, a great deal of resentment had been generated among the Congress rank and file. Without pacification by the senior Congress leadership, a split appeared inevitable, the paper warned.[54]

A second and equally important issue was whether the government whip, Satya Narain Sinha, was entitled to canvas opposition to the bills and personally vote against them. According to reports circulating in the assembly lobby, League members of the government had already begun to regard him as a party whip and not the government

49	*Hindustan Times*, 10 March 1947, p. 1.

50	*National Herald*, 11 March 1947, p. 8.

51	*Bombay Chronicle*, 13 March 1947, p. 1.

52	The Progressive Group was a non-party, cosmopolitan organization based in Bombay. Its chairperson at the time was R.K. Karanjia, who was the founder-editor of the tabloid Blitz, started in 1941.

53	*Bombay Chronicle*, 15 March 1947, p. 3.

54	*Pioneer*, 16 March 1947, p. 16.

whip.[55] It was inevitable, then, that lobby talk would indicate a perceptible difference among Congress and League members in their approach to the finance bill, which was shortly coming up before the central legislature. The recent move in the central assembly for the extension of time for the presentation of the report of the Select Committee appointed to consider the taxation proposals was an indication of this internal disagreement between the two major parties. 'The apparently smooth passage of the Budget demands is no indication that the Finance Bill will have a plain sailing. Indeed indications are otherwise'—this laconic observation made by a prominent office-bearer of the Congress party to the United Press of India representative was a pointer in this direction.[56]

The point was that both the finance member and the League were unwilling to accept the Rajagopalachari-brokered compromise by which the revenues expected in the budget proposals would be raised by a greater reliance on indirect taxes. In the language of the *Times of India*, they were very particular about the form of taxation and they did not accept as sufficient the Congress party's gesture in agreeing to meet the demands completely with only a little alteration in the form and impact of taxation.[57] Persistent reports had, in fact, for some days been suggesting a split, not only between the Congress and the League in the Select Committee, but also within the Congress Party itself, involving Congress members of the government.[58]

THE CONGRESS RETREAT

The authorities of the Bombay Stock Exchange had stated on 1 March that the exchange would remain closed until they had received satisfactory clarifications on the final shape of the budget proposals. However, even before any official announcement on this question, the Bombay Exchange reopened on 18 March, followed by the Calcutta Exchange the day after, signalling that assurances about crucial concessions had been extracted.[59] The extraordinary phenomenon of the

---

55 *Pioneer*, 16 March 1947, p. 16.
56 *Bombay Chronicle*, 17 March 1947, p. 4.
57 *Times of India*, 18 March 1947, p. 4.
58 *Pioneer*, 19 March 1947, p. 4.
59 *National Herald*, 18 March 1947, p. 6.

Congress accepting the abject role of political negotiator of big business interests had perturbed the *Hindu*'s correspondent. He reported that

[a] prominent Congress member whom [he] asked as to how the Congress happened to adopt almost entirely the proposals of the Federation of Chambers in respect of the Business Profits Tax, retorted that as the tax concerned affected only businessmen, their views as to how it should be levied so that it may be equitable should be respected so long as the exchequer did not suffer any loss of revenue.[60]

By their control of the *Times of India* and the *Hindustan Times*, the main English language papers of Bombay and north India, major industrialists had shown that they could influence middle class opinion effectively and force concessions, even from the leading political party of the national movement.[61]

The Select Committee Report on Business Profits Tax and Capital Gains Tax was finally presented on 19 March, with a dissenting note signed by the Congress members. Although a chartered accountant questioned by the *Bombay Chronicle* found the proposals in the main report acceptable, the business community had evidently struck a very hard bargain with the Congress leadership.[62] On the following day, five members of the Interim Government—Nehru, Patel, Rajendra Prasad, Matthai, and Rajagopalachari—met Liaquat Ali Khan. Following the meeting in the morning, the Congress members were in consultation again that evening.[63]

Liaquat Ali Khan, Nehru, Patel, Rajagopalachari, and Matthai continued the discussions on 21 March in order to resolve differences. These were over entirely technical features of taxation policy, whether borrowings and reserves should form part of the definition of capital, the maximum level of profit on this capital beyond which the tax would be levied, and the rate of the tax. The explicit alignment of S.N. Sinha with the opposition in the Select Committee made it clear that unless an agreement was reached in these

60 *Hindu*, 20 March 1947, p. 4.
61 *National Herald*, 18 March 1947, p. 4.
62 *Bombay Chronicle*, 20 March 1947, pp. 1, 5, and 7.
63 *Hitawada*, 21 March 1947, p. 1.

informal meetings, the points at issue would be referred back to the cabinet.[64]

Although Matthai proposed a wider definition of capital, on the basis of which the rate of profit would be determined to the advantage of businessmen, their public campaign continued during these negotiations.[65] The *Hitawada* reported that it was being freely stated in Delhi that the intentions behind the League finance member's budget proposals were not laudable at all, as they affected Hindu businessmen very seriously. The introduction of this communal consideration into the budget was being vehemently criticized.[66] On the other hand the *Hindu* reported that it was no secret that the rank and file members of the Congress Party did not wish the Congress to precipitate a showdown on issues which, whatever Congress' reasons for its stand, would make the Congress appear as the champion of business interests. These Congressmen felt that by agreeing to the changes already made by the Select Committee and those agreed to in the informal meetings, the finance member had met the major criticisms of Congress members.[67]

On his last day as viceroy on 22 March, Wavell met Liaquat Ali Khan. After long talks, he persuaded the finance member to reduce the Business Profits Tax rate from 25 per cent to 16.25 per cent, to define capital as paid-up-capital and reserves, to administer the Capital Gains Tax according to the Congress' dissenting note to the Select Committee Report, and to agree to the appointment of a wide-ranging expert committee on taxation.[68] On Sunday evening Wavell had talks with both Nehru and Liaquat Ali Khan. These, the business lobby reports later indicated, in justification of their tactics, were expected to be of the 'usual preliminary nature', and Nehru was not expected to commit the Congress irrevocably.[69]

64 *Bombay Chronicle*, 22 March 1947, p. 1.

65 *Times of India*, 22 March 1947, p. 1.

66 *Hitawada*, 22 March 1947, p. 4.

67 *Hindu*, 23 March 1947, p. 6. In fact, in two letters to Pethick-Lawrence as late as 19 and 20 March, Wavell suggested that the Congress still faced the threat of a split if there was a vote in the assembly. This threat explained the Congress leadership's anxiety to avoid a vote and its decision to refer the budget proposals back to the cabinet (Great Britain 1980: 991, 995–6).

68 *Times of India*, 24 March 1947, p. 1; Moon (1973), Entry for 22 March 1947, p. 432.

69 *Tribune*, 26 March 1947, p. 8.

However, on Monday morning, 24 March, the papers announced an authoritative Congress–Muslim League agreement on the finance bill as introduced on 28 February, and on the Business Profits Tax as modified by the Select Committee, with the further Matthai-inspired rate reduction to 16.67 per cent from 25 per cent. The distinction between corporations and individuals was removed and the maximum profit eligible for tax exemption was set at 6 per cent of the capital. The definition of capital as amended by the Select Committee remained, as did the Capital Gains Tax, with marginal reduction in tax rates.

According to *Dawn*, having read in Monday's papers that the Congress had agreed to everything except the two points on which the finance member had made concessions, a number of big businessmen took the Congress leaders severely to task. This resulted in the latter taking up an entirely different attitude in their discussions with the finance member on Monday. In their final talks with the finance member, they raised objections to the appointment of a commission for investigation into large private fortunes, which was the subject of a fourth bill. The finance member was adamant and a break followed all along the line. This is what the 'behind the scenes schemers and wirepullers' had been working for, because they wanted the matter to be referred to the cabinet. There, everything might be reopened, and all the taxation proposals remodelled according to the pattern dictated by industrial bosses, by the sheer majority of votes at the disposal of the Congress.[70]

This friction over the budget was just one facet of the political issue which the new, and presumably the last, viceroy would have to tackle. It was pointed out in connection with the demand for the increase of power of the Interim Government that the actual functioning of the Interim Government at that time had hardened the League against collaboration with the Congress in the sphere of central administration.[71]

Confronted with the possibility of a cabinet crisis, Nehru staked his personal prestige to avert it. The Congress group had a prolonged pre-cabinet meeting where Nehru, placed in a minority, was supported by colleagues on the agreement he had reached the previous day. The

70 *Dawn*, 25 March 1947, pp. 1, 8.
71 *Hitawada*, 25 March 1947, p. 4.

Congress, however, had its way as far as the Wealth Inquiry Commission Bill was concerned. The agreement did not cover that bill, which was to be judged on its own merits. An expert committee to consider all taxation proposals was to be appointed with specific reference to the Business Profits Tax and the Capital Gains Tax.[72]

Several newspapers mentioned that Nehru looked dejected and depressed when he came to the assembly on the morning of 25 March. According to the *Pioneer*, however, the meeting of Congress cabinet ministers had brought reality home to him. Presumably referring to the Sunday evening talks with Liaquat Ali Khan and Wavell, the paper advised Nehru that if he wished to lead his party, he would have to be more responsive to their wishes. The paper also asserted that the decisive opinion in the assembly lobbies was that government-by-consultation would have to be substituted for the then government-by-dictation.[73]

It was not surprising that a Muslim League member of the assembly was quoted as saying that the capitulation, which was en bloc, left him with mixed feelings.[74] For a comparison between the demands of the Indian industrialists and those made, either by the Congressmen in the Select Committee or by the Congress high command, revealed that not even on one occasion was a new proposal made by the Congress. The entire basis of discussion was provided by the elaborate and carefully prepared demands of the industrialists; Congressmen appeared only in the political role of exerting pressure on the finance member for a 'compromise', and this too, on the threat of a split in the *cabinet*![75] It was only appropriate that M.A. Master, the then President of FICCI, should ask industrialists two days later to take account of what the 'man in the street' thought of them. The philosophical gulf between government and industry must be bridged, he warned.[76]

* * *

72 *Bombay Chronicle*, 26 March 1947, p. 7.

73 *The Bombay Sentinel, Bombay Chronicle,* and *Pioneer* dated 26 March 1947, amongst others.

74 *Bombay Chronicle*, 26 March 1947, p. 5.

75 *Independent India*, 6 April 1947, p. 182.

76 *Times of India*, 28 March 1947, p. 9.

There were several extraordinary features of the political play enacted in the three weeks after the 1947–8 budget proposals were announced. The most obvious was, in the words of the *National Herald*, the 'rampage' that characterized the behaviour of FICCI and associated big business, led by figures of the stature of G.D. Birla.[77] The second was the capitulation of the Congress leadership in the face of FICCI's opposition to the proposals, even though there was substantial evidence that the Congress legislators supported the proposals, as did numerous newspapers, let alone the positive public response. The third feature, associated with the Congress capitulation was the spectacle of the senior leadership of the national movement spending many hours in conference on details of revenue raising, normally dealt with at the deputy secretary level in the finance secretariat.

It is argued here that the main feature underlying the extreme reaction was the social engineering that the budget proposed. Intriguing corroboration of this thesis is provided by the reaction of M. Visvesvaraya's All India Manufacturers' Organization, representing small- and medium-scale factory owners. This organization not only supported the budget at the height of the controversy, but somewhat cheekily asserted that the opposition came from 'businessmen' seeking quick profits, not from true industrialists.

> Mr. S.N. Haji said that the proposals [in the budget] for taxing business profits and capital gains were the only means of meeting the huge deficit in a national Budget. He added that a businessman whose only motive was profit could have legitimate grounds for complaint but a manufacturer's only concern was the progress of industries. If the industrialization of the country was assured under the Budget proposals he would support the Finance Bill.[78]

77 It should be mentioned that there were reservations expressed about Birla's tactics by his senior FICCI colleagues, Sri Ram and Purshottamdas Thakurdas. Sri Ram complained to C.M. Kothari, a Madras-based share broker, that Birla monopolized the session FICCI had with the Select Committee. In addition, to Sri Ram's disappointment, Birla did not address the issues raised by members of the Committee in a forthright way, but spoke in a roundabout manner so as to avoid the issue. Thakurdas, himself, seems to have left Delhi early and raised the suspicion among the Birla brothers that he was not sufficiently supportive of their motives (PT Papers, File no. 296, pp. 245–8, 254, 256–60).

78 At a reception hosted by the AIMO executive for members of a delegation on their return from a trip to the UK, the USA, and Europe (*Bombay Chronicle*, 21 March 1947, p. 4).

The *National Herald* grasped another aspect of the social engineering process. The paper noted that the lack of unanimity in the Select Committee was to be expected, considering the controversial nature of the new taxes. Business lobbyists might fudge the issue by various random assertions: that smaller profits would lead to a smaller production level, while bigger profits held out the promise of higher production. For businessmen, payment of statutory minimum wages would only lead to inflation, while payment of taxes on excess profits would have deflationary consequences. Amidst all this specious reasoning, big business had shown where it was sensitive and why it was so. The inquest over unaccounted wealth was crucial, the paper noted, and it was this proposal rather than the new taxation that had upset big business.[79]

Another aspect of the situation that had perhaps genuinely caused panic was the imperviousness of the finance secretariat to budget proposal leaks. According to the *Statesman*'s correspondent, whose coverage of the budget extended over many years, the 1947–8 tax proposals were the best kept secret of any budget within his memory. As he reported, in the middle of the week previous to the budget announcement, everything was going 'as merrily as a marriage bell'. The principal stock and commodity market operators in Bombay had the reputation for knowing most things 24 hours before anybody else, under the earlier regimes led by British finance members. In stark contrast, even the most prominent amongst these figures was taken completely by surprise.[80] The intemperate interviews given by A.D. Shroff, and his active role in preparing FICCI's counterproposals are indicative of this.[81]

It was the *Statesman*'s correspondent, again, who comprehended the full significance of the proposals. He noted that Liaquat Ali Khan's budget was destined to not merely go down in history as the first Indian budget to have kept certain social objectives in view but also the *tone* of his budget speech was designed to mobilize the full force

79 *National Herald*, 22 March 1947.
80 *Statesman*, 3 March 1947, p. 7.
81 In a letter to the Indian Merchants Chamber, A.D. Shroff wrote on Bombay House (Tata Headquarters) letterhead that the Chamber should support the proposals made by FICCI, in formulating which he took an active part (IMC Papers, File 67, p. 165).

of public resentment in support of his new taxation proposals against market speculators.[82] The industrialists' reaction, therefore, raised the fundamental question of whether capitalists could be expected to cooperate with the State in its attempts to restrict speculative profits. This was a condition for social progress and the finance bill was a challenge to them.[83]

Liaquat Ali Khan's condemnation of the stock market and the commodities and bullion exchange had come a little late in the day but the long-term implications of his remarks were unmistakable. Whilst nothing could be done about the speculative activities of the past, it was clear that action would be taken to prevent them in future. Equally, it was doubtful whether his proposed inquiry into the accumulation of war fortunes, and the evasion of taxation could be retrospectively effective. However, his words on the subject were evidently a red light of warning to those who had accumulated enormous wealth during the wartime years by questionable practices.[84] In that sense it was a test budget. For, if the proposals failed owing to non-cooperation from industry, then to prevent a chaotic economic situation, the government would either have to take decisive action or would have to be seen to give in to the very first assault.[85]

In spite of all this mass of evidence indicating the rational basis for big business opposition, explanations at this level ultimately remain unsatisfactory. The true answers must lie in placing the events of March 1947 within the context of the Congress' declining commitment to a united India, and therefore, to running a coalition government in a spirit of partnership. Perhaps these factors can account for G.D. Birla's turn towards an amazing degree of narrow business-centred assertiveness, or to Jawaharlal Nehru's inability to capitalize on the groundswell of public opinion in favour of the budget.

For though the budget was of the Interim Government as a whole, it was presented by the leader of the Muslim League *bloc*, which was not always on cordial terms with the Congress *bloc*. The success of the businessmen's campaign lay in transforming perceptions of the

82 *Statesman*, 1 March 1947, p. 1.
83 *Independent India*, 6 April 1947, p. 140.
84 *Statesman*, 1 March 1947, p. 1.
85 *Independent India*, 6 April 1947, p. 140.

budget. Viewed by most Congress legislators as a welcome effort to introduce social objectives into economic policy, the perception was remarkably stage-managed into its opposite within a week. Their public posture was now that the budget, though ostensibly based on Congress' own ideals, was in reality a sectarian, if not a Machiavellian, drive to destroy the very base of the Indian economy as a prelude to an easy escape to Pakistan.[86] The effort succeeded because the will of the CLP to ensure that the Interim Government functioned relatively cohesively was destroyed by a decision of the CWC. On 8 March 1947, the working committee confirmed the long-advocated proposal of the partition of Punjab as a solution to the political problems created by the Muslim League in that province. This, in effect, conceded the principle of India's partition and reduced the requirement for continued Congress–League cooperation within the Interim Government. With this development, the body of opinion within the CLP led by Nehru, which favoured an accommodation with the Muslim League over the budget, was substantially weakened. Nehru, along with John Matthai, had fully supported the proposals in pre-budget presentation consultations and his capitulation, usually viewed in isolation from larger political events, has been severely criticized.

---

86 Cf. Liaquat Ali Khan's reference to this charge laid against him by MLA Mohan Lal Saksena in the course of the discussion on the Indian Finance Bill, 27 March 1947 in Afzal (1967: 98).

CHAPTER FOUR

Administrative Attempts to Channel Accumulations

The Income Tax Investigation Commission

In the previous chapter, the Government of India's policies on price and distribution controls during the Second World War were discussed. It was evident that accumulations of money capital would be further swollen by wartime speculative activities, and new entrants, enriched by speculation, would join the stratum of proto-capitalists. On the other hand, as the response to the Grady Mission showed, potential entry from these ranks into new industrial ventures was actively discouraged. Facilitated by wartime import restrictions which relieved the pressure from international competition, an opening could have been created for the transformation of this accumulated money capital into industrial capital, provided there was also an assurance of sustained demand by a supportive government. In the event, while some of these accumulations were spent on acquiring managing agencies, others were expended in buying large blocks of company equity.[1]

After Independence, the government embarked on a policy of decontrol.[2] With the partition of the country the one political group

---

1 See Introduction to this volume, fn 4.

2 The process was heralded by the appointment of the Purshottamdas Thakurdas Committee on Food Grains Policy in October 1947 (D.R. Gadgil, Foreword to Sovani 1949: vii). The following paragraphs are selected and resequenced from Gadgil (1949: 117–18).

that had shown itself capable of withstanding the pressure of Indian capitalists had vanished from the scene.[3] The new policy was thus oriented towards liquidating government commitments as soon as possible. Towards this, controlled distribution and price control of foodgrains was restricted to a few industrial centres.[4] The prices of sugar, refined and raw, were also decontrolled shortly thereafter, and decontrol of cloth and yarn prices followed within a couple of months. The country passed, as a result, from a state of *suppressed* inflation to one of open inflation.[5]

If political circumstances forced on the wartime government a policy of appeasement of industrialists, the post-Independence government gave no indication of a desire to change this policy.[6] Its attitude is best illustrated by reference to the detached indifference it exhibited to questions concerning cloth production and prices. During the war, when manufacturers had the main voice in determining the prices of cloth, there were many complaints regarding the general level at which prices were fixed and the manipulation of individual prices. In spite of many attempts by government officers and committees, the manufacturers successfully resisted all attempts at standardizing production and rationalizing the price-fixing system. On the evidence of the industry itself, the absence of standardization of production in individual units resulted in the disruption of official plans for cloth production and cotton consumption. It was, therefore, the unanimous opinion of all who reported on the problem that revision of cloth prices and standardization and rationalization of cloth production should take place simultaneously. Despite this awareness, in the first two post-war years, manufacturers were prevented from obtaining an increase in the price of coarse cloth only by pressure of public opinion, but they succeeded in evading control over production. Subsequently came complete decontrol and some months of hectic profit-making.

3 D.R. Gadgil, Foreword to Sovani (1949: vii).

4 Vakil (1946); Patvardhan (1958).

5 This process is documented in Sovani (1949: 46–57).

6 In the agricultural sphere, the choice of Purshottamdas Thakurdas to chair the Committee on Foodgrains Policy was a pointer; in the industrial sphere, the handling of the December 1947 Conference on Industrial Development, and more so, the 1948 Industrial Policy Resolution made clear the government's inclinations.

All the commodities whose prices had been decontrolled were essential consumer goods for which there were steady demands and whose supplies were inelastic. Speculators and traders had accumulated large liquid funds and upper income groups of consumers had, during 1946–7, obtained considerable increase in their money incomes.[7] Decontrol was, therefore, followed by speculative activity on the part of traders and attempts at increased purchases by consumers. During the war, the governments of the provinces had built up food grain procurement and distribution systems on a more or less elaborate scale, depending on whether they had a deficit or surplus of food grain production. The operation of these systems had depended on imports of foodgrains arranged by the central government. The aim of the whole system, developed after the Bengal famine, had been to guarantee everyone a minimum supply of food grains at controlled prices.[8] In the absence of controlled distribution in the post-Independence period, the government faced a continuous rise in the prices of food grains; its attempt to prevent a recurrence of conditions such as in Bengal in 1942 involved an even larger import of food grains from abroad than in previous years.[9] The rising trend of prices generated serious resentment within the country.

The policy of decontrol was, therefore, abandoned. Control over the prices and distribution of cloth was completely restored; however, when control was resumed, the prices fixed were once again negotiated prices and the government acquiesced in the industry's

7 While the Excess Profits Tax had been abolished in March 1946 and thus enabled large accretions to profits, the Pay Commission proposals, which were made retrospectively effective from January 1947, increased official salaries substantially. Gadgil's views on the central role of government salaries in determining the pattern of income distribution and consumer expectations are in 'Memorandum on scales of salaries submitted to the Central Pay Commission' in Gadgil (1955: 61–72).

8 There is a detailed account of the later wartime and immediate post-war policy on foodgrain procurement and distribution in the 'Report on Prices of Rabi Grains and Pulses for 1947–48' in Sovani (1948: 1–7).

9 Imports of foodgrains, which began in 1945–6 at 9.31 lakh tons, at a cost of Rs 26 crore, rose to 26.58 lakh tons in 1946–7 costing Rs 88.70 crore. For the nine-month period from April to December 1944, estimated imports were of 19 lakh tons at a cost of Rs 77.97 crore (Sovani 1949: 47, Table 21).

demand that it be left alone to produce what it chose. The new system of controls adversely affected all small retailers of cloth but assured manufacturers a market at guaranteed prices for whatever cloth (of whatever quality) they wished to produce.[10] An understanding was arrived at with sugar manufacturers for some reduction in the inflated prices of sugar; and it was decided that by November 1949, all food controls that had existed in November 1947 would be reintroduced. The inevitable cost of the decontrol experiment was that price levels had moved upwards and the resumption of controls could not bring them to their former levels. In fact, except in a few cases, like those of cloth and sugar, there was almost no reduction in prices from the peaks reached in the middle of 1948. The finance minister declared in December 1948 that the immediate aim of the government could only be the stabilization of prices and not their reduction from 1948 levels.[11] The fixing of prices of other products—coal, cement, iron, and steel—had equally demonstrated the desire to appease industrialists. The finance minister evidently thought in terms of stabilizing prices at the high levels attained in 1948 in the belief that industrialists could be induced to produce at full capacity only if they were assured substantial profits.

When industrialists pressed for decontrol during 1947, they were concerned with consumer goods of which they were producers; the control of prices and distribution of producer goods like cement, coal, iron, and steel, initiated in wartime, continued without any protest from them.[12] Thus, fairly complete regulation of the import and export trade continued. Imports of the more important producer goods had always required licenses and the possession of sufficient currency to pay for the imports. All important exports were subject to license. In most cases the total quota of exports was distributed annually amongst a limited number of persons. It was the satisfactory

10 'Utility cloth', produced under an early wartime scheme, had been pronounced to be futility cloth (Thakkar 1949: 185).

11 Gadgil (1949: 117–18).

12 With the expiry of the Defence of India Act in September 1946, the government allowed the majority of wartime-induced controls to lapse except for those over capital issues, imports and exports, foreign exchange, and the production, supply, and distribution of food stuffs and textiles (Sovani 1949: 30–1).

allocation of coal, cement, and transport facilities, and the ability to obtain an import license that determined the possibilities of maintaining or enhancing productive capacity; and export licenses enabled those influential enough to get them enormous profits. Indian businessmen evidently wanted the maintenance of this regime of controls. What they protested against was its logical extension, either to government control of international trade so that profits flowed to the exchequer or to the regulation of final product prices which was enabled by the existing control system.[13]

Profits in Indian industry during the war and post-war periods remained high, occasionally, as for example in 1948, reaching record levels. Indian industrialists were evidently exacting in their demands. Only profits such as those enjoyed in 1948 would spur them to productive effort, and the government appeared to have no means other than the profit incentive of regulating their production. The government allowed private enterprise a free field in industry but withheld controls over prices or production as would have been deemed essential even in countries such as the United States.[14]

Despite the record profit levels, tax evasion by industrialists and traders continued. The level of taxation on personal incomes and business profits was high, though no more than that in the United Kingdom and the British Dominions.[15] These evasions led to growing concentration of wealth and accumulation of larger and larger fortunes in the hands of a few. It was reported that the Sassoon Textile Mill empire in Bombay had changed hands for a consideration of Rs 4.8 crore; the A.F. Horsman interests in Kanpur were sold 'for a few

13 'The reaction to the proposal [for State trading] from member-bodies [of FICCI] when it was first made in 1949 was furious. In general, the business community was not unwilling to reconcile itself to the State's presence in industry, but found the proposal for its presence in trade simply intolerable. Industry could be a privilege, but trade was its prerogative' (Venkatasubbiah 1977: 80).

14 Gadgil (1949: 123–4).

15 A calculation by the finance department showed that the effective tax rate for a family of four was 42.7 per cent in India for an income of Rs 80,000 as compared to 54 per cent in Britain; 26 per cent in India for an income of Rs 40,000, and 41 per cent in Britain; and 6.6 per cent in India for an income of Rs 12,000 compared to 21 per cent in Britain. Statement by Liaquat Ali Khan at the end of the 1947 budget discussion in Afzal (1967: 104).

crores'.[16] Speculators and traders had developed evasion of regulations into a fine art.[17]

The phenomenon of widespread tax evasion was all the more serious because among the names under investigation by the income tax authorities were many of the most prominent leaders of Indian business.[18] Examples of the methods employed to evade taxes mentioned later provide insights into the problems confronting the state in attempting to channelize accumulations sourced from various activities, often extralegal, into industrial accumulation. The 1948 Industrial Policy Resolution, through which businessmen had clawed a preponderant role for the private sector, required that large investments be made. On the basis of their post-war proclivities, there were not many grounds for optimism.

The operation of controls to meet socially acceptable goals required the adjudication of several competing claims, both between businessmen themselves as a group, and between them and their suppliers and customers. The wartime government, in furthering its policy of appeasing industrialists, had delegated the adjudication process to institutions such as the Textile Control Board, to which it nominated representatives of textile manufacturing interests alone. After Independence, these decisions were placed within the province of the concerned ministry. The consequences of this soon became evident, as is apparent from a letter written by Jawaharlal Nehru to the then minister for industry and supply, Hare Krushna Mehtab. Nehru warned that there was a perception that in these decisions, the ministers did not count. It was the bureaucracy that distributed the favours.[19]

Ironically, Mehtab had, at this time, a file before him concerning precisely bureaucratic favours to a large business house. In late 1949, Murugappa and Sons of Madras were given permission to set up

16 Mehta (1954: 208).

17 According to the finance department's estimate, a tax assessee with an income of Rs 30 lakh a year or Rs 1.5 crore over the quinquennium 1941–2 to 1945–6, during which the Excess Profits Tax was in force, would have had an after-tax income of Rs 21 lakh. With this, the extravagant payments for managing agency rights or the block purchase of shares witnessed in the previous few years would not have been possible. See Liaquat Ali Khan's budget speech in Afzal (1967: 85).

18 Gadgil (1949: 121–2).

19 Secret and personal letter dated 27 September 1950 from Nehru to Mehtab, JN Papers, File no. 56, p. 237.

T.I. Cycles to manufacture Hercules-brand bicycles in collaboration with the British firm, Tube Investments, with an installed capacity of 1,00,000 cycles a year.[20] They were required to buy parts from Indian suppliers subject to adherence to quality standards and adequate production levels. While the imports of complete bicycles were controlled by half-yearly quotas distributed amongst various classes of importers, imports of complete bicycles was not contemplated in the case of T.I. Cycles.

Despite this, in May 1950, in the course of their application for complete bicycle imports, the firm referred to the existing policy for the motor vehicle industry, where traders with an approved manufacturing programme were permitted to import complete vehicles until they had achieved manufacturing capabilities. This analogy, though accepted by the industry and supply ministry, had been initially opposed by the commerce ministry on the grounds of its harmful impact on competing small-scale indigenous cycle manufacturers. Finally, a consensus was reached that T.I. Cycles would be permitted to import cycles up to the value of Rs 2.5 lakh during the period July–December 1950 and January–June 1951. After the amalgamation of the two ministries, the ministry of commerce and industry allowed them to expand their imports up to 20,000 components and tubes during July–December 1950 and 50,000 components and tubes in January–June 1951. Though this license was subsequently cancelled in March 1951, the visit by the secretary of the ministry the same month to the T.I. plant led to the issue of oral instructions that import of 20,000 cycles should be permitted. This change in the nature of the quota was also lobbied for by Ramaswamy Mudaliar, prominent politician of the Justice Party, and Chairperson of T.I. Cycles. Not only was this oral order by a senior civil servant contrary to declared policy, but it was also found to be irregular because no formal application had been made, it had bypassed the minister, and the finance ministry had not been involved.

Tax evaders included senior members of both the Birla and Tata groups. In March 1950, the Bengali weekly *Yuga Bani* published a fea-

---

20 'A Note on the licenses granted to the T.I. Cycles Ltd., Madras, for complete Bicycles and Parts' by D.P. Karmarkar, Deputy Minister for Commerce and Industry in Harekrushna Mehtab Papers, Subject files (A) Political and Administrative, File no. 20, vol. II, pp. 259–65.

ture on the connivance between the West Bengal sales tax department and the G.D. Birla Group, by which the Birla-owned Kesoram Cotton Mills evaded payment of a substantial quantum of sales tax. Material from the article was republished in *Current*, a Bombay-based English periodical. Later in the year, at the Nasik session of the Indian National Congress, the distribution of a book—*Mystery of Birla House*—led to a cause célèbre, and forced the Government of India to take special notice of the matter.[21]

In September 1950, Nehru had brought to Mehtab's notice the resentment amongst businessmen over the partiality shown towards Birla Group companies in the allocation of import and export licenses. The letter to Mehtab was written when Nehru had experienced the ambivalence shown by the West Bengal chief minister, B.C. Roy, in investigating the sales tax matter more fully.[22] The incident had become notorious because the West Bengal government had transferred the official who had been asked to deal with the Kesoram Cotton Mills tax cases, and correspondence exchanged between this official and his senior colleagues had been leaked to the press. In essence, the Bengal government was intent on investigating the source of the leak. Nehru was equally concerned to prevent continuation of the connivance that had led to the leak in sales tax revenue.

In his initial response to the articles in *Current* sent to him by Nehru, B.C. Roy responded by sending him official notes prepared by the sales tax commissioner and the finance secretary. The finance secretary stated that the question of tax evasion did not arise as during the post-war years of 1944–5, 1945–6, and 1946–7, no assessment of the tax payable had been undertaken by the sales tax department. In other words, the sales figures provided by the company had been accepted at face value and the tax paid by them treated as the amount leviable. Thus, no tax could be said to have been evaded. It was the Central Board of Revenue which had initially alleged tax evasion, but they were unable to find evidence on which evasion could be proved, and had also accepted tax payment from the company, presumably based again on data provided by the Mills. The assistant commissioner

21 Burman (1950).

22 Birla was reported as having 'excellent personal relations' and was on first name terms with the then finance minister of West Bengal, Nalini Ranjan Sarkar (Kudaisya 2003: 205).

in the sales tax department had worked for two years attempting to obtain information on which to base an independent assessment of sales and the tax payable. He had not progressed in this, and when he persisted in attempting to complete the assessment, he was transferred. His replacement, in contrast, had successfully completed assessments from 1945 to 1950 within a year.[23]

This explanation did not convince the finance ministry in Delhi, nor Nehru himself, that the Bengal government had taken adequate steps to realize the full tax due. He reminded B.C. Roy that there was a great deal of prejudice in the public mind against important business and commercial concerns, particularly in their propensity to evade taxes.[24] The fact that when the official asked for the manufacturing records of the Mills, they had termed it unreasonable and expressive of harassment, was telling. Their response, at a later stage when it was claimed that the records had been destroyed, was unacceptable and led to doubts about their bonafides. The sales tax commissioner's report which stated that the assistant commissioner was biased against the Birla Group revealed the way in which the sales tax department had internalized the viewpoint of the commercial community. Nehru reasserted that the case had entered the public imagination and both the state and the central governments would have to consider how the matter could be taken further.

The Central Board of Revenue presented a detailed appreciation of the situation.[25] Rich and influential taxpayers were known to complain about alleged harassment whenever an assessing officer began to initiate inquiries deemed inconvenient. Every complaint of harassment was investigated and appropriate action, including a transfer, was taken if the complaint was established. On the other hand, if the complaint was unfounded, suitable orders were passed and a copy was given to the officer concerned. This procedure was important in sustaining the morale of officials in the face of the opposition and criticism by influential taxpayers. If taking the line of least resistance

23 Secret letter no. 661 C.M. dated 24 August 1950 from B.C. Roy to Jawaharlal Nehru, JN Papers, File no.52, p. 319.

24 Secret letter no. 1413 P.M. dated 28 September 1950 from Jawaharlal Nehru to B.C. Roy, JN Papers, File no. 56, pp. 303–7.

25 Secret letter no. 1413 P.M. dated 28 September 1950 from Jawaharlal Nehru to B.C. Roy, JN Papers, File no. 56, p. 304.

was to be discouraged, the unpopular and thankless task of assessing and collecting taxes had to be actively supported by the government, rather than merely not blaming an official against whom false and malicious charges had been made. In fact, the board of revenue's experience was that if senior-level support was made evident for the demand by an assessing officer for specific documents, there was prompter compliance.

The board also noted that no investigation of the affairs of important and influential assessees could be completed quickly in the absence of their cooperation. In such cases, no time limit could be laid down as it was impossible to know beforehand which line of enquiry would be successful. Unless, therefore, it was officially ordered that a particular investigation should be abandoned or by other means the scope of the enquiry had been limited, there could be no basis for complaints about the slowness of the process of completing an assessment.

About two weeks later, Nehru wrote again.[26] He had referred the matter to the attorney general and had shown him a copy of the book *Mystery of Birla House*. The attorney general had reacted strongly and recommended that a judicial enquiry should be instituted into the circumstances which led to the transfer of the assistant commissioner. The Bengal government was urged by Nehru to accept the attorney general's advice. Nehru mentioned to B.C. Roy that a public judicial enquiry might have to follow. A copy of this letter was also sent to the central home minister, making the issue into a potential controversy between the central and state governments.

Kesoram Mills had initially stated that their manufacturing accounts were of no relevance in an assessment of sales tax, and had claimed that the assistant commissioner's demand for these amounted to harassment. When the Bengal government supported the assistant commissioner in this, the Mills changed their position to claim that these records had been destroyed. Interestingly, the Bengal government took the position that '[w]hether this statement was malafide or bonafade is more than we can know'.[27]

---

26 Secret letter dated 11 October 1950 from Jawaharlal Nehru to B.C. Roy, JN Papers, File no. 59, pp. 128–31.

27 Secret letter no. 780 C.M. dated 13/14 October 1950 from B.C. Roy to Jawaharlal Nehru, JN Papers, File no. 59, p. 276.

The report in *Current* had mentioned the fact that goods bought from army surplus stores, and subsequently traded, had not been mentioned in the tax returns of the Mills. On enquiry, it was found that the stores (parachutes made in Canada) had been sold in three exactly equal quantities to three registered dealers. Even though the Bengal commissioner for commercial taxes had earlier been of the view that valuable evidence had been suppressed, the Bengal government offered the explanation that as sales from one registered dealer (the Mills were registered as such) to others were not taxable under their act, no tax revenue was lost from this practice.[28]

B.C. Roy responded to the suggestion that a judicial enquiry be conducted into the circumstances of the assistant commissioner's transfer by arguing that there was no case for further investigation.[29] The commissioner in the department had recommended the transfer and this had been accepted by the government. The commissioner claimed that this decision was not based on any representation made by the Kesoram Mills, but solely on the assistant commissioner having been found guilty of disobeying orders and hampering the progress of the case. In other words, the West Bengal government was not going to be pressurized into sitting in judgement on its own actions.

The matter, however, was not to remain at the level of a contest between the prime minister and the chief minister. As Nehru wrote on receiving this last expression of B.C. Roy's opinion of the matter, public charges of administrative impropriety had been made and the case had gained a status of high notoriety.[30] A centrally sponsored high-level inquiry was necessitated, whose focus would be the evasion of taxes by Kesoram Mills, together with the manner in which government officials had connived in this. The assistant commissioner's alleged obstreperousness would be scrutinized in the course of this inquiry.

Evidently, in order to prevent such an inquiry, the Bengal government moved swiftly, not only to ensure the completion of assessments

28 Secret letter no. 1413 P.M. dated 28 September 1950 from Jawaharlal Nehru to B.C. Roy, JN Papers, File no. 56, p. 305; Secret letter no. 780 C.M. dated 13/14 October 1950 from B.C. Roy to Jawaharlal Nehru, JN Papers, File no. 59, p. 275.

29 Secret letter no. 784 C.M. dated 14 October 1950 from B.C. Roy to Jawaharlal Nehru, JN Papers, File no. 59, p. 277.

30 Secret letter no. 1597 P.M. dated 16 October 1950 from Jawaharlal Nehru to B.C. Roy, JN Papers, File no. 59, p. 389.

for 1944–5, 1945–6, and 1946–7[31] but also, more significantly, they managed to get production data from Kesoram Mills, measured in terms of bales of cloth. The Mills continued to maintain that as they were unable to convert bales into yards of cloth, their earlier plea that production data were unavailable was not compromised. With this data, and bale–yard conversion ratios obtained from the textile commissioner, the sales tax department was able to identify serious discrepancies in the figures of production given to them and to the textile commissioner. Over a three-year period, unreported production of the value of Rs 70 lakh was identified and an additional tax of Rs 2.7 lakh levied. B.C. Roy did not explain how the production figures were made available, given that the earlier position of the Mills was that the manufacturing data had been destroyed. Four of the six pages of his letter were devoted to a re-recital of the circumstances that led to the assistant commissioner's transfer. Although the details of subsequent events are not available from the records, it would seem that the Bengal government, by acting swiftly, had averted the ignominy of a central judicial probe into the business–government nexus.

In an early retort to Nehru, B.C. Roy had mentioned that the book *Mystery of Birla House* was as little worthy of attention as were the many scurrilous books and pamphlets circulating about Nehru himself.[32] Some years later, M.O. Mathai, personal assistant to Nehru, expressed concern that the assiduously created perception by Tata employees of the close proximity of senior board members of the Tata group to Nehru prevented the central board of revenue from taking firm action against tax evasion in the Tata group companies.[33] In particular, J.R.D. Tata, P.A. Narielwala, and Nehru were all known to address one another by their first names; J.R.D. Tata was invited to a meal every time he was in Delhi, and Narielwala was 'in and out' of Nehru's house and had free access to him without an appointment. The Tata Iron and Steel Company Limited (TISCO) case was said to be the single largest case of evasion in the entire history of Indian

31 Secret letter no. 872 C.M. dated 25/27 November 1950 from B.C. Roy to Jawaharlal Nehru, JN Papers, File no. 65, pp. 197–202.
32 Secret letter no. 780 C.M. from B.C. Roy to Jawaharlal Nehru, JN Papers, File no. 59, p. 274.
33 Secret note attached to top secret and personal memo by M.O. Mathai dated 31 December 1955 to Jawaharlal Nehru, JN Papers, File no. 410, pp. 197–200.

income tax administration. During 1940–6, the board had identified Rs 3.5 crore of unreported profit, implying an evasion of Excess Profits Tax (EPT) of Rs 2.25 crore and an income tax of Rs 50 lakh on the EPT. Together with penalties and interest this amounted to Rs 7.75 crore, of which Rs 4.5 crore were still leviable. According to the revenue board, they had evidence of J.R.D. Tata and Ardeshir Dalal (former member of the viceroy's executive council) personally recommending courses of action leading to tax evasion, despite written protest from their auditors. The methods of tax evasion were ingenious: undervaluation of stocks, stores, and raw materials in illegal ways; charging capital expenditure to revenues by illegal methods; and claiming excessive tax relief for deferred repairs through false statements and the misrepresentation of facts.

The general point was stated in a note prepared by the income tax authorities. They argued that tax evasion by manufacturing concerns had existed in most countries during and after the war, the least affected being Switzerland and the Scandinavian countries. The problem had in all cases been dealt with by special schemes which had one common feature that accounted for their success: this was the criminal prosecution of the most glaring cases. Tax experts were unanimous that this was the only possible method. It was not possible to detect more than a handful of cases, and tax evasion would continue unless there was evidence of very severe consequences. The deterrent moral effect of even one serious prosecution would be far reaching.[34]

Apart from resort to the manipulation of accounts as a means to tax evasion, as shown in the Birla and Tata cases, post-war shortages which encouraged widespread blackmarketing by both traders and manufacturers had led to abnormal accumulations of money capital.[35] As discussed earlier, the budget of the Interim (Congess–Muslim League) Government had, in fact, in February 1947 announced the institution of an Income Tax investigation commission. While the more general budget proposals had to be considerably diluted because of concerted opposition led by the Federation of Indian Chambers

---

34 JN Papers, File no. 410, p. 197, enclosure to note by M.O. Mathai, 31 December 1955.

35 So much so, that Merchant (1953) wrote an interesting analysis of the root causes of blackmarketing.

of Commerce and Industry (FICCI), the concept of the investigation commission survived into Independence and also formed part of the budget passed in independent India in late 1947.

The commission was not successful in bringing offenders to book speedily, and it was decided to get at least something for government revenues by inducing the suspects to reach a settlement. However, the commission trod a very cautious line in estimating the degree of concealed income and the quantum of revenue and penalty payment due to the government.[36] Although it was not explicitly mentioned, it seems clear that the concealed income could be shown to be nominal because of the difficulty in tracing financial transactions between firms that were interconnected through having a common managing agent.[37] The cases of two prominent businessmen of Uttar Pradesh (UP), Padampat Singhania and Ram Ratan Gupta, both of Kanpur, illustrated the problems in achieving a satisfactory investigation in the absence of legislated disclosure norms.[38] Both of them were not only well-known offenders but had a poor public reputation.[39] Political wisdom and policy, however, required that the government's dealings with them should be seen to be above criticism.[40] The situation in UP had been brought to Jawaharlal Nehru's personal attention after reports from the intelligence agencies had warned of large-scale

36 This was evident from their estimate, in 1951, of the concealed income of the Dalmia-Jain Group which amounted to Rs 4.58 crore over the eight-year period from 1939–47. During the same period, the Dalmias increased their controlling interest over share capital in both acquired and new enterprises from Rs 3.93 crore to Rs 16 crore (JN Papers, File no. 81, p. 260, 'Gist of the Report by the Income Tax Investigation Commission on the Dalmia group of cases' enclosure to letter No 640-PSF/51, 20 April 1951 from C.D. Deshmukh, finance minister, to Jawaharlal Nehru).

37 In the stock taking after the financial crises faced by the 'Miracle Economies' of East Asia, four concepts entered the economic research sphere: the better known is that of 'crony capitalism'; however, 'pyramids', 'tunneling', and 'propping' have been fruitful areas for academic excursions. See Bertrand et al. (2002), Bertrand and Mullainathan (2003), Chakrabarti and Chatterjee (2006), Friedman et al. (2003), Johnson et al. (2000).

38 Secret and urgent letter from H.P. Mody, governor of UP, dated 27 June 1950 to Jawaharlal Nehru, JN Papers, File no. 46, p. 312.

39 Secret letter nos 779 P.M. and 780 P.M. dated 30 June 1950 from Jawaharlal Nehru to C.D. Deshmukh and S. Varadachariar, JN Papers, File no. 46, p. 315.

40 Secret letter dated 3 July 1950 from S. Varadachariar to Jawaharlal Nehru, JN Papers, File no. 47, p. 321.

smuggling in Meerut. The UP government had taken some action but the results seemed to be inconclusive.[41] Curiously, Padampat Singhania's case had been settled by the UP government on payment of what amounted to a token penalty of Rs 2.5 lakh. It was proposed to follow a similar course of action with Ram Ratan Gupta on the grounds that protracted investigations had failed to build up a case which would hold in court.[42] This course of action was strongly opposed by both the finance minister and the chairperson of the Income Tax Investigation Commission; both felt that for the government to settle without launching a prosecution was morally indefensible and legally open to objection in that it amounted to compounding a crime.[43]

In the case of Ram Ratan Gupta, whose case was before the Income Tax Investigation Commission, his undisclosed income between 1940 and 1948 was estimated at Rs 129 lakh. Much of this had been invested in shares, which had depreciated in value. Because the finance ministry had agreed to reduction in assessable value on account of depreciation of assets, the commission had settled on an assessment of Rs 75 lakh, on which the tax was Rs 51 lakh. As he was already due to pay Rs 55 lakh on the normal assessment by the income tax department, the commission had left it to the central board of revenue to permit Gupta to pay in instalments.[44] In Padampat Singhania's case, the home ministry had faced major obstacles in proceeding with a case in Bombay, because all the witnesses had allegedly been bought up by Singhania.[45]

The Income Tax Investigation Commission, in the course of its enquiries into the affairs of Surajmull Choteylal, provided evidence of the ways in which intra-group transfer of funds allowed for tax evasion.[46] Surajmull Choteylal was a prominent figure in the Calcutta

41 Memo dated 2 May 1950 from Jawaharlal Nehru to his Personal Private Secretary, JN Papers, File no. 43, p. 75

42 H.P. Mody, letter dated 27 June 1950.

43 Secret letter no. 5280-PSF/50 dated 7 July 1950 from C.D. Deshmukh to Jawaharlal Nehru, and S. Varadachariar letter dated 3 July 1950, JN Papers, File no. 47, pp. 321 and 322.

44 S. Varadachariar, letter dated 3 July 1950.

45 Secret and personal letter no. 880-PM dated 8 July 1950 from Jawaharlal Nehru to H.P. Mody, JN Papers, File no. 47, p. 325.

46 Top secret letter no. 725-PSF/51 dated 8 May 1951 with enclosures from C.D. Deshmukh to Jawaharlal Nehru, JN Papers, File no. 83, pp. 401–7.

hessian trade and vice chairperson of McLeod and Company, who managed tea estates, jute mills, and other enterprises. Beginning his independent business career in Benares in 1929 as a Commission Agent for Standard Vacuum, he moved a little later to trading in hessian and gunny. With the outbreak of war in 1939, he had a meteoric rise made possible by contravening control regulations while trading in jute and jute goods. By 1944, he had acquired sufficient shareholding in McLeod to be elected vice chairperson. While his assets in 1940 were about Rs 5 lakh, by 1947 he was on the board of 47 companies. It was the size of his assets that drew the attention of the commission to Surajmull Choteylal.

It was found that Choteylal had concealed income of about Rs 55 lakh through creation of a number of Jaipur-based companies which were profit-making, while he showed a loss through creation of fictitious loans and by showing incomplete account books. When he understood the implications of the commission's inquiry, he asked for some time to settle his affairs. However, he used this time to fabricate further fictitious evidence and his statement of assets was found to be incomplete and unreliable. Complicit with Choteylal were senior public figures: J.R. Walker, chairperson of McLeod and wartime jute controller with the Government of India, and Mandhata Singh, former dewan of Bikaner. While Walker had allowed Choteylal to keep *benami* assets of Rs 5 lakh in his name, Mandhata Singh had lent his name to fictitious loans made ostensibly by himself and close relations. These amounts were, actually, part of Choteylal's concealed income.

In this case, diligent ferreting by commission officials had led to a sufficiently strong case; so Choteylal had to agree to a 'settlement' amounting to 75 per cent of the evaded tax and a penalty of Rs 2.8 lakh. To this was added a figure of Rs 5 lakh for concealed income dating from before 1939. However, as Nehru noted in a letter to C.D. Deshmukh, beyond summoning Walker and Mandhata Singh and conveying the government's displeasure, there was little more that could be done to penalize their connivance in tax evasion.[47]

In other words, the efforts of the Income Tax Investigation Commission, however fruitless in gaining for the government the revenue

47 Top secret letter dated 8 May 1951 from Jawaharlal Nehru to C.D. Deshmukh, JN Papers, File no. 83, p. 409.

which was its due, brought sharply into focus the varied methods by which funds could be diverted and excess profits earned without leaving evidence of extralegal practices. The full implications of the formation of interlocking groups of companies, first noted by Ashoka Mehta in 1940, began to come to the notice of the Government of India in 1949.[48] Calling it a public menace, Jawaharlal Nehru singled out the Dalmia group, and suggested that the Companies Act should be amended to prevent intra-group transactions which were clearly against the spirit of the law.

The prospect of stable economic progress in India depended on the extent to which the decision to develop the resources of the country through private enterprise was reconciled with the aims and expectations placed before and entertained by the mass of the people.[49] Such reconciliation could come about only if the government showed considerable intelligence and firmness in controlling the exploitation by private enterprise of the opportunities that government policies offered. In the Indian case, despite the provisions of the Voluntary Disclosure Scheme of 1951, whose terms implied prosecution of those who did not declare their concealed income, not a single prosecution had taken place by the end of 1955. It was estimated that Rs 100 crore was evaded every year or an aggregate of Rs 500 crore during a plan period.[50]

48 Secret letter from Jawaharlal Nehru to K.C. Neogy, minister for commerce, dated 8 August 1949, JN Papers, File no. 27, p. 162.

49 Cf. A. Mehta (1949).

50 JN Papers, File no. 410, p.197, enclosure to note by M.O. Mathai, 31 December 1955.

CHAPTER FIVE

Sholapur Mills and the Initiation of Social Engineering

DEVELOPMENTS DURING THE WAR AND EARLY POST-INDEPENDENCE YEARS

As discussed at the end of Chapter 1, the Government of India did not agree in 1936 to the demand for the abolition of managing agencies. However, various restrictions were imposed by the Indian Companies (Amendment) Act passed that year. Besides prescribing the duration of managing agency agreements, specifying their duties, liabilities, and the remuneration of managing agents, the Amendment Act prohibited firms from granting or guaranteeing loans to their agents. Intra-firm investment of funds by managing agents when they had several companies under the same management was also forbidden. Similarly, the employment of the funds of a company in the purchase of the shares and debentures of another company under the management of the same managing agent was prohibited. Managing agents were also prevented from carrying on, on their own account, business which was of the same nature as and directly competed with the business of the managed company. Finally, the practice of managing agents filling the board of directors with their own nominees was discouraged by the directive that no managing agent should be allowed to nominate more than one-third of the total number of directors.

These changes introduced by the Amendment Act were criticized by businessmen as violating the fundamental principle of the sanctity of contract. It was asserted that existing contracts were being interfered with and a company was being prevented from choosing the form of management, and also the basis of remuneration, which it considered to be the best in its own interests. It was stated that '....undue legislative restrictions like those embodied in the Act would kill a system which had rendered such splendid service to industry in the past'.[1] It was also mentioned that limiting the period of managing agency agreements to twenty years was shortsighted in view of the fact that industrialization in India was still in a nascent stage. It stated:

> It takes about ten to fifteen years for any industry to be established on a profitable and economic basis and it would not, therefore, be sufficient inducement to the managing agents to develop an industry if they are to relinquish the fruits of labour so soon after they have succeeded in developing it.... Further, the restrictive clauses, by dissuading managing agents from embarking on new industrial ventures, would only retard the industrial development of the country.[2]

In actual fact, not only had there been no relaxation of the grip of the managing agency system since 1936 over private industrial enterprise, but there had also been a further extension of its application. The advantages of the system were evidently so great that despite widespread public criticism, the percentage of companies controlled by managing agency firms increased from 75 in 1935 to over 95 in 1955—a considerable rise.[3] Despite the clause inserted by the 1936 act that required managing agents to be appointed after the passing of a resolution at a general body meeting of the company, the situation remained such that it could be asserted that the managing agency was the active agent and the associated joint-stock companies merely operating arms of the agency.[4]

1 Circular Letter No. 193/1936 of 20 June 1936, from the Bengal Chamber of Commerce, Calcutta, on the bill to amend the Indian Companies Act of 1913, quoted in Das (1956: 89).

2 Memorandum of the Federation of Indian Chambers of Commerce and Industry (FICCI) on the on the bill to amend the Indian Companies Act of 1913, quoted in Das (1956: 89).

3 Das (1956: 76–7), based on data contained in the Investors' India Year Book for the relevant years.

4 Brimmer (1955: 555).

Although glaring malpractices which were widespread before 1936 were prevented, businessmen's acumen was soon able to find ways and means of circumventing the legal restrictions imposed. Many managing agency firms were advised by lawyers and chartered accountants familiar with company law, and they devised ways of remaining within the letter of the law and at the same time continuing their manipulative practices in a disguised form.[5]

The continuance of these practices was facilitated by the ineffectiveness of the procedure in administering the act. Despite the amendments, the Indian Companies Act had a number of loopholes which became obvious as the years passed. Large changes had taken place in the organization and working of joint-stock companies, and, over a wide sector that was dominated by new entrants in trade and industry, the ethos of company management had changed. Conventional methods of company management were replaced by unorthodox and more speculative techniques, which the existing company law was unable to control adequately. More serious than the obvious loopholes was the inadequate and perfunctory manner in which the act was administered.[6] This was due to a number of reasons. First, although both the legislative and executive authorities in respect of the regulation and inspection of joint-stock companies were vested in the Government of India, in practice, the central government had very little to do with the administration of the Companies Act. The central government delegated all its functions under the act to the provincial governments. The delegated powers were so extensive that for practical purposes the responsibility for the administration of the act rested with the state governments.[7] The reasons for such delegation were both financial and based on the doctrine of the minimal state. As a result, the social implications of company law as the moulder and channeler of business behaviour was not recognized and the administration of the act was regarded as the negative function of preventing the joint-stock companies from contravening statutory requirements. This negative

5 Das (1956: 89).

6 According to the Company Law Committee, the Indian Companies Act was perhaps the most under-administered of all the central acts relating to trade and industry (India 1952: 179).

7 For a statement showing the nature and extent of the powers delegated, see India (1952: 180–1).

Table 5.1 Growth of Corporate Sector

Year	No. of Companies	Paid-up Capital (Rs crore)
1922	5,189	230.5
1932		285.9
1939	11,114	290.4 (excludes Burma)
1945	14,859	389.0
1947	21,853	487.7 (before Partition)
1955	29,779	983.1

Source: Das (1956: 125–6).

function could be performed as easily by the provincial governments. Additionally, on the plea of observing economy in administration, the power to appoint registrars of joint-stock companies was delegated to the provincial governments. Very little importance was placed on the administration of Company Law with the result that in 1952, barring Bombay and West Bengal, none of the provinces had full-time registrars. Elsewhere, the registrar's duties were performed by officers of the provincial government in addition to their other duties, although the number of joint-stock companies at work in India had exceeded the figure of 22,000 since 1947.

The total budget in respect of the establishments of the registrars of joint-stock companies in all the provinces did not exceed Rs 5 lakh per annum.[8]

The continuance of the malpractices which the 1936 company law amendments were designed to prevent was again the focus of attention after the Second World War. As a first step towards formulating reform, the Government of India in 1946 appointed Tricumdas Dwarkadas, a Bombay solicitor, as an officer on special duty. He was to indicate comprehensively the lines on which the Indian Companies Act should be revised, in the light of the developments in trade and industry since 1936, taking also as a guide the amended provisions of the English Companies Act. Between 1946 and 1947, Dwarkadas submitted his recommendations in three parts, but was unable to

8 India (1952: 183).

complete his assignment on account of his other preoccupations. The Government of India thereupon appointed V.T. Thiruvenkatachari, advocate general of Madras, to carry out some further studies in the matter and to advise the government. Thiruvenkatachari completed his task in October 1948. Dwarkadas' and Thiruvenkatachari's reports were subjected to a detailed departmental scrutiny in the ministry of commerce.[9] The proposals formulated as a result of this scrutiny were embodied in a memorandum circulated to all state governments and organized industrial and commercial bodies in December 1949.[10]

In response, a series of startling disclosures were made by the Bombay Shareholders' Association exposing the loopholes in the 1913 Indian Companies Act and placing the subject of managing agencies in the forefront of public attention.[11] These loopholes, together with the absence of an effective organization to administer the provisions of the act, had enabled businessmen and financiers to misuse and distort these provisions to serve their personal ends.[12] In the case of a large number of companies, the managing agency had been used to undertake a variety of corrupt practices.

An important development in company law took place when the Government of India promulgated the Indian Companies (Amendment) Ordinance, 1951, on 21 July 1951. By this ordinance, the government for the first time assumed extensive powers to intervene directly in the affairs of a company and also greatly extended the powers of the court to take suitable action when the affairs of a company were being conducted in a manner prejudicial to its interests or in a manner oppressive to some part of its members. It was intended to prevent the passing of well-established and reputable joint-stock enterprises into unscrupulous hands who wished to acquire control over them for their personal advantage, to the detriment of the investors and the

9 N.K. Majumdar, a former registrar of joint-stock companies, West Bengal, was placed in charge of this work.

10 India (1952: 3).

11 As mentioned earlier, Bombay Shareholders' Association (1949: 74–82) lists questionable practices by managing agencies owned by Birla Brothers, Dalmia-Jain, Karamchand Thapar, Jaipuria, Walchand, Surajmull Nagarmull, Sarupchand Hukumchand, Kamanis, and Bajoria amongst the more prominent business groups.

12 India (1952: 19). See also 'The Congress Party in Parliament, Indian Companies Bill', 1955 (mimeo), note in JN Papers, File no. 367, pp. 79–113.

interest of the companies themselves. The ordinance was replaced with some changes by the Indian Companies (Amendment) Act, 1951. This book began with the discussion on the bill introducing the amending legislation.

The Advisory Commission on Company Law, appointed by the Government of India in October 1951, had, by February 1952, disposed of 92 out of 122 cases referred to it. The cases referred mostly covered changes in the controlling interests of companies which required the prior approval of the central government. The references included changes that were proposed to be made in the boards of directors or the managing agencies of firms, transfer of shares, constitution of the managing agencies, appointments of managing agents, increase in the directors' remunerations, appointments of new managing agents, changes in the articles of association of a company relating to remuneration of managing agents, and changes in the constitution of a company.[13]

THE SHOLAPUR MILLS CASE AND THE INITIATION OF SOCIAL ENGINEERING

The political imperative for drastic revision of company law was made clear by the legal infirmities under which government functioned. These were dramatically displayed by the Sholapur Mills episode, which also exhibited the vagaries of management that industrial enterprises faced under the managing agency system. The Mills were managed by the managing agency of Morarji Gokuldas and Company, based in Bombay.[14]

In 1931, important changes in the partnership of the managing agency firm led to the financial crises which culminated in the

13 *Economic Weekly* (1952a).

14 The cotton textile industry in the Sholapur hinterland was consolidated in the 1860s through two developments: the construction of the Ekruk irrigation tank assured sufficient water for cotton cultivation leading to an increase in the area under cultivation, and a railway connection provided a link to both internal and export markets. Thus, complementary to the existing hand-spinning and weaving industry, a steam-spinning and weaving mill—the Sholapur Spinning and Weaving Company Limited—began operating at Sholapur in March 1877. Directories (Industry & Web Directory), http://www.solapurcorporation.com/dir_industry_web_dir.asp/, accessed on 7 April 2012.

termination of their managing agency.[15] In 1930, the Mills had faced financial difficulties and was threatened by the prospect of a winding-up petition by a creditor. To avoid this, it was essential for the Mills to secure additional finance. As it was the customary practice for joint-stock companies to rely on managing agents for finance, the Mills' management approached Morarji Gokuldas. However, as the three existing partners were not able to provide the money themselves, they entered into negotiations with two Calcutta firms, the Jhajharias and Dhandhanias. Eventually, it was agreed that these two Calcutta firms would be admitted as partners in the firm of Morarji Gokuldas as a precondition for their advancing Rs 12 lakh to the Mills. In addition, they were to be appointed as selling agents for the Mills. Critically, for the future, under the hypothecation agreement, the two Calcutta firms were to act as managing partners as long as the loan extended to the Mills was outstanding.

On completion of these negotiations in early 1931, three agreements were finalized. First, there was one between the existing partners in Morarji Gokuldas and these two Calcutta firms, by which the latter two were admitted as partners in Morarji Gokuldas. The second was a hypothecation agreement between the Mills and the two Calcutta firms, by which an advance of Rs 12 lakh to the Mills on certain security was agreed on, and finally, there was an agreement between the Mills and the Calcutta firms by which these firms were appointed selling agents. There was no specific agreement between the Mills and Morarji Gokuldas appointing the reconstituted firm of Morarji Gokuldas as managing agents of the company.

Immediately after, in February 1931, differences began to arise between the managing partners, Ramdhandas Jhajharia and Lokenathprasad Dhandhania, both principal partners of their own firms. These differences ultimately led to the passing of a resolution by the directors of the Mills at a board meeting in January 1933 which ended the term of the managing agency of Morarji Gokuldas.

The managing agency of the Sholapur Mills then passed into the hands of Morarka and Company, whose partners were also partners in a separate firm engaging in moneylending and speculation in sil-

15 Morarji Goculdas and Company vs Sholapur Spinning and Weaving Company Ltd 1943 Law Suit (Bom) 32.

ver and shares.[16] Through this firm, which started business in August 1942, Morarka had, by 1948, bought 99 ordinary shares and 6,780 preference shares of the Sholapur Mills.[17] However, internecine differences of opinion continued to plague the management of the Mills. One of the partners of Morarka held a controlling interest. For a long time, these differences between him and his partner, Ramkumar, had seriously affected the working of the Mills to an extent that the balance sheet as on 31 March 1948 showed an enormous loss of Rs 33 lakh.

The director's report for the year admitted that the balance sheet and profit and loss account had not been signed by the managing agents, Messrs Morarka and Company, nor had they certified the inventory of the stock-in-trade and stores. The board had to ask the manager to go through the valuation of the stock-list on the basis of the previous year's method and to certify the stock-list. Mr Ramkumar Shrinivas Morarka, ex-officio director and a member of the managing agents' firm, who was present at the board meeting, was asked if the managing agents would sign the balance sheet and profit and loss account but he declined to answer the question. In July 1948, due to the inability of the managing agents to cooperate amongst themselves in managing the affairs of the company, a deadlock was created. The secretary of the company had to report this to the chairperson, who asked the agents to ensure that their disagreements were resolved immediately. The managing agents expressed their regret at the state of affairs created by their neglect and undertook to clear the deadlock within a week (which they did at the time) and to see that similar problems did not reoccur. In spite of this undertaking, the board had to admit to serious lapses in the annual report, which were echoed in the auditor's comments.

At the annual general meeting held in December 1948, allegations and counter-allegations were made by the partners of the managing

16 Dwarkadas Kesardeo Morarka vs CIT(SC) 44 ITR 529(SC), available at http://www.indiankanoon.org/doc/276037/, accessed on 24 September 2012.

17 The authorized capital of the Mills was Rs 48,00,000 divided into 1,590 fully paid-up ordinary shares of Rs 1,000 each, and 20 fully paid-up ordinary shares of Rs 500 each, and 32,000 partly paid-up redeemable cumulative first preference shares of Rs 100 each. The then current paid-up capital of the company was Rs 32,00,000, Rs 16,00,000 being fully paid-up ordinary shares and Rs 16,00,000 being partly paid up preference shares, Rs 50 being unpaid on each of the 32,000 cumulative preference shares.

agents' firm, so much so that they very nearly came to blows; due to the chaos, the chairperson dissolved the meeting. Mr Ramkumar Shrinivas Morarka, while admitting that he had not taken part in any substantive managerial work and had confined himself to signing cheques, charged the chairperson with adopting a partisan attitude.[18] At the adjourned meeting held in January 1949, the chairperson, E.B. Ghaswala, made it clear that owing to sharp differences amongst the partners of the managing agency, the management of the Mills was at a standstill during part of the year which resulted in a large loss to the company. He said he was unable to bring about a satisfactory solution to the present problem as there were only four directors, including himself, on the board, and three of them were connected with the managing agency.[19]

The Sholapur Mills were then one of the largest in Asia, employing 13,000 workers.[20] Per shift, they produced 25 to 30 thousand pounds of yarn, and 100,000 yards of cloth. Prior to 1947, the highest dividend paid by the company was Rs 525 per share and the lowest Rs 100. In 1948, while other textile companies had been able to show very substantial profits, the accounts of the Sholapur Mills showed a loss of Rs 30 lakh. On 27 July 1949 the directors of the company gave a notice to the workers that the Mills would be closed, and the Mills were in fact closed on August 27.[21] They were working on two shifts when they closed down. The closure of the mill meant a production loss of 25 lakh yards of cloth and 1.5 lakh pounds of yarn per month.

The managing agents had acquired control over the majority of the shares of the company, and a large number of minority shareholders felt powerless as they could not make their voices heard. A representation was made on behalf of a section of these shareholders to

18 In reply to a query from a shareholder as to who conducted the affairs of the Mills, Mr Ramkumar Morarka was reported to have said that 'Thakorji', that is 'God', was conducting the Mills' affairs (*Bombay Samachar*, 31 December 1948, quoted in BSA 1949: 174).

19 *Times of India*, 7 January 1949, quoted in BSA (1949: 174).

20 Chiranjit Lal Choudhuri vs The Union of India and Others on 4 December 1950, 1951, AIR 41; 1950 SCR 869, http://indiankanoon.org/doc/4354, accessed on 24 September 2012.

21 Dwarkadas Shrinivas of Bombay vs The Sholapur Spinning and Weaving Co. Ltd and others on 18 December 1953, 1954, AIR 119; 1954 SCR 674 http://indiankanoon.org/doc/1880952, accessed on 24 September 2012.

the registrar of joint-stock companies in Bombay against the conduct of the managing agents, and the government of Bombay ordered a special inquiry into the affairs of the company. Two special inspectors were appointed by the Bombay government and their report revealed 'certain astounding facts' and showed that the Mills had been grossly mismanaged by the board of directors and the managing agents. It also revealed that the persons who were responsible for the mismanagement were culpable under the law. The Bombay government accepted the report of the inspectors and instructed the advocate general of Bombay to take legal proceedings against persons connected with the management of the company. Thereafter, the Government of India was requested by the state government to take special action to ensure the early reopening of the Mills. However, the Government of India found that they had no power to take over the management of a particular mill unless its efficient functioning could only be ensured through the existing management acting under the direction of a controller appointed under the Essential Supplies Act; thus, in October 1949, the government appointed a controller under the act. In November 1949, the controller asked the directors of the company to make a call on the amount remaining unpaid on each of the preference shares of Rs 50 per share. As the directors refused to comply with this requisition, the government found that a peculiar situation had been created where the managing agents themselves were unwilling to conduct the affairs of the company in a satisfactory and efficient manner. Because of their voting strength, the managing agents made it impossible for a controller under the Essential Supplies Act to function, and they also made it difficult for the company to run smoothly under the normal law. Finally, the Government of India, in January 1950, promulgated an ordinance under Section 42 of the Government of India Act. This ordinance not only enabled the government to take over the control of the Mills but also empowered the delegation of all its powers to the government of Bombay; under these delegated powers the government appointed new directors.

These newly appointed directors passed a resolution in February 1950 making a call of Rs 50 on each of the preference shares payable at the time stated in the resolution. In April 1950, the ordinance was repealed and an act was passed by the parliament, known as the Sholapur Spinning and Weaving Company (Emergency Provisions)

Act which re-enacted in close terms all the provisions of the ordinance and provided that all actions taken and orders made under the ordinance should be deemed to have been taken or made under the corresponding provisions of the act. The preamble to the ordinance was not, however, reproduced in the act.[22]

The Government of India placed the case before the standing committee of the Industrial Advisory Council, where a large number of leading industrialists of the country were present. Here it was agreed that this was a case where the government could rightly and properly intervene and there would be no occasion for any criticism coming from any quarter. From the discussion on the floor of the House it was clarified that the total number of weaving and spinning mills which were closed down for one reason or another was about thirty-five. Some of them were said to have closed due to insufficient cotton supply, some due to overstocks, some due to shortage of working capital, and some on account of demonstrated mismanagement. What distinguished the case of the Sholapur Mill from the other mills against whom there might have been similar charges of mismanagement were the simultaneous fulfilment of four criteria: the undertaking related to an industry of national importance; the firm was of proven viability; a technical report on the condition of the plant and machinery showed that they could be properly utilized as they stood or after necessary repairs and reconditioning; and finally, a proper enquiry had been held which showed that the managing agents had so misbehaved that they were no longer fit and proper persons to remain in charge of such an important undertaking.[23]

Despite the debate in parliament and consultation with industrialists, apparently signifying a consensus on the necessity of government intervention, the act was challenged in the Supreme Court on two occasions. In the first case, a five-member division bench of the Supreme Court held by a majority of three to two that the act was in

22 It was stated in the preamble to the ordinance that 'on account of mismanagement and neglect, a situation has arisen in the affairs of the Sholapur Spinning and Weaving Company Limited which has prejudicially affected the production of an essential commodity and has caused serious unemployment amongst a certain section of the community', and it was on account of the emergency arising from this situation that the promulgation of the ordinance was necessary.

23 Parliamentary Debates, 3(14): 2394–5; 31 March 1950.

accordance with the Constitution. A second challenge was, however, successful and another division bench of the Supreme Court held that the property rights of shareholders had been 'eroded' by the act and the government's subsequent appointment of a board of directors which was not accountable to the shareholders.[24] Essentially, the distinction between a temporary takeover of a firm from manifestly corrupt and incompetent managing agents and nationalization without compensation was evidently not sympathetically viewed by the court. The inconsistency between the two rulings of the Supreme Court, which in themselves have entered the lore of commonwealth legal history, was evidently based on differing conceptions of property and thus the type of actions that constituted an attack on property rights.[25]

Even before the second judgement was delivered, the tone of the remarks made by the bench had warned the government that their most ambitious attempt to legislate measures to 'save capitalism from the capitalists' was not going to withstand legal scrutiny. This realization, with its implications for the administration of the Industrial Development and Regulation Act, the Land Acquisition Act, and the Insurance Act amongst others, led the government to consider appropriate constitutional changes in the fourth amendment to the Constitution in 1953.[26]

CONTEST OVER THE LEGITIMACY OF THE MANAGING AGENCY SYSTEM

Together with the Bombay Shareholders' Association, scrutiny by the Fiscal Commission, the Income Tax Investigation Commission, and the Planning Commission had raised a general discussion on several

---

24 Chiranjit Lal Choudhuri vs The Union of India and Others on 4 December 1950, 1951, AIR 41; 1950 SCR 869, http://indiankanoon.org/doc/4354, accessed on 24 September 2012; Dwarkadas Shrinivas of Bombay vs The Sholapur Spinning and Weaving Co. Ltd and others on 18 December 1953, 1954, AIR 119; 1954 SCR 674 http://indiankanoon.org/doc/1880952, accessed on 24 September 2012.

25 Allen (2000: 150–1).

26 Letter no. 982/CIM/53 dated 13 November 1953 from T.T. Krishnamachari, the then minister for commerce and industry, to Jawaharlal Nehru, TTK Papers, correspondence with Jawaharlal Nehru, 1953, p. 120.

aspects of company law.[27] In October 1950, the Government of India set up a committee, with C.H. Bhabha, a former commerce minister of the Government of India and a prominent businessman, as chairperson, which reported in 1952. Although government officials in their memorandum had been in favour of abolishing the managing agency system, the Company Law Committee continued to hold that the system could be reformed.[28]

In Chapter 1, it was argued that managing agencies were the central institutional feature by which the city of London controlled the Indian economy. It was also the reason the system remained impervious to reform and, more insidiously, to effective regulation. It was a remarkable testimony of this proposition that the British chancellor of the exchequer himself, in early 1955, raised one of the very first of the influential voices in support of managing agencies. He protested against the wide sweep of the reform proposals, which were to cover all managing agencies (both British and Indian) and not merely those found engaging in fraudulent activities (supposedly, largely Indian).[29] The narrow time frame within which the restrictions were to come

27 The main points that were discussed concerned company promotion, shareholders' control over management, powers of directors, appointment of managing agents, government authority over investigations, audit, liquidation proceedings, rights of minority shareholders, and administration of the Company Act.

28 India (1949: 8, para 27).

29 In this context, *Economic Weekly* under the title 'Irregularities in Company Accounts' had this to say:

McLeod and Company is one of the important managing agency firms of long standing having interest in jute, tea, engineering, shipping, etc. It has a reputation for the efficient administration of industries under its control and for clean and straightforward dealings. The statement of its chairman, Mr A.J. Peppercorn, and the report of Lovelock & Lewes, the auditors of the firm—which are embodied in the report and statement of accounts of the company for the year that ended on 31st December 1950 submitted in April 1952—therefore, come as a great surprise. The Chairman reports, 'As a result of the investigations that I undertook, it was ascertained and confirmed that during 1951, certain of the transactions, as recorded in the books of the various Jute Mills Companies, Baling Companies and in the books of McLeod & Co., Ltd., were irregular. Some of these transactions were fictitious in that no actual transactions took place, while in other cases, although there were actual transactions, the dates on which they took place had not been correctly shown, thereby transferring profits by charging incorrect prices.'

According to the auditors, either some of the transactions were not entered in the company's register of contracts maintained under section 91(a) of the Indian

into force was also a matter of objection. The most ingenious, however, of his complaints was that the ownership of a managing agency agreement was itself a property right and thus to be treated as quite distinct to the financial interests that the agreement may have been based on. It was in this context that the Government of India's proposed amendment to Article 31 of the Constitution, which ensured private property rights, was arousing uncertainty amongst would-be investors.[30]

It was at this stage that the trajectories of company law reform, the role of foreign capital, and the specific malpractices of the managing agencies converged, and the discussion now turns to a consideration of these issues. There was a clear understanding amongst policymakers that the purpose of company law was to manage the behaviour of promoters and managing agents, rather than that of the companies they controlled. In pleading for Jawaharlal Nehru's intervention in ensuring that the Companies Bill, introduced into the parliament in September 1953, received sufficient attention for the bill to become law by the middle of 1954, the finance minister raised important issues.[31] Emphasizing that the bill was premised on the necessity of reforms, he emphasized that it was designed to check abuses and malpractices amongst some promoters and managements, which not only brought them discredit but also generated widespread distrust and suspicion amongst investors. This had hindered capital formation in the private sector in the early post-war years, and this impression persisted in good measure. The Fiscal Commission, the Income Tax Investigation Commission, the reports of the Industrial Finance Corporation, and the Planning Commission had all emphasized the need to curb gambling on the stock exchanges and other management malpractices affecting the companies themselves.

Companies Act or false entries were made in the books of account and provisions of the Indian Companies Act contravened.

The fact that a British firm of such a long standing and reputation as that of McLeod & Co., should also have stooped to practices which have been associated generally with financiers who have captured a number of industrial enterprises in this country in the post-war period and used them to their own personal ends, augurs ill for the future. (*Economic Weekly* 1952b.)

30　Letter from R.A. Butler, Chancellor of the Exchequer, to Jawaharlal Nehru dated 14 February 1955, JN Papers, File no. 320, pp. 159–60.

31　Letter no. 297-PSF/54 dated 15 February 1954 from C.D. Deshmukh to Jawaharlal Nehru, JN Papers, File no. 235, pp. 132–6.

The arena for the contest for supremacy between the political forces favouring the continuation of the managing agency system and those opposing it was the Joint Select Committee, established to scrutinize the bill, particularly within the Congress group. These proposals were passed after strenuous opposition and pressure on the Congress members of the Select Committee. A letter from the All India Congress Committee (AICC) complained to Jawaharlal Nehru that despite a compromise reached within the Congress after the Indian National Trade Union Congress (INTUC) leader Khandubhai Desai had met the finance minister, it was still felt within the AICC that the managing agency system was the feudal equivalent, within industry, of zamindari. The implicit argument was that if one of these had been abolished on the grounds of social engineering in the agrarian sector, so should the other be to cleanse the field of industrial management.[32] On the other hand, Amrit Kaur, the health minister wrote a hand-written letter to Nehru offering a novel argument in support of the managing agency. She said that G.D. Birla had reported a conversation that he had with Gandhi, where Birla had asked what capitalists could do to reduce the palpable hostility evident towards them. Gandhi reportedly informed Birla that the only means to do this was for the capitalists to work for the country's prosperity. In this context Amrit Kaur appealed to Nehru that the industrialists should be given a chance to do precisely this, presumably in this context by retaining the right to run managing agencies.[33] H.P. Mody asked Nehru to arrange a meeting with the members of the Select Committee.[34] Of concern were provisions by which the government could, while requiring that all agency agreements would be subject to scrutiny, prohibit managing agencies in specific industries. Also contemplated was the prohibition of the practice by which managing agencies could be inherited.[35]

The opposition to reform measures also came in the guise of reminders that it was the managing agency system that allowed

32 Letter dated 22 November 1954, JN Papers, File no. 297, p. 46.
33 Letter dated 23 November 1954, JN Papers, File no. 297, pp. 112–13.
34 JN Papers, File no. 297, pp. 229–30.
35 Congress Party in Parliament, Indian Companies Bill, 1955, pp. 35–6. See also the note signed by the finance minister enclosed with his letter No. 1169/PSF/55 dated 2 April 1955 to Jawaharlal Nehru in JN Papers, File 331, pp. 188–90.

industrialists to donate generously to political funds. B.C. Roy, the chief minister of West Bengal, linked the Income Tax Investigation Committee and changes in Company Law to increasing difficulties in raising election funds.[36] Perhaps coincidentally, G.D. Birla repeated the same point in a letter to M.O. Mathai. The ingenious argument here was that while the managing agents were able up to the present time to make contributions for political- or disaster-related appeals from the funds of a company, they would henceforward have to obtain the agreement of the shareholders in a general body meeting. This was likely to arouse 'controversy' and deny any grace to the giving of the contribution. While Mathai was asked to bring the 'dangerous' move to the prime minister's notice, Birla also intended to approach T.T. Krishnamachari, the then commerce and industry minister, directly.

In his response to these apprehensions, the finance minister explained that through his own intervention the new provision of 'Secretaries and Treasurers' had been introduced. His explanation is worth quoting in detail:

> They [Secretaries and Treasurers] ... [would] ... not be in a position to control the affairs of companies as managing agents ... [had] ... often done in the past, but ... [would] ... be able to exercise almost all the powers needed to manage the companies in their charge subject to the effective supervision, management and control of directors. In other words, like the managing agents they ... [would] ... be able to place at the disposal of the managed companies all the economies of large-scale management, which ... [had] ... hitherto constituted the principal justification of the managing agency system. The Select Committee did not place any limit to the number of companies which Secretaries and Treasurers, as such, could manage. What it objected to was the undesirable concentration of economic power in the hands of a few managing agents and the provision limiting the number of companies which a managing agent, as such, could manage to ten was designed to secure this object.[37]

It is likely that the introduction of this provision formed the basis of the compromise reached between Khandubhai Desai and the

---

36 JN Papers, File no. 299, p. 50. Personal and confidential letter dated 9 August 1955, JN Papers, File no. 369, pp. 209–11.

37 Paragraph 4 of the finance minister's note enclosed with his letter 1169/PSF/55 dated 2 April 1955 in JN Papers, File no. 331, p. 191.

finance minister which sought to pave the way towards the consensus mentioned earlier. However, Congressmen were emboldened by the Lok Sabha's declaration of the objective of a socialistic pattern of society. According to them, this proviso would allow the back-door entry, if not the perpetuation, of managing agencies. Speculation within the press on this new offensive detrimental to the interests of the managing agency led to another intervention by the British government through its High Commission, which sought reassurance from Nehru that the provision of permitting secretaries and treasurers would not be diluted. Similar protests had been made by Indian businessmen to the secretary of the Department of Company Administration but it was the diplomatic initiative, even if 'informal', that led the cabinet secretary to forward the British representation to Nehru.[38]

There is another point worthy of note. British interests were concerned about preserving the managing agency system as a way of ensuring their existing asset base, for they had little interest in investing in the new ventures for which the Second Five-Year Plan was to create opportunities for private investment.[39] However, Indian firms, who favoured planned economic growth precisely because of the opportunities of new areas of investment, were directly affected by the clause by which the government could prohibit managing agents in specific new industrial sectors. The paper circulated to Congress members of parliament gave three examples by which this proviso could be bypassed through the device of diversifying into these new fields by existing enterprises managed by agencies. These were the Jiyajeerao Cotton Mills with Birla Brothers as managing agents which had issued preference shares of value Rs 1 crore in order to set up a soda ash factory, while the Birla Jute Mills was in the process of constructing a cement factory with an investment of Rs 2 crore. Dhrangadhra Chemicals were establishing a soda ash plant with investment of Rs 3 crore.

Using his access to M.O. Mathai, special assistant to Nehru, G.D. Birla, who had managed to acquire a copy of the Congress Parliamentary Party (CPP) paper, objected that the Jiyajeerao Cotton Mills

38 The press report titled 'Company Law Changes' in the *Times of India*, 16 July 1955, was enclosed together with the High Commission representation in the cabinet secretary's note dated 3 August 1955 in JN Papers, File no. 367, pp. 223–5.

39 Cf. Tomlinson (1978, 1981).

ventured into the soda ash plant project at the specific and persistent pleading of the Saurashtra government. What was revealing in this case was that, initially, Birla claimed that the problem of raising capital would make the project infeasible. However, when the Saurashtra authorities offered to provide Rs 1 crore as a loan sourced from the Government of India, Birla apparently found no difficulty in raising the capital through Jiyajeerao Cotton Mills, for a venture in an entirely distinct field. In other words, the circumstances by which the Saurashtra authorities entreated the Birla Group to establish the soda ash plant were neatly interpreted as an invitation to diversify an existing cotton mill on the rationale that its reputation would enable capital to be raised. It is intriguing that neither Nehru nor Mathai chose to grasp the point of the CPP paper, that such practices sidestepped proposed controls on managing agents in new branches of industry. As the report of the Industrial Licensing Policy Inquiry Committee (the Dutt Committee) was later to show, this subterfuge was the principal way in which established business houses increased their hold on the industrial economy.[40] Both took the path of viewing the objection to be in the nature of ideological nitpicking at *any* manifestation of growth of existing big business.[41]

Within the CPP the main issue underlying the opposition to managing agencies was institutional framework which the agencies provided for the concentration of capital and, consequently, of economic power. The CPP paper started its argument by stating that the Second Five-Year Plan placed emphasis on the growth of the public sector, where an investment of Rs 1,000 crore was envisaged in the five years, while the private sector was expected to invest Rs 500 crores. This was counterposed to the total investment of Rs 1,400 crores over the entire industrial era in India. The investment was to take the form of either the floatation of new joint-stock companies or the expansion of existing enterprises. Thus, the paper argued, given both the constitutional injunctions against the concentration of income and wealth and the Lok Sabha resolution on the socialistic pattern, company law

40 India (1969).

41 Birla's initial letter of protest, Nehru's chiding letter to the secretary of the Congress party in parliament, Nehru's 'no objection' note to Mathai, and Mathai's reassuring response to Birla are in JN Papers, File no. 367, pp. 114–19.

should rightfully consider the implications of these on economic policy and prohibit those practices of 'company formation, promotion, management and administration which were conducive to undesirable economic consequences'. The chief instrument for this was the managing agency system, and, by implication, subsequent lobbying within Congress circles against the provision of secretaries and treasurers was on the same basis.

Although this provision did ultimately appear in the new company law, the economic consequences of cartelization through the interlocking of companies continued to cause concern to the administrators of company law. That they had reason to do so was made evident in a representation that G.D. Birla sent on behalf of fellow businessmen, including Vitthal Chandavarkar, J.R.D. Tata, Modi, and others. After a meeting with U.N. Dhebar, the then Congress president and Morarji Desai, the then chief minister of Bombay State, the representation was forwarded to Dhebar and Nehru through M.O. Mathai.[42] The note was suffused with objections to the way in which clauses of the bill had linked firms, and the individuals 'associated' with any given firm: that is, towards its attempts to pin down the mechanisms of interlocking. According to the note, there were four objections to the specific powers likely to be at the disposal of the government if it chose to investigate the internal affairs of a company. First, the affairs of an associate could be included in the scope of investigation; second, the restrictions on managing agencies holding the right to buy or sell on behalf of the firm applied also to associates; third, loans to associates were restricted in the same way as they were to the managing agent; and, finally, when a managing agent was debarred from acting in this capacity, the same prohibition would apply to the associate. Particular objection was taken to the inclusion of first cousins and spouses as 'relatives', and thus associates.[43] There were numerous other objections about the treatment of 'proxies', who would be entitled to attend company meetings on behalf of shareholders, of government's much expanded powers of intervention, and of its demurring

---

42 Letter 353-PMO/55 dated 18 August 1955 from Nehru to the finance minister, explaining the context of the Mumbai meeting and the note, in JN Papers, File No. 371, pp. 193–4.

43 'Note on Company Law' enclosed with letter dated 16 August 1955 from G.D. Birla to M.O. Mathai, File no. 371, pp. 1–4.

to recognize managing agents as legitimate, and so on. However, it was clear from that the specification of the concept of 'associate', with all its implications of identifying interlocking arrangements, was the chief feature causing anxiety to businessmen.

In the context of the distinction between the two organizational forms of operation of foreign capital, the managing agency and the Transnational Corporation (TNC) subsidiary, it is important to note that the TNCs were not in favour of forming new managing agencies even in their joint ventures with Indian firms. This opposition was sufficiently strong to threaten at least one joint venture. In the case of dyestuffs, Imperial Chemical Industries (ICI) refused to accept that their joint venture with the Kasturbhai Lalbhai–owned firm of Atul could continue to be operated as a managing agency, and insisted that the board of directors have full powers. This became a matter of sufficient concern to lead to a swift exchange of telegrams between the Indian High Commission in London and the ministry of commerce and industry.[44] Significantly, ICI also refused Lalbhai's suggestion that the powers and remuneration of the managing agency would be determined by the board of directors. It will be recalled that this was the substance of the reforms suggested by the Select Committee on company law reform.

It was then left to the Parliamentary Joint Select Committee, which was formed to scrutinize the 1953 Companies Bill, to suggest the first major inroads into the system. While the government itself had rejected the Companies Law Committee's recommendation for a statutory authority to administer the act in favour of a departmental authority, the Select Committee made other modifications, particularly in relation to managing agencies and the mechanisms by which companies were to be managed. Most importantly, the Joint Select Committee reinserted a provision by which managing agents could be prohibited in specific industries, as suggested by the official memorandum of 1949. Further, it recommended that all new agreements between agents and managed companies would be subject to the government's approval. The momentum had finally been gained by which the all-permissive regime of the managing agency system

---

44 Telegram no. 1855 dated 23 July 1956, from H.V.R. Iengar to L.K. Jha, and reply in Telegram no. 09236 dated 24 July 1956, JN Papers, File no. 457, pp. 16 and 71.

and a complacent company law was dismantled and the framework for effective social engineering put in place.

Unless these steps were taken, the finance minister urged, large-scale investment by the private sector envisaged in the Second Five-Year Plan would fail to be achieved due to avoidable leakages and waste. It was recognized that the reform of company law could only create the conditions for the efficient functioning of private enterprise, but in the absence of these basic conditions no measure of positive assistance to trade and industry would be effective.[45]

It was in the same line of reasoning that Nehru later explained the rationale of the curbs on managing agencies and the amendment to the Constitution which had allowed the government to establish managerial control of enterprises which were found to be mismanaged.[46] The legislation on managing agencies had aroused suspicion of the government's intentions to nationalize these firms eventually. Nehru reiterated to Vijayalakshmi Pandit, high commissioner in London, that the legislation and constitutional amendments were means of social engineering (the term used here explicitly perhaps for the first time). Nehru claimed that the concept of property now defined by the Constitution was exactly in line with the view that he and others had held in the Constituent Assembly, but the courts had interpreted property rights differently and put government's attempts at zamindari abolishment in jeopardy.

45 Letter no. 297-PSF/54 dated 15 February 1954 from C.D. Deshmukh to Jawaharlal Nehru, JN Papers, File no. 235, pp. 132–6.

46 Letter no. 619-PMH/55 dated 3 April 1955, from Jawaharlal Nehru to Vijayalakshmi Pandit, JN Papers, File no. 333, pp. 192–3.

CHAPTER SIX

Private Industry and the Second Five-Year Plan

The Dalmia-Jain and Mundhra Episodes

PROTECTING INDUSTRY FROM PREDATORY CAPITALISTS

In early 1955, at its annual session held at Avadi, near Madras, the Indian National Congress passed a resolution declaring its aim to take India towards a socialist pattern of society. Even before this resolution, it was becoming apparent to British interests operating in the form of managing agencies that the halcyon days of their unhindered business activities were not likely to last much longer. Although they supported a determined effort to retain the managing agency system which ultimately continued for the next 15 years, repatriation of capital was clearly a major preoccupation.[1]

In the middle of 1954, the Dalmia Group attempted to use this moment of vulnerability by attempting to buy a substantial block of shares in one of the major British managing agencies in Uttar Pradesh—the British India Corporation (BIC). Although this effort failed, a year earlier, the Dalmia Group had provided evidence that the managing agency system enabled financial manipulations that even the most demanding financial analyst could not fault on legal grounds.[2] It was a Dalmia financial company, Bharat Insurance, that

---

1 As discussed in Chapter 5.

2 'Proceedings against Messrs Dalmia-Jain Airways Ltd and other Dalmia's Concerns' typewritten, undated, unsigned note, C.D. Deshmukh Papers, Subject file 1.

was subject to scrutiny by a specially appointed professional auditor. On the basis of his report, a change in management was recommended by the relevant authority, the controller of insurance. However, the group appealed for a rehearing of their case with the government and, finally, the matter was resolved by a method that left the Dalmias in an advantageous situation.[3] There were four charges made against the firm: first, that the company transmitted large funds from time to time to Ramkrishna Dalmia's son-in-law, Shanti Prasad Jain, and the Dalmia Cement and Paper Marketing Company for the ostensible purpose of investment, but really in order to allow them to make illegal use of the money; that government and other approved securities supposedly to be held under the Insurance Act were never actually bought; that large investments were made in related Dalmia enterprises at inflated prices; and that property was bought from other Dalmia firms, also at inflated prices. Of these charges, the first two were the most critical in that they alleged a straightforward diversion of funds. However, precisely because of the leeway for financial manipulation that the managing agency system provided, they could not be proved. In effect, Dalmia's only penalty was the requirement that they buy back from Bharat Insurance valuable urban property (the *Times of India* building in Mumbai) within 10 years *at the same price* at which it had been sold.

At the end of the following year, a representation made by the employees union of the *Times of India* and Allied Publications alleged that benami share transfers had taken place from Ramkrishna Dalmia to Shanti Prasad Jain. By this time the government, frustrated by five years of attempts to pin down the mechanisms through which the Dalmia Group's financial manipulations were undertaken, had begun to consider the option of an enquiry under the Commissions of Enquiry Act.

After the failure of even the Income Tax Investigation Commission, it had dawned on the government that its own concerns of safeguarding its sources of revenue were directly linked to issues of shareholder democracy, that is, to the manipulations made possible by the managing agency system. Without the legally prescribed disclosure of

3 Letter no. 853-PSF/54 dated 21 April 1954 from the finance minister to Jawaharlal Nehru, JN Papers, File no. 298, pp. 83–6.

the operational results of firms, it was impossible for investigators to trace the means by which company managements could manipulate records, set up dummy directors, and transfer funds from publicly held companies to the promoter's closely held companies. While auditor's reports occasionally provided evidence of these practices, the provisions of civil law, when invoked to identify and collect concealed income, could be challenged. The only control on corrupt practices was through shareholders' vigilance, but while company management could win over cantankerous elements amongst them, the bulk of shareholders were inclined to be apathetic. Thus, shareholder's interests and government revenues could be better protected by changes in company law which would require greater disclosure of all operational results. Although the commission of enquiry would not meet either the shareholders' or the government's purposes directly or quickly, the public would be educated about the kinds of manipulations that managements engaged in and it would equally allow the government to identify the precise ways in which company law required to be changed.[4]

The essential feature of the devices that the Dalmia Group used was that of interlocking of companies, clearly through the mechanism of the managing agency system.[5] Thus, Dalmia-Jain Airways, a major company in the group, was amalgamated with Dalmia-Jain Aviation after it had suffered major losses due to mismanagement. Records of the company were subsequently destroyed through a board resolution at which only three board members, all Dalmia employees, were present. Dalmia Cement and Paper Marketing Company, entirely owned by Ramkrishna Dalmia, was used as the clearing house of the group, with all speculative profits accruing to Dalmia while losses were transferred to other group companies. Dalmia's personal expenses were also debited to the company. Shriyans Prasad Jain (Shanti Prasad Jain's brother) was appointed to a tax-free salary of Rs 4,000 per month and shortly thereafter, when this appointment was termi-

4 JN Papers, File no. 392, pp. 248–9, letter no. O117-PSF/55 dated 17 October 1955 from the finance minister to Jawaharlal Nehru. Nehru's concurrence with the proposal to institute a Commission of Enquiry is in the same file, p. 250, in his letter no. 1945-PMH/55 also dated 17 October 1955.

5 JN Papers, File no. 443, p. 80, letter no. 0365-PSF/56 dated 15 May 1956 from the finance minister to Jawaharlal Nehru.

nated, a compensation of Rs 7 lakh was paid to Jain. The Shapurji Broacha Mills and the Madhowji Dharamsi Manufacturing Company, both profitable and well-established firms, were cornered by Dalmia, and his closely held companies made sales agents for them. When these arrangements were ended, a total of Rs 114 lakh was paid as compensation by the Mills, which accrued to the selling agents. The decision to terminate the selling agencies and authorize the payment of compensation was taken by two directors, both Dalmia employees. Ultimately, the Mills were taken into liquidation. Funds of Bharat Insurance were placed at the disposal of Shriyans Prasad Jain and though they had been given for investment in shares and securities they were used to acquire or to retain control over other companies.

The general pattern appeared to be the same in all companies of the group. Funds were not used for the purpose for which the firms had been established and for which public subscriptions had been enlisted.[6] They were invested in other companies of the group. As these shares were not dividend-paying, the funds were available free of interest. After a few years, the shares would be transferred to the closely held group companies as a security for loans, and an agreement would be reached between debtor and creditor companies that the loans would be repaid without interest, in a number of yearly instalments. Sometimes the loans were adjusted against compensation payable to the closely held firms to terminate their agency agreements.

The point was that taken by themselves, and isolated from the chain of events in the group as a whole, many of the actions appeared to be within the letter of the law, or at worst, trivial offences.[7] It was then considered essential to probe into the affairs of the group as a whole and obtain an overall picture of the state of affairs within the Dalmia Group and the ways in which the investing public had been duped by the opportunities to appropriate public funds that the interlocking of the group companies had provided. However, given that the powers of

---

6 JN Papers, File no. 443, p. 79.

7 As early as 1949, the memorandum of the Bombay Shareholders' Association had pointed to the Dalmia-Jain Group, and to other similar cases, and demanded an ordinance to prevent interlocking of companies. See Bombay Shareholders' Association (1949: 206–11).

a commission of enquiry were limited to those of a civil court, it was proposed to modify the rules of procedure to give the commission powers similar to the Income Tax Investigation Commission.[8]

The Dalmia-Jain Group was self-evidently not the only group which was known to have evaded taxes on a gross scale. To take two of the most obvious ones, as described in Chapter 4, there had been protracted correspondence over the Birla Group, in particular, their operations in West Bengal where the state government was unwilling to concede that the failure of efforts to identify evidence of widely surmised malpractices required deeper investigation using innovative means. More spectacularly, in what the Central Board of Revenue described as the biggest case of concealment in income in the history of tax collection, the board of Tata Sons, the managing agents of Tata Iron and Steel, were directly accused of conniving in enormous concealment of taxable income.

The crux of the argument of this book, however, is that these were straightforward cases of managing agents using loopholes available in accounting practices to lower the degree of taxable income chargeable to firms in their control. This practice, however reprehensible, is a normal characteristic of capitalist enterprise and the cat and mouse features of the attempts by the revenue authorities to identify the practices by which evasion is concealed a standard component of actual political life, and of fiction.[9] What made the Dalmia-Jain practices *qualitatively* different was that they represented in quintessential form the unreconstructed activities of merchant capital and usurer capital operating through the legal forms of joint-stock enterprise and the institution of the managing agency. As the examples of their operations briefly outlined earlier show, they are characterized by a total absence of concern for industrial accumulation through manufacturing operations. Their utility lay in the possibilities of access to centralized blocs of capital, subscribed by a dispersed and managerially

8 Letter no. 0365-PSF/56 dated 15 May 1956 from the finance minister to Jawaharlal Nehru, JN Papers, File no. 443, p. 78. Nehru's concurrence with the procedure suggested is in the same file (Letter no. 1172-PMH/56 dated 16 May 1956, p. 81).

9 Pages 9 and 39 of the petition by Shanti Prasad Jain quoted by Homi Daji, MP, in the course of the Lok Sabha debate on the motion, Re: Report of the Commission of Enquiry into Dalmia-Jain Companies, on 6 May 1963. col. 14030 of Lok Sabha Debates, 1963, vol. XVIII.

ineffective group of shareholders; the image the firms had earned as profitable and dividend-paying companies, for whom raising further resource would not be difficult; and the safeguards of limited liability, which ensured that speculative and extralegal operations remained within financially manageable bounds for their owners.

Given the vast array of economic offenses requiring the attention of the finance ministry, from political economy considerations, it was the correct decision to focus and examine Dalmia-Jain operations. This would enable the identification and prohibition of the parasitical operations of merchant capital in joint-stock industrial enterprises.

The momentousness of the step was shown by the decision after approval in principle by the cabinet to refer the matter to a cabinet subcommittee so as to enable the examination of the terms of reference, with the recommendations to be referred back to the cabinet.[10] Significantly, it was decided that this subcommittee was to be chaired by the home minister, G.B. Pant, with the ministers of defence, works, housing and supply, food and agriculture, legal affairs, and V.K. Krishna Menon, then without a portfolio, as members. The composition of the sub-committee is an indication of the seriousness with which the matter was to be taken. After two meetings of the subcommittee, the cabinet approved the terms of reference of the commission in November 1956.[11]

However, while it is true that the home minister was probably the most appropriate choice, his proclivity to treat corporate misconduct benignly was displayed almost 20 years earlier. In a discussion of the amendments to the Companies Act in the Central Legislative Assembly, Pant had attempted to narrow the grounds on which a managing agent could be removed. This was opposed by the law member who asserted that the shareholders had the right to dismiss managing agents on any number of grounds and that limiting this would not

10 Minutes of the meeting of the cabinet held on Wednesday, 25 July 1956 at 5.30 pm, Case no. 180/39/56 on 'Alleged Mismanagement of a large number of Dalmia Group of Concerns', JN Papers, File no. 457, p. 353.

11 Letters nos 1702-PMH/56 dated 5 August 1956, and 1707-PMH/56 dated 6 August 1956 from Jawaharlal Nehru to Shah, and letter dated 5 August 1956 from S.P. Jain to Jawaharlal Nehru in JN Papers, File no. 462, pp. 42, 132, and 141, respectively. Minutes of the meetings of the subcommittee are in JN Papers, File no. 467, pp. 68–70 and File no. 470, pp.111–13. The cabinet approval is in JN Papers, File no. 486, p. 120.

be in their interests.[12] It may be of note that Krishna Menon did not attend either of the subcommittee meetings. Also, neither Nehru nor M.C. Shah, minister in charge of revenue and civil expenditure, were informed of the first meeting, though Shah, at Nehru's urging, was present at the second meeting. Soon after the cabinet meeting establishing the subcommittee, a Lok Sabha question asked for a confirmation of this fact, which was followed by a letter to Nehru from S.P. Jain. In this, he declared that after the split that had taken place in 1948, there was no such entity as the Dalmia-Jain Group. The Sahu Jain Group, which he was now in charge of, had no links with Dalmia. Consequently, he wanted an opportunity to explain that he was apprehensive of the undeserved adverse publicity that the investigation would entail. Nehru instructed Shah to meet Jain and hear his case.

THE MUNDHRA CASE: SHARE SPECULATION AS A FINE ART

A year later Haridas Mundhra, who had successfully obtained control of British firms in the Calcutta area in the tea industry and engineering firms such as Jessop and Company, also wrested control of BIC.[13] Expressing his anxiety at the ability of Mundhra to do as he pleased right under the nose of the Government of India, T.T. Krishnamachari,

12 Bombay Shareholders' Association (1949:149).

13 Starting in the tea export trade, Mundhra kept both the sales proceeds and profits in sterling in London, and used that to raise further finance in India. Gradually, he began buying British Indian companies such as Jessops, Richardson and Cruddas, Duncan and Stratton, the Brahmaputra Tea Company, and the Oslers Electrical Concerns, apart from a few collieries. However,

the main appeal which he has—as a potential purchaser—in the British market is *his preparedness to refrain from general interference with the internal workings of the companies he buys* ... at least one big insurance company in the United Kingdom is prepared to support him ... it is difficult to see how he has been able to do all that he has without the knowledge of the U.K. exchange control authorities. The support which the U.K. exchange banks give him would necessarily mean at some stage or other a guarantee with the head offices of the exchange banks for Mundhra's loans in India and for that purpose some kind of approval or acquiescence by U.K exchange contro. would be necessary. [Emphasis mine.] (Letter no. 084/PSF/55 dated 21 September 1955 from the finance minister to Jawaharlal Nehru, JN Papers, File no. 385, pp. 116–17.)

See also India (1958a, 1958b) and *Free Press Journal* (1958).

minister for commerce and industry, asked C.D. Deshmukh, finance minister, to have procedures examined which would allow the government to examine the bona fides of an acquirer of any large block of shares in a company whose capital and other assets were valued at Rs 20 lakh or more in then current prices.[14]

Mundhra's large-scale acquisitions had reached the stage where they had attracted the attention of the US newsmagazine *Time*. A message, presumably about Mundhra and probably intercepted by the revenue intelligence authorities was forwarded to Jawaharlal Nehru who, mystified by the then unknown name, also wrote to C.D. Deshmukh to ask whether there was any material in the finance ministry about Mundhra's origins.[15] Deshmukh's reply, sent three days later, was full of information, and given the importance of Mundhra to later events, is worth examining in detail.[16] Mundhra was, according to Deshmukh's information, a 'self-made man', though as subsequent details show, with a considerable network of support, both in Marwari business circles and amongst the tea export traders. With finances of Rs 50 lakh each provided by the firm of Bansilal Abhirchand of Nagpur and Vallabhswami, a Vaishnavite guru from Rajasthan, he started with tea exports before the Second World War, subsequently building up his capital base in Britain by retaining both the sales proceeds and profits there.[17] With this collateral, he was able to gain further resources in India, buying up not only Jessops but also Richardson and Cruddas, Duncan and Stratton, some collieries, the Brahmaputra Tea Company, and Oslers Electrical concerns. His most

14 Secret letter D. O. no. 349-CIM/55 dated 23 August 1955, TTK Papers, Subject file 8(B), p. 16.

15 Secret letter no. 177-PMH/55 dated 18 September 1955, JN Papers, File no. 384, p. 190.

16 Secret letter no. 084/PSF/55 dated 21 September 1955, JN Papers, File no. 385 pp. 116–17.

17 Rai Bahadur Bansilal Abhirchand's firm had come to the notice of the Central Provinces Banking Enquiry Committee, which submitted a report in 1929–30. At that time the Abhirchand firm was the only indigenous bank in the province. It had eight branches in the province and seventeen outside. Although not operating under the Companies Act, it transacted business like modern banks, with payment by cheques. However, unlike banks, it also engaged in trade and advanced loans against the security of immovable property. *The Central Provinces Banking Enquiry Committee 1929–1930* Vol I: 98, quoted in Levkovsky (1966: 231).

recent acquisitions were the Assam Tea Company and BIC. Throughout 1954 and 1955, Mundhra was in touch with large shareholders in the Assam Tea Company, and the resulting share price fluctuations were remarked on by the British financial press. The existing board of directors, as a defensive measure, had created a large number of shares worth one shilling each, with voting rights equivalent to the existing pound valued shares. Mundhra had been trying to obtain foreign exchange to finance the purchase of these shares, but Deshmukh claimed that his officials had been instructed not to allow foreign exchange outgo on this account.

In the case of BIC, although Mundhra had bought a small number of shares, the McRobert Trust owned the controlling block and Mundhra had worked hard to persuade the trustees in England to sell their holdings to him. The Singhania Group, which already held a substantial number of shares, was prepared to buy Mundhra's block if he was unable to persuade the McRobert Trust. With this, the Singhanias would have gained control. However, Deshmukh wrote, that very day's edition of the *Statesman* newspaper had reported that Mundhra had succeeded in his effort, on condition that he, in turn, did not sell off. Mundhra's own managing agency, the S.B. Industrial Development Company Limited, managed many of his acquisitions in name, but his main appeal as a potential buyer in the British market lay in his preparedness to refrain from detailed interference in his managed companies.

Mundhra had extensive support. One large British insurance company, at least, was behind his acquisitions. Even with all this, Deshmukh noted, and with his reputed 'phenomenal' luck, he could not have succeeded without the knowledge of the British exchange control authorities. British exchange banks would have required a guarantee from their head offices in London before extending loans to him in India and this could not be provided without approval or acquiescence of the exchange controllers. What was clear was that Mundhra had very satisfactory arrangements with the exchange banks and large overdrafts against the shares he lodged with them.

By the mid-1950s, Mundhra's wealth (presumably his personal assets) was reputed to be about 1–1.5 crore. Apart from the Vaishnavite guru, Mundhra was also rumoured to have access to the resources commanded by Shanti Prasad Jain, chairperson of the Punjab

National Bank. He was also a 'bull' operator both for the shares of companies under his control and for those he wished to acquire. He was reputed to have a 'thoroughly dishonest attitude', and the judge who had disposed of one of his appeals concerning income tax matters in 1954 had gone so far as to record that, given Mundhra's past record, he would have used his discretion to refuse any writ filed by him.[18]

From Krishnamachari's and Deshmukh's accounts, it appears that at least three of the Marwari business groups, Dalmia, Singhania, and Mundhra, with the support of a fourth business interest, S.P. Jain, were vying to gain control of major firms involved in the tea, textile, and engineering industries, in the vacuum created by the repatriation of British interests. There were several points of concern here. First, whatever the failures of the British managing agencies, there was a vast difference between their professionalism and that of the Indian groups who were engaged in taking them over.[19] In fact, the differential quality of industrial management that the British and Indian managing agencies represented went beyond any normal range in capabilities. The Indian firms were either representative of trading and speculative capital (Mundhra) or, as in the other two cases of Dalmia and Singhania, they represented capital accumulated through trade and usury, painfully attempting the transition to industrial capital, a transition made doubly difficult because of the constraints placed on industrial investment by the very recently concluded colonial period of India's history.

The consequences of such a pedigree were well described by Bettelheim.[20] Basing his analysis on the Reserve Bank of India (RBI)–conducted All India Rural Credit Survey of 1951, he argued that an overlooked feature of the effect of the high rates of return to rural

18 Remark made by Justice S.R. Tendolkar while disposing of an appeal by Mundhra in an income tax case, quoted by C.D. Deshmukh in his letter to Jawaharlal Nehru (Letter no. 084/PSF/55, 21 September 1955, JN Papers, File no. 385 p. 116).

19 Brimmer (1955: 556–9).

20 Bettelheim (p. 76) quotes the Majority Report of the Indian Central Banking Enquiry Committee (p. 99), which stated in 1931 that '....commercial banks ... occupy a significant place in the financial superstructure that is available to the village moneylender, the urban moneylender, the indigenous banker and the trader in agricultural produce'. Given that all the major groups had large-scale commercial banks within their fold, the link between '....big monopoly and financial capital with rural moneylending capital' was quite apparent to Bettelheim (p. 78) (Bettelheim 1971: 74–9).

moneylending capital was the drain on urban capital stocks. This differential was the cause of a continuous drain on newly formed industrial capital, taking it not only into financial and commercial operations, but also into the rural areas. This led to a situation where capital accumulated in the industrial process was degraded into an accumulation of debts—an extraordinary transformation of capital into income in the hands of landlords and previous debtors.

Even if this flow could be reduced (by, for instance, the creation of the State Bank of India with an extended network of rural branches), there was the second point of concern for the State. This lay in the predilections of these businessmen: rather than using their accumulated capital in greenfield investments, they were engaged in the takeover of existing companies. This practice enabled them to evade evolution into industrial capitalists. Finally, and perhaps most dangerously, stock market operations, explicitly visible in the case of Mundhra, were driving the stock market forward and encouraging other businessmen to similarly engage their resources in speculation on the markets.

The entire plan of industrial development which the Second Five-Year Plan was to lay out was threatened by these activities of private capital. The 1948 Industrial Policy Resolution, soon to be replaced by the more clearly focused resolution of 1956, had laid out new industrial areas which were open for fresh investment by the private sector. It was within these bounds that private resources were expected to be channelled. For the representatives of merchant and usury capital, however, widespread forms of pre-industrial capital—the traditional textiles, sugar, and other light industry—were the preferred area of activity. With capacity in large-scale cotton mills limited by the policy measures designed to increase handloom production, acquisition of existing firms in textiles, tea, and engineering, the last assured of market demand by planned expansion of public sector activity, were far more attractive, being known quantities with production processes well understood and demand assured.

It was these considerations that led T.T. Krishnamachari to address the finance minister only a couple of months later on the inexplicable boom in the stock market.[21] Curiously, the beginning of the boom

---

21 Secret letter dated 26 October 1955, copied to Jawaharlal Nehru on the same date. TTK Papers, correspondence with Jawaharlal Nehru 1955, pp. 145–6.

seems to have coincided with announcement of the 'Socialist Pattern of Society', implying, perhaps, that the stock market realized that private industrial profits were going to rise in the foreseeable future. However, Krishnamachari was apprehensive about the degree of appreciation in share prices, which was qualitatively of a higher order as compared to worldwide trends. Such an increase would mean, as earlier mentioned, that fewer resources would be available to take up shares in new companies floated in order to establish industrial capacities in areas hitherto untapped. Krishnamachari suggested that measures should be explored to channel investments into these newer areas, possibly by asking banks through the Reserve Bank of India to discontinue lending for investments in shares of existing companies.

It was not only British interests which were contemplating repatriating their holdings in India. In a letter to T.T. Krishnamachari, G.D. Birla explained the mysterious circumstances by which he was approached by 'quite an important' man, who, coming straight to the point, wished to know whether Birla would be interested in buying out Neville Wadia's holdings in Bombay Dyeing, the major textile mill in Bombay.[22] The deal was to include the managing agency which would be transferred to the Birla Group. From the trend of Birla's letter, it appeared that he was expected to show an interest and name a suitably inflated price, which would then be used to bargain with the Calcutta or Ahmedabad buyers who were reputed to have offered double the then Bombay Dyeing share price of Rs 500. Birla reportedly advised the intermediary that if the Ahmedabad offer came from Kasturbhai Lalbhai, that should be accepted as that would offer the prospect of far better management than would be provided by the Calcutta aspirers. Birla ended his letter by saying that he felt sorry at the prospect of industrialists selling off their interests. Birla mentioned Haridas Mundhra, Chiranjilal Bajoria, and Shanti Prasad Jain as likely buyers who would pay a 'fancy' price but who were not, presumably, in his estimation, industrialists. He also expressed the politically correct statement that at the age of 62, he wished only to create employment opportunities and wealth, neither of which could be realized by buying an existing company. This then was the defining

22 Personal and confidential letter dated 17 February 1956, TTK Papers, correspondence with G.D. Birla, pp. 33–5.

element of an industrialist, at least in that early period of industrial development in India.

Foremost amongst the capitalists whose outlook did not accord with those of industrialists were the jute mill owners of Bengal. T.T. Krishnamachari had remarked, nearly three years earlier on the Marwaris being 'notoriously indifferent to the efficient working of the industrial apparatus, mechanical as well as human'.[23] This was in one of the earliest expressions of concern about the consequences of British interests selling out to the Marwaris. This was a colourful yet acute portrayal of the attitudes of representatives of merchant and usurer capital to issues of industrial management, plant maintenance, and modern systems of industrial relations. As Nehru noted, even B.C. Roy, chief minister of West Bengal, and no 'socialist' ideologue, had spoken rather strongly about the jute mill employers and felt that steps should be taken to make them behave.[24] This was presumably a reference to their cavalier attitude, along the lines of absentee agrarian landlords, towards laws regulating labour conditions in their plants.

To summarize the situation as it appeared to the Government of India at the beginning of the Second Five-Year Plan, businessmen who had accumulated large funds through grey areas of economic activity had found that the stock market, buoyed by the prospects of high returns to industrial investment, was a source of high short-term returns. Simultaneously, established British industrialists and even some Indian ones, whether motivated by fatigue or uncertain prospects within a controlled economy, were keen to liquidate their stock market–based assets. There was then the prospect that well-established and well-managed firms would fall into the hands of unknown figures, some of whom had the reputation of being adventurers.[25] Apart from their own proclivities on the stock exchange, their manipulation of the market through insider trading was proving a lure to

23 Secret letter No. 1001/CIM/53 dated 24 November 1953 from T.T. Krishnamachari to Jawaharlal Nehru, JN Papers, File no. 216, p. 92.

24 Letter no. 605-PMO/56 dated 17 November 1956, to Khandubhai Desai, labour minister, JN Papers, File no. 489, p. 34.

25 Deshmukh in his letter to Jawaharlal Nehru referred to Mundhra as someone willing 'to take risks—and heavy risks involving his personal fortune too...' (Secret letter no. 084/PSF/55 dated 21 September 1955, JN Papers, File no. 385, pp. 116–17).

other capitals which might have been invested in new enterprises. With ambitious plans for private investment, the Government of India could not be indifferent to these phenomena.

SOCIAL ENGINEERING THROUGH FISCAL POLICY

Even before he became finance minister in September 1956, Krishnamachari was playing an important role in introducing innovative ideas into Indian fiscal policy. After a meeting with Nicholas Kaldor in March 1956, he wrote to Jawaharlal Nehru mentioning that he agreed with Kaldor that the existing taxation system took no account of human factors and presumed that by increasing the rate of tax the desired redistribution would take place.[26] He also emphasized that Kaldor's proposals, with which he was familiar, having read his book on expenditure tax and his minute of dissent to the British Royal Commission on Taxation, formed parts of an integrated scheme and could not be introduced piecemeal. However, given the novelty of the scheme, Krishnamachari felt that considerable propaganda efforts would be necessary, both with MPs and within the Congress. He asked Nehru if he was agreeable to have a meeting in the Lok Sabha, to which Nehru agreed.[27]

Two months later, when a group of Congress MPs submitted a memorandum on taxation policy, a copy was sent to Krishnamachari.[28] The substance of their argument was that with the adoption of the 'socialist pattern of society'[29] (by both the Congress and the Lok Sabha), the recommendations of the Taxation Enquiry Commission had been made obsolete. So the proposal to tax basic items

26 Secret letter D. O. no. 96-CIM/56 dated 15 March 1956, TTK Papers, correspondence with Jawaharlal Nehru 1956, pp. 38–9.

27 Confidential letter no. 115-OMO/56 dated 15 March 1956, TTK Papers, correspondence with Jawaharlal Nehru, 1956, p. 40. It was presumed by both that C.D. Deshmukh, the titular finance minister, would be consulted only as regards the details of the meeting.

28 Members of Parliament's letter dated 27 April 1956, to the prime minister enclosed with Jawaharlal Nehru's confidential letter no. 1180-PMH/56 dated 16 May 1956, TTK Papers, correspondence with Jawaharlal Nehru, 1956, n.p.

29 The actual resolution referred to a 'socialistic pattern'. The distinction is important as there was opposition within the Congress to the full-blooded term 'socialist', but these MPs, on the left politically, probably wanted to assert themselves.

of consumption in use by the poor, so as to raise resources for the Plan, was not valid. The group presented a list of items which they indicated should not be taxed, but measures taken to ensure stable prices prevailed despite resort to measures of deficit finance. For this, not only price controls, but also a system of buffer stocks in strategic locations had to be established. The resources foregone because of the exemptions on tax of these basic items could be balanced by increasing taxation levels of the higher income groups, whose income and wealth would necessarily increase with a 'high pressure development programme'.[30]

Concerned by the implications of these trends in economic ideology, the World Bank took the opportunity of Krishnamachari's formal appointment as finance minister to deliver a few home truths.[31] Emphasizing that it was his conviction that India's interest lay in giving private enterprise, both Indian and foreign, every encouragement, Eugene Black, president of the World Bank, disparaged the intrusion of ideology into policy matters. He singled out the Industrial Policy Resolution in this regard, and argued that the targets for public sector investment were far too large. The deficit financing necessary to support this investment were sure to lead to unacceptable inflationary pressures and create financial instability. As far as external finances were concerned, the bank wanted a change from the existing policies that discouraged exports of textiles and vegetable oils to the active support of these and other traditional exports.[32]

30 The quoted phrases are from a letter written by 11 members of Parliament to the prime minister, 27 April 1956, enclosed with Jawaharlal Nehru's confidential letter no. 1180-PMH/56, 16 May 1956, TTK Papers, correspondence with Jawaharlal Nehru 1956, n.p.

31 Letter dated 5 September 1956 circulated with Planning Commission Circular No. PC/CDNo9/1/56 dated 1 October 1956, distributed widely within the Planning Commission, JN Papers, File no. 477, pp. 5–8.

32 In fact, in December 1956, a committee of secretaries set up to make recommendations for increasing exports identified sugar, cotton, vanaspati, groundnuts, and salad oil as commodities for special attention. There was opposition to exporting groundnut oil from the ministers in charge of agriculture, food, and commerce and consumer industries. 'Recommendations of the Committee of Secretaries for Increasing Exports', Ministry of Finance, Department of Economic Affairs, and, enclosure to secret letter dated 28 December 1956 from T.T. Krishnamachari to Jawaharlal Nehru, JN Papers, File no. 498, pp. 94–8. Chakravarty (1989: 16) claims that in the case of cotton textiles, exports were not encouraged not

Reiterating the bank's willingness to support India's plan, Black cautioned that the quantum of aid would necessarily depend on India's success in attracting foreign investment (phrased as '... external financial assistance ... [which did not entail] ... fixed foreign exchange commitments'). A specific area of policy reform, with which the letter ended, noted that Indian reliance on the expansion of the rail network, while welcome, should not ignore the importance of road and coastal shipping, a problem of transport 'which has particularly engaged the attention of the Bank, as well as of your own Government and of private interests throughout India'.

The impact of this letter was evident a short time later, when the cabinet met to consider the subject of the financial resources required for the Second Five-Year Plan.[33] The terse minutes merely recorded that after consideration of a finance ministry paper on the subject, there was broad agreement on the approach. However, it was decided that for the time being only the three proposals of a capital gains tax, an increase on tax rates on dividends, and controls on companies' reserves were to be implemented.

This was certainly a retreat from Kaldor's integrated scheme. However, the significance of the controls on the use of reserves by companies needs to be emphasized. From the 1930s, observers had noted the tendency of managing agencies to use these reserves as cheap sources of finance for a variety of purposes, with the concomitant that depreciation reserves were perpetually inadequate to meet replacement costs, particularly at times of technological change, or even of unusual levels of inflation.[34] Ensuring that reserves not intended to

---

because of considerations of maximizing internal supplies but because of the regional concentration of the industry and the political issue of supporting particular groups of industrialists at the expense of others. If this was also true of vegetable oils, another regionally concentrated industry, this would amount to a serious indictment of the political management skills of the cabinet. It is significant that in an undated note in 1957, Krishnamachari suggested to the commerce and industry, food and agriculture, and steel, mines, and fuel ministers that distribution and export organizations should be established on a statutory basis for the sugar, textiles, cement, and iron and steel industries (TTK Papers, correspondence with Jawaharlal Nehru 1957, pp. 17–19).

33 Meeting of the cabinet held on Thursday, 15 November 1956 at 9 am, Financial Resources for the Plan, Case no. 308/66/56, JN Papers, File no. 488, p. 204.

34 See, for instance, Samant and Mulky (1937: 167).

be utilized for upgradation of plant and equipment would not be eligible for tax rebate was an important step in social engineering, discouraging non-industrial forms of utilization of company resources.

Another controversy that erupted at this time was that created by the resignation of the RBI governor, B. Rama Rau.[35] The substantive issue was the government's proposal to increase the stamp duty levied on money market transactions. The RBI felt that the large increase in stamp duty, a 'fiscal measure with monetary implications' in Krishnamachari's words, infringed on the prerogative of the bank to determine monetary policy. Apart from the government's action, Rama Rau was also incensed at the characterization of the bank as a department of the government and offended at Krishnamachari's personal behaviour towards him. Nehru supported Krishnamachari, and various commentators have noted and generally deplored the era of subordination of the RBI to the government that this episode inaugurated. What has not been remarked on is the fact that this institutional subordination was the expression of the primacy given to industrial policy over monetary policy.[36] As a measure of social engineering, this was even more critical than the controls on reserves. Basing himself on the empirical results of the RBI's All India Rural Credit Survey,

35 The Reserve Bank's view of these developments is in Balachandran (1998: 715–24). While this account is largely framed as an account in interpersonal and inter-institutional issues, later, on pp. 729–30, Balachandran comes close to the present discussion, although it is framed in a Keynesian-cum-structuralist-cum-'modernist' versus monetarist policy perspective. The present account is also based on the following documents—JN Papers, File no. 494: Secret and immediate letter no. 2816-PMH/56 dated 6 December 1956, from Jawaharlal Nehru to T.T. Krishnamachari, p. 157; Secret letter no. G.8-300/56 dated 10 December 1956, from B. Rama Rau to H.M. Patel, enclosing Secret memorandum no. B-34, Memorandum to the Central Board Implications of Certain Provisions of the Finance Bill, 1956 dated 10 December 1956, pp. 172–6; Letter dated 11 December 1956, from T.T. Krishnamachari to Jawaharlal Nehru, p. 177; Secret letter no. 689-PMO/56 dated 12 December 1956 from Jawaharlal Nehru to B. Rama Rau, pp. 307–8. Also JN Papers, File no. 498, Secret letter no. G.8-311/56 dated 29 December 1956 from B. Rama Rau to Jawaharlal Nehru, pp. 102–8 with enclosure 'Extract from the statement by Shri B. Rama Rau, Governor, Reserve Bank of India, at the Bank Annual Report Discussion (25 September 1956) on p. 101.

36 It is significant to note in this context that thirty-five years later, the Economic Survey of the Ministry of Finance for 1992–3 noted explicitly a reversal of this situation: henceforward, industrial policy would be complementary to trade, fiscal, and exchange rate management policies.

Bettelheim had remarked on the large difference between the interest rates in the urban money markets and those in rural moneylending (the bank rate rose to a maximum of about 5 per cent in 1958 as compared to agricultural moneylending rates of between 25 per cent in Bihar and 40 per cent and above in Bengal, Orissa, and Himachal).[37] The tightness of the money market and requests for steps to ease controls were one, constantly repeated, theme in all of G.D. Birla's correspondence with Krishnamachari.[38] Shrewdly, he linked the market conditions affected to the difficulties it created in financing industrial expansion plans.[39]

THE MUNDHRA EPISODE

The resignation of T.T. Krishnamachari from the finance ministership in early 1958 was the culmination of three developments that evolved concurrently, but were distinct in their historical significance. The first was the actual sequence of events that led to Jawaharlal Nehru accepting Krishnamachari's resignation. This has been detailed in the public record, in the open proceedings of the M.C. Chagla Commission of Enquiry and notably, in G. Balachandran's account in the volume of the history of the RBI authored by him.[40] The second, little noticed, is the way in which the 'Mundhra episode' was media-managed with the encouragement, if not at the behest, of industrial interests who found that the controls established as part of the industrialization drive accompanying the Second Five-Year

37 Bettelheim (1971: 82–3).

38 See, for instance, his letter dated 28 February 1956 (in which he mentions that he had voiced the same concern in an earlier letter), TTK Papers, correspondence with G.D. Birla, pp. 36–7; see also, letter dated 8 June 1957 where the money market is mentioned twice with reference to Mundhra's increasingly serious 'fix'; letter dated 8 June 1957 from G.D. Birla to T.T. Krishnamachari, TTK Papers, correspondence with G.D. Birla, pp. 78–80.

39 In asserting that Krishnamachari's controls on the use of reserves needed to be relaxed, he warned that a collapse of the Mundhra edifice would further aggravate the tight money situation. Fresh share issues by Tata Steel and Indian Iron and Steel required substantial resources for the call money to be payable, and Birla argued that investment prospects in both public and private sectors were being jeopardized by the reserve deposit scheme. Letter dated 8 June 1957, TTK Papers, correspondence with G.D. Birla, n.p.

40 Balachandran (1998), Appendix D, 'The Bank and the Mundhra Affair'.

Plan made serious and unacceptable inroads in private capitalist deci-sion-making. These were felt to be of an order that justified, in their minds, a multi-pronged political response, as will be seen. The third development, involving social engineering, was a concerted effort to push the bearers of merchant and usurer capital towards industrial capital norms. It will be argued that it was an uneasy coalition formed by opponents of each of these developments that coalesced and led to Krishnamachari's resignation.

In May 1957, as large quantities of shares of the Mundhra firms were held by commercial banks in the country, including the State Bank of India (SBI) and several exchange banks, H.V.R. Iengar, gov-ernor of the Reserve Bank had convened a meeting to take concerted action to prevent a sudden or haphazard unloading of these shares on the market.[41] However, this meeting was abortive and by June 1957, Mundhra was in serious trouble. He had approached G.D. Birla for help in liquidating a part of his holdings, but Birla felt that with the tight conditions in the money market no one would be prepared to buy the shares. Birla suggested that Mundhra should meet Krishna-machari and ask for his advice.[42] By this time, the Punjab National Bank, which had been accommodating Mundhra, was pressing him to repay and Birla felt that Mundhra risked losing control of Turner Morrison.

Following a further meeting between the SBI, Life Insurance Cor-poration (LIC), and T.T. Krishnamachari in June, it was decided that LIC would attempt to reduce the pressure of the market by buying a large block of Mundhra's shares. The proposal was conceived as a short-term measure to maintain share prices in the market but this step proved incapable of restoring confidence in the share market.[43]

Later in the year, SBI and LIC, both with very heavy stakes in the matter, had reviewed the situation and, in consultation with Krishnamachari, had agreed that SBI should take urgent action.[44] In November 1957, it was the turn of H.V.R. Iengar, then governor of

41 Secret note by D.L. Mazumdar dated 5 December 1957, U.O.D. No. 1600/SCLA/57 dated 6 December 1957, TTK Papers, Subject file 21, p. 51.

42 Letter dated 8 June 1957, TTK Papers, correspondence with G.D. Birla, pp. 78–80.

43 Secret note by D.L. Mazumdar, TTK Papers, Subject file 21, p. 50.

44 Secret note by D.L. Mazumdar, TTK Papers, Subject file 21, p. 51.

the RBI, to report to Krishnamachari. The managing director of BIC was reported to have confided to Sachin Chaudhuri, member of the SBI's Calcutta local board, that in payment for dues from Mundhra's mills, BIC had received Richardson and Cruddas shares. These shares had been supposedly held by the Punjab National Bank which had sold them. However, confidential enquiries with the bank showed that the endorsement for transfer had been forged; the shares neither belonged to the bank nor had they transferred them. The managing director of the BIC had lodged the shares in safe custody and Mundhra was now demanding that they be returned. Although both the SBI and the LIC were taking steps to ensure the security of their advances and investments in Mundhra's various firms, Iengar felt that the time had certainly come to stop Mundhra in his share certificate forging orgy.[45] Iengar followed with another letter two days later, informing Krishnamachari that the managing director of BIC had also lodged the share transaction form with the SBI, with an RBI lock installed for double protection. In the meantime a large block of Mundhra's shares pledged to the Punjab National Bank were offered for sale because Mundhra had not been able to pay his dues and his cheques were not being honoured. It was uncertain how many of these shares were forged.[46]

Events moved quickly after this. On 5 December, Iengar wrote to say that LIC and SBI would jointly present a petition asking the court to appoint a manager for Richardson and Cruddas and BIC, which were to be taken possession of under the hypothecation agreement they had entered into.[47] A criminal case was to be filed concerning the forged shares in the possession of the Punjab National Bank. Finally, an investigation under the Company's Act was to be initiated into the affairs of all the Mundhra companies. In his secret note, D.L. Mazumdar, then Secretary, Department of Company Affairs, added that LIC was also keen to change the management of Jessop and Company and was seeking the cooperation of other large shareholders, Punjab

45 Secret letter D.O. no. G.8-309/57 28 November 1957 TTK papers Subject file 21, pp. 29–30.
46 Secret letter D.O. no. G.8-317/57, 30 November 1957, TTK Papers, Subject file 21, pp. 35–6.
47 Secret letter D.O. no. G.8-329/57, 5 December 1957, TTK Papers, Subject file 21, pp. 37–8.

National Bank and the engineering firm Burn, Brathwaite, Jessop and Co.[48] If this cooperation did not materialize, LIC wished to take action under the Companies Act with its 20 per cent shareholding, but it was felt that no minority shareholder could bring about a quick and non-disruptive change in management. Mazumdar also reported that he was informed that at the time when LIC came to Mundhra's help in June 1957, no special powers of intervention had been sought from Mundhra, so that if the situation did not improve, LIC could decisively intervene in company management. In the event, before the Mundhra case became a cause célèbre, the Department of Company Law, SBI, LIC, and RBI had agreed on the takeover through court action of the management of BIC and Richardson and Cruddas, police action against the share forgeries, and an investigation into the affairs of the Mundhra companies by the Department.[49]

In the context of the controversy over the LIC purchase of the Mundhra shares, whether the shares should have been bought from Mundhra himself, or whether Krishnamachari or H.M. Patel browbeat the chairperson and managing director of LIC to buy these shares against their better judgement, the most critical factor seems to have fallen by the wayside. This was emphasized by a comparison of the two notes written by D.L. Mazumdar, secretary of the Department of Company Law Administration in September 1957 and the second in December 1957. The first was addressed to Jawaharlal Nehru, at a time when Krishnamachari was in the United States.[50] Pointing out that the share purchases by LIC seemed not to have had any lasting results, with the share prices continuing to fall, Mazumdar suggested two options to the government. The first was an investigation into the affairs of the Mundhra Group under provisions of the Companies Act; the second was action against the management of specific companies of the group for contravention of articles defining sound principles of corporate governance. Mazumdar suggested that any process of formal investigation would be long-drawn-out, subject to judicial scrutiny, and would be detrimental not only to the 'interests of investors but also of employees and, indeed, of production as such'.

48 Secret note by D.L. Mazumdar, TTK Papers, Subject file 21, pp. 53–4.
49 Secret note by D.L. Mazumdar, TTK Papers, Subject file 21, p. 56.
50 Secret and Priority note, U.O.D. no. 1390/SCLA/57 dated 18 September 1957, JN Papers, File no. 587, pp. 273–4.

As for action against specific companies, the department was considering feasible action.

Curiously, the note did not suggest the takeover of at least those
companies in the group in which the SBI had a decisive stake through
the hypothecation agreements accompanying the loans advanced to
both the BIC and Richardson and Cruddas, a step that was taken finally,
three months later. Similarly, the provisions under the Industrial Development and Regulation Act (IDRA), allowing action by the government
in the public interest, were not considered at any time. According to
Mazumdar, it was the evidence of Mundhra's widespread use of forged
share certificates which made the governor of the Reserve Bank feel
that urgent action was demanded. It was also the combined resolve of
the RBI, SBI, and LIC that led to the agreement by Krishnamachari in
late November of these initiatives to gain managerial control.

What is being suggested is that in a long-term historical perspective, the issues that gained public attention at the time of the Mundhra
episode were irrelevant. The question that needs to be asked is why
these steps could not have been taken earlier. The conventional reasons offered, both by the commissions of enquiry and later commentators, of a short-term nexus between Mundhra as an individual and the
Congress Party's requirements of funds for the 1957 elections seems
inadequate.[51] As has been mentioned, Mundhra had long-standing
connections with the British exchange banks and even with the British Government. The significance of the reluctance of Mundra's creditor banks to take combined action to protect their own interests at
the meeting called by the RBI governor in May 1957 has already been
noted. Also, there was the marked reluctance of the Punjab National
Bank, which, together with the LIC, was a major shareholder in BIC,
to initiate police action even when it was discovered that the share
certificates it held as surety were forgeries. It will be recalled that the
then chairperson of the bank, Shanti Prasad Jain, was one of the persons under scrutiny in the Dalmia Jain case. What is then suggested
is that action to divest Mundhra of control of his companies, until
a stage was reached where action became imperative, was actively

51 See the views of the Vivian Bose Board of Inquiry, quoted by Balachandran
(1998), Appendix D, 'The Bank and the Mundhra Affair', pp. 803–4. See also the issue
of the *Salivati Newsletter*, published from Bombay, vol. 1, no. 25, 27 December 1957, JN
Papers, File no. 580, p. 66.

discouraged because Mundhra belonged precisely to the category of short-horizon businessmen who were so entrenched in the political economic nexus that presided over at least a significant part of the Indian political economy.

If this was indeed so, then a more promising area of enquiry is raised by the brief mention of the controversy surrounding Mundhra in the *Salivati Newsletter*, a broadsheet published from Bombay and evidently in the know of Bombay share market gossip.[52] According to this account, in March 1957, the Union commerce minister was alerted by the chief minister of Uttar Pradesh to the accumulation of stocks at the BIC mills and the imminent threat of closure of the mills leading to unemployment of 20,000 workers. After a visit to Lucknow and discussions with the chief minister and Mundhra, Union government officials advised Mundhra to reduce the labour force by dismissing a section of workers. He was also offered financial help, but after the refusal of the National Industrial Development Corporation, the SBI, and the exchange banks to advance further funds, attention was to focus on LIC. According to the *Salivati Newsletter*'s sources, between four and six members of the Union cabinet were in favour of extending financial help to Mundhra and, quite contrary to the predominant view that the financial improprieties were the result of a series of ill-considered and unsound directives issued by Krishnamachari, it was held that actually he was guilty of an inability to withstand the pressure from his cabinet colleagues and was merely an instrument in the decision that LIC would purchase the shares.[53]

OPPOSITION TO THE SOCIALIST PATTERN: THE FORUM OF FREE ENTERPRISE AND THE DEMOCRATIC RESEARCH SERVICE

Almost simultaneously with the adoption of the resolution on the socialistic pattern of society in January 1955, and its endorsement by

---

52 *Salivati Newsletter*, published from Bombay, vol. 1, no. 25, 27 December 1957, JN Papers, File no. 580, p. 66.

53 It is significant that Balachandran gives some credence to the opinion that Krishnamachari's decision to deny any knowledge of the LIC deal at the public hearings conducted in the course of the Chagla Commission was on the advice of the home minister, G.B. Pant (Balachandran 1998: 802).

the Lok Sabha soon afterwards, Bombay businessmen began to voice their dissatisfaction with the trend in economic policies. As a result, the government agreed to a series of consultations with major figures in the industrial field. In 1955, the major concern was the Companies Act, and a meeting was held with the Congress president, U.N. Dhebar, Morarji Desai, chief minister of the then Bombay state, G.D. Birla, J.R.D. Tata, and Gujarmal Modi amongst others. The discussion began with a general discussion about the socialist pattern. While both Tata and Modi were very gloomy and felt that the future held out little hope, Birla and some others took the line that adaptation to changing conditions and acceptance of major policies laid down by the government was essential if private industry was to function properly. Ultimately, both Tata and Modi, though probably not wholly convinced, toned down their criticism.[54]

By February 1956, with the imminent announcement of the new Industrial Policy Resolution, the feelings of apprehension were quite apparent to G.D. Birla, who reported the mood at a lunch hosted by Tata. Birla's attempt to inject some optimism apparently entirely failed.[55] Led by the Tata Group these misgivings materialized in the Forum of Free Enterprise.[56] According to its manifesto, which was published in the Bombay edition of the *Times of India* in July 1956, the forum was to be a non-political and non-partisan organization, disseminating authoritative information to educate public opinion on the achievements of private enterprise, and the manner in which it could contribute to the economic development of the country.[57] It called for support from those in service, profession, agriculture, trade, and industry. However, in its far-flung effort to explain the purpose of its establishment, A.D. Shroff, one of its chief organizers, clarified that the forum would have its political activity in the shape of

54 Confidential letter no. 353-PMO/55 dated 18 August 1955 from Jawaharlal Nehru to C.D. Deshmukh, JN Papers, File no. 371, p. 194.

55 Personal letter dated 28 February 1956, from G.D. Birla to T.T. Krishnamachari, TTK Papers, correspondence with G.D. Birla, pp. 36–7.

56 Kochanek (1974) discussed the Forum of Free Enterprise in some detail. See pp. 204–8. A.D. Shroff's presentation reported in 'Minutes of the Meeting of the Departmental Heads of Tata Companies convened by the Chairman on the 23 April 1957', TTK Papers, Subject file 10, pp. 13–15.

57 Top secret note, 'Forum of Free Enterprise', undated, JN Papers, File no. 485, p. 97a.

organizing public opinion against the government's economic policy, including the threat of nationalization implicit in the takeover of the airlines, the Imperial Bank, and the life insurance sector. The 1956 Industrial Policy Resolution was responsible for creating apprehensions in businessmen's minds, as also in the minds of middle class investors.[58] M.R. Masani, founder of the Democratic Research Service, spoke more explicitly at Bangalore: lovers of freedom, he said, should be alert enough to shift their fire and their aim from one source of the centralization of power and privilege to another.[59] In his opinion, the social forces represented by industrial management, trade, organized labour, the professions, industrial proprietors, and religion could provide the checks and balances necessary to curb power. Morarji Vaidya, president of the Indian Merchants' Chamber, in an article in the *Times of India* criticized both the nationalizations, but extended the basis for opposition by referring to the 'attitude' adopted by the State Trading Organization.[60] Further activity was reported: contact was established in the course of five meetings in July 1956 with 120 trade organizations in Bombay, with 50 members of parliament in Delhi in September 1956, with members of the Mysore Chamber of Commerce and the Indian Institute of Culture at Bangalore, also in September.[61] Meetings in Calcutta were held with 'prominent citizens, with the Upper India Chamber of Commerce in Kanpur, and the Gujarat Chamber of Commerce in Ahmedabad. Finally, an All India Essay contest was organized for students on the subject "Free Enterprise and Economic Progress"', and, under the auspices of the magazine *Trend*, a meeting for women was held at the Taj Mahal hotel, where the audience was reminded that as consumers of domestic goods, they provided adequate regulation of the industry, thereby making state regulation superfluous.

So as to make the aim of the forum plain beyond any doubt, according to another intelligence report, A.D. Shroff, speaking to the

58 A.D. Shroff's speeches in Calcutta to a group of businessmen in September 1956 and, in Bombay, to the Commerce Graduates Association in October 1956. Top Secret note, 'Forum of Free Enterprise', undated, JN Papers File no. 485, p. 97a.

59 Top secret note, 'Forum of Free Enterprise', undated, JN Papers, File no. 485.

60 Top secret note, 'Forum of Free Enterprise', undated, JN Papers, File no. 485, p. 96.

61 Secret note, 'A note on the "Forum of Free Enterprise"', undated, JN Papers, File no. 492, pp. 34–9.

Commerce Graduates Association in October 1956, referred to the letter from Eugene Black, president of the World Bank, to T.T. Krishnamachari, criticizing the direction of recent economic policy. Black was,
according to Shroff, a 'real and sincere' friend of India. By December
1956, the ambitions of the sponsors of the forum, perhaps fortified by
the response to their campaign, had extended to the overtly political.
Japan Singh, an MP of the Jharkhand Party, was approached to gain
his support for the candidatures of M.R. Masani, A.D. Shroff, H.P.
Mody, and Leslie Sawhney, J.R.D. Tata's brother-in-law, in the 1957
parliamentary elections from the Jharkhand area of Bihar.[62] Tulsidas
Kilachand, another industrialist-MP, had joined the 'Tata crowd' who
were simultaneously in touch with N.C. Chatterjee, extending support to fifteen candidates in constituencies where the Hindu Mahas-
abha and Jan Sangh had a political base. The Democratic Research
Forum and the Forum of Free Enterprise, having collected Rs 10 lakh,
were in need of more money. A political attaché in the US Embassy,
'...working directly under the orders of Mr. Allen Dulles...'(director
of the CIA) had offered considerable financial assistance from secret
service funds.[63]

Apart from the broader relevance of these developments to India's
political trajectory and the increasing pressures towards modifying
economic strategy, by April 1957, it was clear that the immediate target
of attack was T.T. Krishnamachari. H.V.R. Iengar informed Krishnamachari of a conversation he had had with Shroff.[64] To a query about

---

62 It is interesting to note that it was G.D. Birla who suggested to H.P. Mody, in
February 1956, that if he wished to contest the Lok Sabha election, he should stand
from an area near Jamshedpur, rather than from Bombay. Personal letter dated 28
February 1956, from G.D. Birla to T.T. Krishnamachari, TTK Papers, correspondence
with G.D. Birla, p. 36.

63 Personal note by M.O. Mathai dated 1 December 1956, JN Papers, File no.493,
p. 29. Nehru sent the substance of this note to U.N. Dhebar, Congress President, in
his secret letter (no. 676-PMO/56 dated 6 December 1956, File no. 494, p. 121). In a
secret note to the secretary general of the ministry of external affairs written on the
same day (to which, significantly, he attached a copy of Mathai's note), he suggested
that at the impending talks with the US Government 'some general reference might
be made to these reports of American funds being offered for election purposes here'
(File no. 494, p. 103).

64 Strictly personal letter dated 4 April 1957, TTK Papers, correspondence with
H.V.R. Iengar, p. 10.

whether Shroff was aware that he was doing a great deal of injury by the reckless manner in which he was attacking the government, Shroff immediately turned the conversation towards Krishnamachari personally, and to his supposed open hostility even to any legitimate criticism of his policies. While reiterating that Shroff's idiosyncrasies were well known to Krishnamachari, Iengar warned that the broader intent of Shroff's criticism was being shared with some of his colleagues in the cabinet. This aspect of Shroff, of allowing bitterness towards policies affecting him in relation to unrelated areas of government's functioning, was noted by Nehru too.[65]

'RIGHT REACTION' WITHIN AND OUTSIDE THE CONGRESS: KRISHNAMACHARI'S EXIT, RE-ENTRY, AND THE BATTLE REJOINED

After the presentation of the 1957 budget, it seemed as if the campaign to create a fear psychosis amongst the middle class had reached such proportions that Nehru, while strongly reiterating his support for the fiscal measures, had to warn Krishnamachari of the prevailing current of opinion.[66] Almost simultaneously, Krishnamachari was told by the old established Congressman and the then governor of Bombay State, Sri Prakasa, of his own misgivings about the budget proposals.[67] Sri Prakasa specifically pointed towards the opportunities for harassment, not only directed at businessmen but also to the middle class who would, reportedly, be required to maintain records of expenditure. In the fortnightly report that state governors were to send to the president, Sri Prakasa elaborated his concerns, a copy of which he sent to Krishnamachari. On his part, Nehru pointed out that it was the business of government, without sacrificing its principles, to carry every shade of opinion with it. He emphasized that even when a policy was opposed by clearly sectional interests, it was important to '....hurt ... [the individuals involved] ... as little as possible, that

65 Secret letter no. 585-PMH/59 dated 11 March 1959 to Fazl Ali, governor of Assam, JN Papers, File no. 676, p. 257.

66 Secret and personal letter no. 1357-PMH/57 dated 2 August 1957, JN Papers, File no. 543, pp. 137–8.

67 Secret and personal letter dated 1 June 1957, TTK Papers, correspondence with Jawaharlal Nehru, 1957, pp. 80–7.

is, to put it ... [crudely, to deal with the problem] ... in a politician's way'. Not only had the Congress party in the Lok Sabha to be taken along in support of these measures, but the people generally. 'Running down' of the propertied classes, though often justified, ended in demoralizing not only them, but also the large middle class and even the lower middle class.

In his reply to Nehru's letter of warning about the currents of opposition created by the 1957 budget, Krishnamachari made an astute point.[68] While agreeing that all the major moulders of public opinion in the press were sharply critical of the fiscal measures proposed, Birla was singled out as a friend. But even 'he feels hurt because the prospect of running the type of business as he has been doing in the past will not be possible in the future'. While Birla could adjust to the new circumstances, other businessmen, presumably deeply enmeshed in the usurious, speculative, and commercial modes of operation could not easily do so. According to Krishnamachari, Birla was thus torn between his loyalty to the Congress (his friends) and to his 'clan'—this latter breed of businessmen.[69]

Where Krishnamachari's shrewdness seems to have failed him was in his unwittingly creating an alliance between Birla's 'clan' and the modern Bombay-based supporters of the Forum of Free Enterprise.[70] While the former reacted to his measures of social engineering, the latter objected to the institution of controls that, in their opinion, impinged on their sources of authority and power. Together, they created the situation that forced Krishnamachai's exit from the cabinet.

After the 1962 elections, Nehru offered a re-elected Krishnamachari any cabinet post of his choice except finance (held by Morarji Desai after a brief interval following Krishnamachari's resignation in 1958). In a bitter letter to Nehru, Krishnamachari claimed that it was Morarji Desai who had played a major role in ensuring a situation in which his resignation became inevitable. His charges were formidable:

68 Nehru's secret and personal letter no. 1357-PMH/57 dated 2 August 1957, JN Papers, File no. 543, pp. 137–8. Krishnamachari's secret letter no. 344/FM/57 dated 3 August 1957, JN Papers, File no.543, pp. 192–4.

69 Kochanek (1974), dealing with the situation within the Federation of Indian Chambers of Commerce and Industry (FICCI) in the mid-1960s, has an interesting discussion on the size of Birla's 'clan' (pp. 170–93).

70 Kochanek (1974) has discussed these differences on p. 216 and pp. 220–2.

....you are a mature politician and the Prime Minister of a great country. In the course of the discharge of your obligations, therefore, it does happen that you might have to walk over the corpses of your friends. I realize it might be necessary & I for my part have no grievance. But I cannot be a good friend and unilateral though it might be I consider myself to be one ... if I did not tell you that you do wrong. It is for you to decide whom you are keeping as helmsman of the economic affairs of this country. You will appreciate also that I cannot serve in any ministry charged with some economic mission with the present FM as economic director. There are two angles to it—one personal and the other a matter of principle. Mr M[orarji] D[esai] had a fair share in the launching of the campaign against me when I was F[inance] M[inister]. I know more of it after I left. His minions in the Lok Sabha & outside did the dirty work. You knew that he brought Moulana [Abul Kalam Azad] into it at one stage. He suborned the loyalty of officials whom I had trusted & even specially favoured by offers of preferment and made them give false testimony before the [first Vivian] Bose Commission. His agent[,] a journalist at the time[,] lobbied with the UPSC and got rewarded as news editor in A[ll] I[ndia] R[adio]. The nasty speeches in the discussion on Bose's report etc. were made by his agents—known to be such to all members of the Lok Sabha. On the public issues he was the apostle [of] all that I was against. The Finance Ministry has become a veritable paradise of the vested interests these last few years. My tax measures were drastically amended & such that remain have been made dead letters administratively...I hear that the Central Board of Revenue has been asked to prepare a paper supporting a scheme to abolish the wealth tax & expenditure tax. Tax evasion during these four years has gathered momentum and officers are afraid of Bombay vested interests ... The Swatantra Party against which you have been fighting is not really led by Rajaji [C. Rajagopalachari] but by the big guns of industry & trade and the FM & another in your cabinet are their firm supporters. At the appropriate time they would change the band wagon....[71]

The message of this emotional outburst was clear: the era of social engineering through innovative fiscal measures was over and private enterprise would increasingly set the terms on which it wished to negotiate with the government.

---

[71] Handwritten letter dated 24 March 1962, TTK Papers, correspondence with Jawaharlal Nehru 1962, pp. 11–14.

CHAPTER SEVEN

Denouement

The Final Abolition of Managing Agencies

The commission of inquiry appointed by the government to examine the operations of the Dalmia-Jain Group submitted its report in 1963 after delays due to court cases filed by the Dalmia-Jain Group, which were first heard and dealt with. The report was the subject of extensive debate in the Lok Sabha, where the members generally responded to the revelations contained in the commission's report with a degree of resignation. The methods by which the group had defrauded shareholders and the government might have been new in detail, but the MPs were evidently at a loss on how precisely these practices were to be prohibited. Shanti Prasad Jain's plea that his group had only employed the same procedures that were common to big business operations neatly summed up the situation, although this was not an accurate description.[1] As has been suggested earlier, by using the frame of joint-stock companies as a means to aggrandizement, the group had behaved in a qualitatively different way to the 'straightforward' cases of tax evasion of Tatas, Birlas, and even the stock market speculation of Haridas Mundhra.

---

1 Pages 9 and 39 of the petition by Shanti Prasad Jain quoted by Homi Daji, MP, in the course of the Lok Sabha debate on the Motion, Re: Report of the Commission of Enquiry into Dalmia Jain Companies on 6 May 1963. Column 14030 of Lok Sabha Debates, 1963, Vol. XVIII.

When the report on the Dalmia-Jain Group was released in 1963, its quite startling revelations gave pause to even those members of the government long inured to the ways of the business world. Its implications were such that Krishnamachari, finally back in the cabinet, felt that a carefully chosen official would need to be appointed to examine the report and suggest remedies. He feared that the forces which would oppose action were so powerful and resourceful that nothing might conceivably be done at all.[2] D.R. Gadgil, in an unsigned note in response to a request from Pitambar Pant, head of the perspective planning division of the Planning Commission, set out in clear terms the reasons why the controls instituted by the government had failed to deal with determined efforts to prevent activities which, though not technically illegal, had serious implications for society.[3]

> The problem posed by the findings of the Commission may be described as follows. It has been found that a group of businessmen has acted together in the past, in all kinds of devious, patently unfair or even illegal ways and has, as a result, not only made large gains for its members, but has enabled them to attain to such dominant economic position that a part of the old group, as such, and most of its members individually, today are amongst the most powerful and prosperous of business concerns and businessmen in India.[4]

Discussing the possible ways of preventing similar occurrences in the future, Gadgil argued that the two principal legislative enactments, the Industrial Development and Regulation Act (IDRA) and the Companies Act, were inadequate to deal with such situations. The Industrial Development and Regulation Act was framed so as to promote industrial development, to maintain continuity and efficiency in production, and for the conservation of resources. Only one subsection, added in 1953, enabled the government to initiate an investigation when any enterprise was seen to be managed in a manner highly

2 Letter no. 49/MEDC/63 dated 28 January 1963 to Jawaharlal Nehru, TTK Papers, correspondence with Jawaharlal Nehru 1963–4, p. 22.

3 Gadgil note, p. 1. In a letter to Pitambar Pant (No 736/-PMH/63 dated 19 March 1963), Jawaharlal Nehru acknowledged that the (unsigned) note came from Gadgil, JN Papers, File no. 743 p. 288. TTK Papers, correspondence with Jawaharlal Nehru 1963, File no. 743, pp. 60–4. Also JN Papers, File no. 743, pp. 277–81.

4 Gadgil note, p. 3.

detrimental to the industry as a whole, or to public interest. However, Gadgil noted, the addition of this subclause had not made any difference to the rest of the act: public interest remained a fifth wheel in the structure of the act.[5] In the case of the Companies Act, Gadgil pointed out that following the example of British Company Law, the Indian act abstracted from economic policy and, more critically, the courts in India had examined proposals for corporate action that came before them in a narrow framework, and public interest again was entirely absent in their consideration of a case.[6] Turning to international experience in dealing with economic offenses of the Dalmia-Jain type, Gadgil pointed out that only in post-war West German legislation did offences include those which 'violate[d] the interest of the State in the conservation and integrity of the economic order as a whole or in individual branches'. Moreover, he added, in relation to this new classification of economic offence, the measurement of the gravity of the offence was also innovative: the yardstick was not only the gravity of the interest that had been injured, but also the *mens rea* (degree of criminal intent) of the offender.

Gadgil concluded that the sphere of action by which such cases could be prevented was not that of legal remedies. Only when public interest was invoked and the approach defined as that relating to the totality of the economic system that a solution to halt, if not reverse, a 'steadily worsening situation' would be possible. Concretely, he suggested that the group's managing agency control over public companies should be forcefully broken, there should be expropriation of the assets of the group, and the firms under their control should be taken over by the government. Finally, the persons indicted were to be prohibited from holding office in any joint-stock company whether closely or widely held.[7]

Despite the generalized revulsion of Dalmia-Jain business practices expressed in the Lok Sabha debate, the supporters of the managing agency system fought a determined rearguard action.[8] When the Managing Agency Enquiry Committee was announced by the

5 Gadgil note, p. 2.
6 Gadgil note, p. 1.
7 Gadgil note, pp. 3–4.
8 This was apparent from the publicity given to the special pleading on behalf of the Dalmias contained in documents such as Mittal et al. (1963?).

government in 1966, it was asked to confine its attention to the utility of the system to enterprises in 'established' industries. The appointment of such a committee was mandatory if action had to be taken under Section 324 of the Companies Act, which enabled the government to ban managing agencies in specific industries. It will be recalled here that the Imperial Chemical Industries (ICI) had objected to Kasturbhai Lalbhai's insistence on a managing agency for the joint venture with Atul Products. As is well known, almost all the firms in the new industries were formed with foreign collaboration with TNCs which were unlikely to differ from ICI's unwillingness to incorporate the managing agency. The injunction to the enquiry committee to confine itself to the established industries is evidence of the perception that the system provided some advantages in these new ventures, situations where uncertainties might be expected to be greater. It is also of some interest that the committee, having chosen as its traditional industries, cotton textiles, jute textiles, cement, paper, and sugar, decided without explanation that managing agencies should be abolished in all except jute textiles and paper. Even given the existing, residual, British interests in jute, it is not overly speculative to conclude that the special attention given to this, one of the two oldest and most well-established industries, was due to their continuing influence on industrial policy. The Committee also fell in line with the go-slow policy, which had been pursued since 1956 in the area of industrial management reform. It recommended continuance of the policy of individual-application-wise rather than industry-wise consideration of appointment and re-appointment of managing agents.

However, the government in 1967 decided to terminate the managing agency system in five industries—cotton, sugar, cement, jute, and paper—effective from 1970. This momentous step was taken by a low-key administrative order, under Section 324 of the Companies Act. Notice was also given, in effect, that abolition in other established industries would follow soon. As a commentator in the *Economic and Political Weekly* noted, this rare fit of courageous decision-making was perhaps inspired by the need to improve the government's image after the ignominy it faced with the 1966 devaluation. However, in another comment a few years later, the journal reported that G.D. Birla had himself suggested that the penultimate rites for the system be performed, that is, that big business had itself conceded that the managing agency system was now proving dysfunctional.[9] Subsequently, as a part of the wide-ranging reforms in industrial finance, which included bank nationalization, the Government of India decreed the total abolition of the managing agency system from 1970.[10] This happened after more than ten years of the passage of the 1956 Companies Act, nearly fifty years after the criticism voiced by the Indian Industrial Commission, and three-quarters of a century or more after the first stirrings of protest in Bombay in the 1890s.

Although, largely as a result of the outrage provoked in the Lok Sabha by the revelations of the Dalmia-Jain Commission's report, the managing agency system was finally abolished and there was never a return to the range of social engineering policies that Krishnamachari had introduced in the 1957 budget.[11] The strategy then adopted seemed to be one that curtailed businessmen's proclivities in the financial sector (for instance, by nationalizing channels of delivery of funds for agriculture through takeovers of commercial banks), rather than the explicit measures that had cost Krishnamachari the finance minister's post in the earlier government.[12]

While detailed company-level analysis would be required to establish the case conclusively, from the extensive documentation over the forty-year period of financial irregularities made possible by the managing agency system, it would seem reasonable to conclude that by the late-1960s, the most backward forms of capital had been removed from the control of industrial enterprises. The tenaciousness of the struggle waged by it is only an indication of the complexity

9 Not surprisingly, the Birla Group proved itself to be amongst those most adept in devising institutional mechanisms by which the financial advantages accruing through the managing agency system would continue (*Economic and Political Weekly* 1967, 1970a, and 1970b).

10 By the Companies (Amendment) Act, number 17 of 1969, passed in May that year, managing agencies were abolished with effect from 3 April 1970.

11 Shirokov (1973) whose close reading of contemporary material is evidenced by his bibliography, notes that the 1956 Industrial Policy Resolution was forced through by 'middle ranking' sections of capitalists. However, further development of capitalist industrialization marked the end of 'bourgeois radicalism' (p. 59).

12 Interestingly, the report which is generally held to be the basis of the decision to nationalize the private commercial banks in 1969 mentions the advantages that nationalization would provide in curbing flows from the banking system to the unorganized rural money market (cf. Bettelheim's comments mentioned earlier). See Congress Parliamentary Party (1967: 65–6).

of the process of development of industrial capital in colonial societies. Equally glaring was the change of rankings of many of the big
business groups, notorious from the days of Ashoka Mehta's pioneer-
ing pre-war pamphlets, and stable amongst the handful which were
synonymous with the term 'big business' for the next thirty years.[13]
Their relative, if not absolute, decline in the industrial arena was an
indication that without the instrumentality of the managing agency
system with which to sustain their financial manipulations, they had
succumbed to the logic of an industrial economy.

13 Thus, the Dalmia-Jain Group and its offshoots were no longer within the group
of the twenty largest industrial houses in terms of assets by the early 1980s. See Table
II.2, p. 24 of Corporate Studies Group (1983), which is based on a reply to a Rajya Sabha
question of 1981.

PRIMARY SOURCES

Private Papers Consulted in the Archives of the Nehru Memorial Museum and Library, New Delhi

C. Rajagopalachari Papers (CR Papers)
C.D. Deshmukh Papers (CDD Papers)
G.L. Mehta Papers (GLM Papers)
Harekrushna Mehtab Papers (HM Papers)
Indian Merchants Chamber Papers (IMC Papers)
Jawaharlal Nehru Papers (JN Papers)
Kasturbhai Lalbhai Papers (KL Papers)
M.A. Master Papers (MAM Papers)
Purshottamdas Thakurdas Papers (PT Papers)
T.T. Krishnamachari Papers (TTK Papers)

Newspapers and Periodicals

Bombay Chronicle
Bombay Sentinel
Dawn
Eastern Economist
Free Press Journal
Hindu, The
Hindustan Times
Hitawada
Independent India

National Herald
Pioneer, The
Statesman, The
Times of India, The
Tribune, The

SECONDARY SOURCES

Adhikari, G., ed. 1982. *Documents of the History of the Communist Party of India*, Volume III C 1928. New Delhi: Peoples' Publishing House.

Afzal, M. Rafique, ed. 1967. *Speeches and Statements of Quaid-i-Millat Liaquat Ali Khan [1941–1951]*. Lahore: University of the Punjab.

Alavi, Hamza. 2002. 'Social Forces and Ideology in the Making of Pakistan'. *Economic and Political Weekly* 37(51): 5119–24.

Allen, Tom. 2000. *The Right to Property in Commonwealth Constitutions*. Cambridge: Cambridge University Press.

Amin, Shahid. 1981. 'Unequal Antagonists: Peasants and Capitalists in Eastern UP in 1930s'. *Economic and Political Weekly* 16(42–3): 19–31.

Anstey, Vera. 1942. *The Economic Development of India*, third edition. London: Longman, Green and Co.

———. 1945. 'A Plan of Economic Development for India'. *International Affairs* 21(4): 555–7.

Azad, Abul Kalam. 1959. *India Wins Freedom: An Autobiographical Narrative*. Calcutta: Orient Longman.

Bagchi, Amiya Kumar. 1972. *Private Investment in India 1900–1939*. Cambridge: Cambridge University Press.

Baker, Christopher John. 1984. *An Indian Rural Economy, 1880–1955: The Tamilnad Countryside*. Delhi: Oxford University Press.

Balachandran, G. 1998. *The Reserve Bank of India*. Delhi: Oxford University Press.

Baru, Sanjaya. 1983. 'State and Industrialisation: Political Economy of Sugar Policy, 1932–47'. *Economic and Political Weekly* 18(5): 2–18.

Basu, Saroj Kumar. 1958. *The Managing Agency System: In Prospect and Retrospect*. Calcutta: The World Press.

Bertrand, Marianne, Paras Mehta, and Sendhil Mullainathan. 2002. 'Ferreting Out Tunneling: An Application to Indian Business Groups'. *The Quarterly Journal of Economics* 117(1): 121–48.

Bertrand, Marianne and Sendhil Mullainathan. 2003. 'Pyramids'. *Journal of the European Economic Association* 1(2–3): 478–83.

Bettelheim, Charles. 1971. *India Independent*. New York: Monthly Review Press.

Bhagwati, Jagdish N. and Padma Desai. 1970. *India: Planning for Industrialisation*. London: Oxford University Press.

Birla, G.D. 1934. *Indian Prosperity: A Plea for Planning*. Speech delivered at the Annual Session of the Federation of Indian Chambers of Commerce and Industry. New Delhi: FICCI.

———. 1944. 'Industrialization in India'. *Annals of the American Academy of Political and Social Science* 233: 121–6.

———. 1946. 'A Critique of Government Planning'. Speech delivered at the Nineteenth Annual Session of the Federation of Indian Chambers of Commerce and Industry. New Delhi: FICCI.

Bombay. 1924. Report of the Stock Exchange Enquiry Committee. Available at http://www.sebi.gov.in/History/HistoryReport1924.pdf. Accessed 10 May 2011.

———. 1937. Report of the Stock Exchange Enquiry Committee. Available at http://www.sebi.gov.in/History/HistoryReport1937.pdf. Accessed on 10 May 2011.

Bombay Shareholders' Association. 1934. 'Written Evidence'. In Cotton Textile Industry, Volume II, Views of the Local Governments, Collectors of Customs, and written statements submitted by Associations and Committees. 180–251.

———. 1936. The Indian Companies Act (Amendment) Bill, 1936: Memorandum Submitted by the Committee of the Bombay Shareholders' Association. Bombay: Bombay Shareholders' Association.

———. 1949. Amendment of the Indian Companies Act: Memorandum of the Bombay Shareholders' Association on Managing Agents. Bombay: Bombay Shareholders' Association.

Bose, Sugata. 1986. *Agrarian Bengal: Economy, Social Structure and Politics*. Cambridge: Cambridge University Press.

Brass, Paul R. 1970. 'Muslim Separatism in United Provinces: Social Context and Political Strategy before Partition'. *Economic and Political Weekly* 5(3–5): 167–86.

Brimmer, Andrew F. 1955. 'The Setting of Entrepreneurship in India'. *The Quarterly Journal of Economics* 69(4): 553–76.

Brown, Hilton. 1954. *Parry's of Madras: A Story of British Enterprise in India*. Madras: Parry and Company Ltd.

Brush, John E. 1949. 'The Distribution of Religious Communities in India'. *Annals of the Association of American Geographers* 39(2): 81–98.

Buchanan, D.H. 1934. *The Development of Capitalistic Enterprise in India*. New York: Macmillan.

Burman, Debajyoti. 1950. *Mystery of Birla House*. Calcutta: Jugabani Sahitya Chakra.

———. 1953. *Mystery of Birla House: Part Two*. Calcutta: Jugabani Sahitya Chakra.

———. 1957. *TTK and Birla House*. Calcutta: Jugabani Sahitya Chakra.

Chakrabarti, M. and B. Chatterjee. 2006. 'Business Conduct in Late Colonial India'. *Economic and Political Weekly* 41(10): 904–11.

Chakravarty, Sukhumoy. 1989. *Development Planning: The Indian Experience*. Delhi: Oxford University Press.

Chapman, S.D. 1985. 'British-Based Investment Groups before 1914'. *The Economic History Review*, New Series, 38(2): 230–51.

————. 1987. 'Investment Groups in India and South Africa: [A Reply]'. *The Economic History Review*, New Series, 40(2): 275–80.

Chattopadhyay, Raghabendra. 1986. 'Indian National Congress and the Indian Bourgeoisie: Liaquat Ali Khan's Budget of 1947–48, Occasional Paper No. 85', mimeo. Calcutta: Centre for Studies in Social Sciences.

————. 1988. 'Liaquat Ali Khan's Budget of 1947–48: The Tryst with Destiny'. *Social Scientist* 181–2, 16(6 and 7): 77–89.

————. 1991. 'Indian Business and Economic Planning'. In *Business and Politics in India: A Historical Perspective*, edited by D. Tripathi. New Delhi: Manohar Publications.

Chibber, Vivek. 2004. *Locked in Place: State-Building and Late Industrialization in India*. New Delhi: Tulika Books.

————. 2005. 'From Class Compromise to Class Accommodation: Labor's Incorporation into the Indian Political Economy'. In *Social Movements and Poverty in India*, edited by Mary Katzenstein and Raka Ray. Lanham, MD: Rowman and Littlefield.

Chhatrapati, A.C. 1956. 'Implications of the Compulsory Company Reserves Deposits Scheme'. *Economic Weekly* 8(51): 1497–500.

Chicherov, A.I. 1971. *India: Economic Development in the 16th–18th Centuries: Outline History of Crafts and Trade*. Moscow: Nauka Publishing House.

Congress Party in Parliament. 1967. *Banking Institutions and Indian Economy: A Critical Review*. Delhi: CPP.

Cornelius, A.R. and T.D. Wickenden. 1943. 'British India'. *Journal of Comparative Legislation and International Law*, third series, 25(1–2): 175.

Corporate Studies Group. 1983. 'Functioning of Industrial Licensing System: A Report', mimeo. New Delhi: Indian Institute of Public Administration.

Dalmia, Ramakrishna. 1948. 'Speculative Profits during War Times'. Extracted in *The Oxford India Anthology of Business History* (2011), edited by Medha M. Kudaisya. New Delhi: Oxford University Press.

Dantwala, M.L. 1937. *Marketing of Raw Cotton in India*. Bombay: Longman, Green and Co.

Das, Nabagopal. 1938. *Industrial Enterprise in India*. London: Oxford University Press.

————. 1956. *Industrial Enterprise in India*, second revised edition. Calcutta: Orient Longman.

Davar, Sohrab R. 1934. *Inefficient Managing Agency System and the Amendment of the Indian Companies Act, 1913*. Bombay: Davars College Publication.

Desai, Ashok V. 1968. 'The Origins of Parsi Enterprise'. *Indian Economic and Social History Review* 5(4): 307–17.

Desai, Ashok V. 1970. 'Evolution of Import Control'. *Economic and Political Weekly* 5(29–31): 1271–8.

Deshmukh, C.D. 1957. *Economic Developments in India 1946–1956: A Personal Retrospect*. Bombay: Asia Publishing House.

Dewey, Clive. 1979. 'The Government of India's "New Industrial Policy" 1900–1925: Formation and Failure'. In *Economy and Society: Essays in Indian Economic and Social History*, edited by K.N. Chaudhuri and C.J. Dewey. Delhi: Oxford University Press.

Dillard, Dudley. 1980. 'A Monetary Theory of Production: Keynes and the Institutionalists'. *Journal of Economic Issues* XIV(2): 255–73.

Dobb, Maurice. 1963. *Studies in the Development of Capitalism*. London: Routledge and Kegan Paul.

Duncan, Ian. 1995. 'The Politics of Liberalization in Early Post Independence India: Food Deregulation in 1947'. *Journal of Commonwealth and Comparative Politics* XXXIII(1): 25–45.

Eastern Economist. 1943. *Principles of Economic Planning*. New Delhi: the author.

Economic Weekly. 1952a. 'Cases Disposed of by Advisory Commission on Company Law'. 4(6): 154.

———. 1952b. 'Irregularities in Company Accounts'. 4(22): 549–50.

Economic and Political Weekly. 1967. 'After Half a Century, an Unnoticed Notification'. 2(6): 349–50.

———. 1970a. 'Change of Labels'. 5(7): 316.

———. 1970b. 'Pass Friend, Halt Bottle'. 5(15): 622.

Enthoven, R.E. 1913 [1966]. 'Managing Agents'. In *Studies in Economic Policy and Development of India (1848–1926)* by Sunil Kumar Sen, Appendix A. Calcutta: Progressive Publishers.

Free Press Journal. 1958. *Mundhra Inquiry: The Full Story*. Mumbai.

Friedman, Eric, Simon Johnson, and Todd Mitton. 2003. Propping and Tunneling NBER Working Paper Series, Working Paper 9949. Available at http://www.nber.org/papers/w9949. Accessed on 26 September 2011.

Gadgil, D.R. 1949. 'The Economic Prospect for India'. *Pacific Affairs* 22(2): 115–29.

———. 1955a. *Economic Policy and Development (A Collection of Writings)*. Poona: Gokhale Institute of Politics and Economics.

———. 1955b. 'Wartime Controls and Peacetime Ends' in *Economic Policy and Development (A Collection of Writings)*, pp. 79–86. Poona: Gokhale Institute of Politics and Economics.

———. 1971. *The Industrial Evolution of India in Recent Times 1860–1939*, fifth edition. Delhi: Oxford University Press.

Gadgil, D.R. and N.V. Sovani. 1943. *War and Indian Economic Policy*. Poona: Gokhale Institute of Politics and Economics.

Gandhi, Rajmohan. 1989. *India Wins Errors: A Scrutiny of Maulana Azad's 'India Wins Freedom'*. Delhi: Radiant Publishers.

Goel R.K. 1961. 'Managing Agents: Their Power and Functions—A Historical Review'. *Journal of the Indian Law Institute* III: 389–414.

Gorwala, A.D. 1952. *The Role of the Administrator: Past, Present and Future.* Poona: Gokhale Institute of Politics and Economics.

Goswami, Omkar. 1982. 'Collaboration and Conflict: European and Indian Capitalists and the Jute Economy of Bengal, 1919–39'. *Indian Economic and Social History Review* 19(2): 141–79.

———. 1985. 'Then Came the Marwaris: Some Aspects of the Changes in the Pattern of Industrial Control in Eastern India'. *Indian Economic and Social History Review* 22(3): 225–49.

———. 1989. 'Sahibs, Babus, and Banias: Changes in Industrial Control in Eastern India, 1918–50'. *The Journal of Asian Studies* 48(2): 289–309.

Grajdanzev, Andrew J. 1943. 'India's Wartime Economic Difficulties'. *Pacific Affairs* 16(2): 189–205.

———. 1944. 'India's Economic Position in 1944'. *Pacific Affairs* 17(4): 460–77.

Great Britain. 1913. *House of Commons Debate, Indian Companies Act, 1913, 25 June 1913* HANSARD volume 54 columns 1052–3. Available at http://hansard. millbanksystems.com/commons/1913/jun/25/indian-companies-act-1913# S5CV0054P0_ 19130625_ HOC _61. Accessed on 21 June 2011.

———. 1974. *Constitutional Relations between Britain and India: The Transfer of Power 1942–1947, Volume V, The Simla Conference Background and Proceedings 1 Sept 1944–28 July 1945.* London: HMSO.

———. 1980. *Constitutional Relations between Britain and India The Transfer of Power 1942–47 Vol IX The Fixing of a time limit 4 November 1946–22 March 1947.* London: HMSO.

Guha, Amalendu. 1970a. 'Parsi Seths as Entrepreneurs'. *Economic and Political Weekly* 5(35): M107–M115.

———. 1970b. 'The Comprador Role of Parsi Seths'. *Economic and Political Weekly* 5(48): 1933–6.

———. 1984. 'More About the Parsi Seths: Their Roots, Entrepreneurship and Comprador Role, 1650–1918'. *Economic and Political Weekly* 19(3): 117–32.

Gupta, Partha Sarathi. 1987. 'State and Business in India in the Age of Discriminating Protection'. In *State and Business in India: A Historical Perspective*, edited by Dwijendra Tripathi (New Delhi: Manohar Publications), pp. 157–216.

Habib, Irfan. 1969. 'Potentialities of Capitalistic Development in the Economy of Mughal India'. *Journal of Economic History* 29(1): 32–78.

———. 1975. 'Colonialization of the Indian Economy, 1757–1900'. *Social Scientist* 3(8): 23–53.

———. 1985. 'Studying a Colonial Economy—Without Perceiving Colonialism'. *Modern Asian Studies* 19(3): 355–81.

———. 1988. 'Processes of Accumulation in Pre-Colonial and Colonial India'. *Indian Historical Review* 11(1–2) reprinted in Habib (1995), pp. 259–95.

Habib, Irfan. 1995. *Essays in Indian History: Towards a Marxist Perception*. New Delhi: Tulika.

Hardiman, David. 1996. *Feeding the Bania: Peasants and Usurers in Western India*. Delhi: Oxford University Press.

Hashim, S.R., K.S. Chalapati Rao, K.V.K. Ranganathan, and M.R. Murthy, eds. 2009. *Indian Industrial Development and Globalisation: Essays in Honour of Professor S. K. Goyal*. New Delhi: Academic Foundation.

Hazari, R.K. 1964. 'The Managing Agency System: A Case for Its Abolition'. *Economic Weekly* XVI(5–7): 315–22.

―――. 1966. *The Structure of the Corporate Private Sector: A Study of Concentration of Ownership and Control*. Bombay: Asia Publishing House.

India. 1927. Tariff Board, Report of the Indian Tariff Board (Cotton Textile Industry Enquiry) 1927 Volume 1 Report.

―――. 1931. The Indian Central Banking Enquiry Committee 1931, Volume I, Part I—Majority Report.

―――. 1932. Tariff Board, Report of the Indian Tariff Board regarding Grant of Protection to the Cotton Textile Industry.

―――. 1934. Cotton Textile Industry, Volume II, Views of the Local Governments, Collectors of Customs, and written statements submitted by Associations and Committees.

―――. 1936. Department of Commerce, Minutes of the Proceedings of the Company Law Amendment Committee (January 1936).

―――. 1938. Agricultural Marketing Adviser, Report on the Marketing of Wheat in India and Burma (Abridged Edition).

―――. 1941a. Agricultural Marketing Adviser, Report on the Marketing of Groundnuts in India and Burma.

―――. 1941b. Agricultural Marketing Adviser, Report on the Marketing of Rice in India and Burma.

―――. 1944. Planning and Development Department, Second Report on Reconstruction Planning.

―――. 1948. Report on the Regulation of the Stock Market in India. Available at http://www.sebi.gov.in/History/HistoryReport1948.pdf. Accessed on 10 May 2011.

―――. 1949. Ministry of Commerce, Memorandum on the Amendments of the Indian Companies Act.

―――. 1952. Report of the Company Law Committee 1952.

―――. 1958a. Commission of Enquiry into the Affairs of the Life Insurance Corporation of India–Report.

―――. 1958b. Report of the Life Insurance Corporation Inquiry (Vivian Bose, Chairperson).

―――. 1960a. Ministry of Commerce and Industry, Department of Company Law Administration, Research and Statistics Division, The Present and Future Role of Shareholders' Associations in India (Author: Raj K. Nigam).

India. 1960b. Ministry of Commerce and Industry, Department of Company Law Administration, Selections from the Debates on the Reform of Company Law in the Central Assembly and Parliament in 1936 and 1954–5: Purposes and Objectives of the Provisions of the Relevant Bills as explained by Government Spokesmen.

————. 1963. Commission of Inquiry—Inquiry on the Administration of Dalmia-Jain Companies, 1956—Report (Chairperson: S.R. Tendolkar, Vivian Bose).

————. 1966. Ministry of Law, Department of Company Affairs, Report of the Managing Agency Enquiry Committee (Chairperson: I.G. Patel).

————. 1969. Department of Industrial Development Report of the Industrial Licensing Policy Inquiry Committee (Chairperson: Subimal Dutt).

Indian Central Cotton Committee. 1928a. Report on an Investigation into the Finance and Marketing of Cultivators' Cotton in Madras (Northerns and Westerns Tracts).

————. 1928b. Report on an Investigation into the Finance and Marketing of Cultivators' Cotton in Middle Gujarat 1927–8.

————. 1928c. Report on an Investigation into the Finance and Marketing of Cultivators' Cotton in Punjab.

————. 1928d. Report on an Investigation into the Finance and Marketing of Cultivators' Cotton in Sind 1927–8.

Indian Central Jute Committee. 1940. Report on the Marketing and Transport of Jute in India: First Report.

Indian Jute Mills Association. 1912. Report of the Committee, 1911. Calcutta: IJMA.

Jain, L.C. 1929. Indigenous Banking in India. London: Macmillan.

Johnson, Simon, Rafael La Porta, Florencio Lopez-de-Silanes, and Andrei Shleifer. 2000. 'Tunneling'. The American Economic Review 90(2): 22–7.

Jones, Geoffrey and Judith Wale. 1998. 'Merchants as Business Groups: British Trading Companies in Asia before 1945'. The Business History Review 72(3): 367–408.

Jalal, Ayesha and Anil Seal. 1981. 'Alternative to Partition: Muslim Politics between the Wars'. Modern Asian Studies 15(3): 415–54.

Kapoor, M.C. 1953. 'Depreciation Policy of Companies in India'. Economic Weekly 5(3): 61–3.

Kamtekar, Indivar. 2002. 'A Different War Dance: State and Class in India 1939–1945'. Past & Present 176(1): 187–221.

Kazimi, Muhammad Reza. 1997. Liaquat Ali Khan and the Freedom Movement. Karachi: Pakistan Study Centre, University of Karachi.

Kidron, Michael. 1965. Foreign Investments in India. London: Oxford University Press.

Kling, Blair B. 1966. 'The Origin of the Managing Agency System in India'. The Journal of Asian Studies 26(1): 37–47.

Kochanek, Stanley A. 1970. 'Interest Groups and Interest Aggregation: Changing Patterns of Oligarchy in the FICCI', *Economic and Political Weekly* 5(29–31): 1291–308.

———. 1974. *Business and Politics in India*. Berkeley: University of California Press.

Krishna, V. 1959. *Indigenous Banking in South India*. Bombay: Bombay State Cooperative Union.

Kudaisya, Medha M. 1998. 'G.D. Birla, Big Business and India's Partition'. In *Freedom, Trauma, and Continuities: North India and Independence* edited by D.A. Low and Howard Brasted, pp. 215–34. New Delhi: Sage Publications.

———. 2003. *The Life and Times of G.D. Birla*. New Delhi: Oxford University Press.

———, ed. 2011. *The Oxford India Anthology of Business History*. New Delhi: Oxford University Press.

Kurian, K.M. 1966. *Impact of Foreign Capital on Indian Economy*. New Delhi: People's Publishing House.

Lamb, Helen B. 1955. 'The Indian Business Communities and the Evolution of an Industrialist Class'. *Pacific Affairs* 28(2): 101–16.

Levkovsky, A.I. 1966. *Capitalism in India: Basic Trends in Its Development*. Delhi: People's Publishing House.

Low, D.A. and Howard Brasted, eds. 1998. *Freedom, Trauma, Continuities: Northern India and Independence*. New Delhi: Sage Publications.

Lockwood, David. 2012. 'Was the Bombay Plan a Capitalist Plot?' *Studies in History* 28(1): 99–116.

Lokanathan, P.S. 1935. *Industrial Organisation in India*. London: George Allen and Unwin.

———. 1945. 'The Bombay Plan'. *Foreign Affairs* 23(4): 680–6.

Markovits, Claude. 1985. *Indian Business and Nationalist Politics 1931–39: The Indigenous Capitalist Class and the Rise of the Congress Party*. Cambridge: Cambridge University Press.

———. 1991. 'Business and the Partition of India'. In *State and Business in India: A Historical Perspective*, pp. 284–307, edited by Dwijendra Tripathi. New Delhi: Manohar Publications.

McQueen, Rob. 2008. 'The Flowers of Progress: Corporations Law in the Colonies'. *Griffith Law Review* 17(1): 383–412.

Mehta, Asoka. 1949. *Economic Consequences of Sardar Patel*. Hyderabad: Chetna Prakashan.

———. 1950. *Who Owns India?* Hyderabad: Chetna Prakashan.

Mehta, S.D. 1954. *The Cotton Mills of India 1854 to 1954*. Bombay: Textile Association (India).

Melman, Sofia. 1963. *Foreign Monopoly Capital in Indian Economy*. New Delhi: People's Publishing House.

Merchant, K.T. 1953. 'Sociology of Blackmarketing'. *Sociological Bulletin* 2(1): 1–17.

Misra, Bhubanes. 1987. 'The Cotton Mill Industry of Eastern India in the Late Nineteenth Century: Constraints on Foreign Investment and Expansion'. *Social Scientist* 15(3): 3–38.

Misra, Maria. 1999. *Business, Race, and Politics in British India* c. 1850–1960. Oxford: Clarendon Press.

———. 2000. '"Business Culture" and Entrepreneurship in British India, 1860–1950'. *Modern Asian Studies* 34(2): 333–48.

Mitchell, Kate. 1942. 'India's Economic Potential'. *Pacific Affairs* 15(1): 5–24.

Mittal, G.P. et al. 1963(?) *Painful Story of Dalmia and the Bose Commission Report*. N.p.

Moon, Penderel, ed. 1973. *Wavell: The Viceroy's Journal*. London: Oxford University Press.

Morris, Morris David. 1974. 'Private Industrial Investment on the Indian Subcontinent 1900–1939: Some Methodological Considerations'. *Modern Asian Studies* 8(4): 535–55.

———. 1982. 'The Growth of Large-Scale Industry to 1947'. In *The Cambridge Economic History of India: Volume 2, c. 1757–c. 1970*, edited by Dharma Kumar. Hyderabad: Orient Longman.

Mukherjee, Aditya. 2002. *Imperialism, Nationalism and the Making of the Indian Capitalist Class*. New Delhi: Sage Publications.

Mukherjee, Mridula. 2005. *Colonializing Agriculture: The Myth of Punjab Exceptionalism*. New Delhi: Sage Publications.

National Council of Applied Economic Research. 1959. *The Managing Agency System: A Review of Its Working and Prospects of Its Future*. Bombay: Asia Publishing House.

Palme Dutt, R. 1970. *India Today*, second Indian edition. Calcutta: Manisha Granthalaya.

Papanek, Hanna. 1972. 'Pakistan's Big Businessmen: Muslim Separatism, Entrepreneurship, and Partial Modernization'. *Economic Development and Cultural Change* 21(1): 1–32.

Papendieck, Henner. 1978. 'British Managing Agencies in the Indian Coalfield'. In *Zamindars, Mines and Peasants: Studies in the History of an Indian Coalfield and Its Rural Hinterland*, edited by D. Rothermund and D.C. Wadhwa, 165–220. New Delhi: Manohar Publications.

Patel, H.M. 1971. 'Oral History Project Transcript No. 91', mimeo. New Delhi: Nehru Memorial Museum and Library.

Patel, Sujata, Jasodhara Bagchi, and Krishna Raj, eds. 2002. *Thinking Social Science in India: Essays in Honour of Alice Thorner*. New Delhi: Sage Publications.

Patvardhan, V.S. 1958. *Food Control in Bombay Province 1939–1949*. Poona: Gokhale Institute of Politics and Economics.

Pavlov, V.I. 1978. *Historical Premises for India's Transition to Capitalism*. Moscow: Nauka Publishing House.

Rangnekar, D.K. 1958. *Poverty and Capital Development in India: Contemporary Investment Patterns Problems and Planning*. London: Oxford University Press.

Rao, V.K.R.V. 1943. *War and Indian Economy*. Allahabad: Kitabistan.

Ray, Amalendu. 1968. *Inconsistencies in Azad*. Howrah: Bangavarati Granthalaya.

Ray, Rajat Kanta. 1979. *Industrialization in India: Growth and Conflict in the Private Corporate Sector, 1914–47*. Delhi: Oxford University Press.

———. 1988. 'The Bazaar: Changing Structural Characteristics of the Indigenous Section of the Indian Economy Before and After the Great Depression'. *Indian Economic and Social History Review* 25: 263–318.

———, ed. 1992. *Entrepreneurship and Industry in India*. Delhi: Oxford University Press.

Reserve Bank of India. 1954. *All India Rural Credit Survey: Report of the Committee of Direction, Volume II, The General Report*. Bombay: RBI.

Rothermund, Dietmar. 1992. *India in the Great Depression, 1929–1939*. Delhi: Manohar Publications.

Rothermund, Dietmar and D.C. Wadhwa, eds. 1978. *Zamindars, Mines and Peasants: Studies in the History of an Indian Coalfield and Its Rural Hinterland*. New Delhi: Manohar Publications.

Roy, Tirthankar. 1999. *Traditional Industry in the Economy of Colonial India*. Cambridge: Cambridge University Press.

Rungta, Radhe Shyam. 1962. 'Indian Company Law Problems in 1850'. *The American Journal of Legal History* VI(3): 298–308.

———. 1970. *The Rise of Business Corporations in India 1851–1900*. London: Cambridge University Press.

Samant, D.R. and M.A. Mulky. 1937. *Organisation and Finance of Industries in India*. Bombay: Longman, Green and Co.

Sanyal, Amal. 2010. 'The Curious Case of the Bombay Plan'. *Contemporary Issues and Ideas in Social Sciences* 6(1): 1–31. Available at http://journal.ciiss.net. Accessed on 26 July 2013.

Satyanarayana, A. 1990. *Andhra Peasants under British Rule: Agrarian Relations and the Rural Economy 1900–1940*. New Delhi: Manohar Publications.

Sen, Sunil Kumar. 1966. *Studies in Economic Policy and Development of India (1848–1926)*. Calcutta: Progressive Publishers.

Sethia, Tara. 1996. 'The Rise of the Jute Manufacturing Industry in Colonial India: A Global Perspective'. *Journal of World History* 7(1): 71–99.

Shah, B.K. 1944. *India Tomorrow: A New Approach to Planning*. Baroda: Padmaja Publications.

Shah, K.T. and K.J. Khambata. 1924. *Wealth and Taxable Capacity of India*. Bombay: D.B. Taraporevala.

Shenoy, B.R. 1944. *The Bombay Plan: A Review of Its Financial Provisions*. Bombay: Karnatak Publishing House.

Shirokov, G.K. 1973. *Industrialisation of India*. Moscow: Progress Publishers.

Sinha, H. 1929. 'Jute Futures in Calcutta'. *Economica* 27: 330–7.

Smith, Wilfred Cantwell. 1963. *Modern Islam in India*. Lahore: Md. Ashraf.

Sovani, N.V., ed. 1948. *Reports of the Commodity Prices Board.* Poona: Gokhale Institute of Politics and Economics.

———. 1949. *Post-War Inflation in India—A Survey.* Poona: Gokhale Institute of Politics and Economics.

Stevens, Bertram. 1941. 'The Eastern Group Supply Council'. *The Australian Quarterly* 13(3): 9–18.

Streeten, Paul and Michael Lipton, eds. 1968. *The Crisis of Indian Planning: Economic Policy in the 1960s.* London: Oxford University Press.

Talbot, Ian. 1994. 'Planning for Pakistan: The Planning Committee of the All-India Muslim League 1943–46'. *Modern Asian Studies* 28(4): 875–89.

Thakurdas, Purshottamdas, J. R. D. Tata, G. D. Birla, Shri Ram, Kasturbhai Lalbhai, A. D. Shroff, and John Matthai. 1944. *A Plan of Economic Development for India Part II (Distribution—Role of the State).* Bombay: Tata Sons.

Timberg, Thomas A. 1973. 'Three Types of the Marwari Firm'. *Indian Economic and Social History Review* 10(3): 3–36.

Tomlinson, B.R. 1978. 'Foreign Private Investment in India 1920–1950'. *Modern Asian Studies* 12(4): 655–77.

———. 1981. 'Colonial Firms and the Decline of Colonialism in Eastern India 1914–47'. *Modern Asian Studies* 15(3):455–86.

Tripathi, Dwijendra, ed. 1987. *State and Business in India: A Historical Perspective.* New Delhi: Manohar Publications.

———, ed. 1991. *Business and Politics in India: A Historical Perspective.* New Delhi: Manohar Publications.

Tyabji, Nasir. 1989. *The Small Industries Policy in India.* Calcutta: Oxford University Press.

———. 2000. *Industrialisation and Innovation: The Indian Experience.* New Delhi: Sage Publications.

Ulyanovsky, Rotislav. 1981. *Agrarian India between the World Wars.* Moscow: Progress Publishers.

Vakil, Chandulal Nagindas, Jashwantrai Jayantilal Anjaria, and Dansukhlal Tulsidas Lakdawala. 1946. *Price Control in India with Special Reference to Food Supply.* Bombay: Popular Book Depot.

Venkatasubbiah, H. 1940. *The Structural Basis of Indian Economy.* London: Allen and Unwin.

———. 1977. *Enterprise and Economic Change: 50 Years of FICCI.* New Delhi: Vikas.

Vicat Turrell, Robert and Jean Jacques Van-Helten. 1987. 'The Investment Group: The Missing Link in British Overseas Expansion before 1914?' *The Economic History Review,* New Series, 40(2): 267–74.

Wadia, P.A. and K.T. Merchant. 1946. *The Bombay Plan: A Criticism,* second edition. Bombay: Popular Book Depot.

———. 1957. *Our Economic Problem.* Bombay: Vora & Co.

Zachariah, Benjamin. 2005. *Developing India: An Intellectual and Social History c. 1930–50.* New Delhi: Oxford University Press.

ABOUT THE AUTHOR

Nasir Tyabji is an economic historian with interests in the areas of technology, innovation, and also the social aspects of industrialization. After some years spent at the Madras Institute of Development Studies, Chennai, and the Nehru Memorial Museum and Library, New Delhi, he taught at the Jawaharlal Nehru University, New Delhi. Subsequently, he moved to Jamia Millia Islamia, New Delhi, and retired as the Director and Professor at the Centre for Jawaharlal Nehru Studies. He continues to edit the centre's journal, *History and Sociology of South Asia*. Nasir Tyabji is the author of *Industrialisation and Innovation: The Indian Experience* (2000), *Colonialism, Chemical Technology and Industry in Southern India, 1880–1937* (Oxford University Press, 1995) and *The Small Industries Policy in India* (Oxford University Press, 1989).

91025143/3-9-15 E.